PRAISE FOR
THE ART OF THE TALE

"Steven and Tom are worldclass crafters of stories and experts at communicating them. The principles they unpack in *The Art of the Tale* will enhance any company or individual's communication strategy and overall effectiveness."

—TONY MARR,
award-winning storyteller and business consultant

"Communication. Connection. Culture. None of these work without storytelling. In this important book, Steven James and Tom Morrisey teach us how to tell superior stories in superior ways by mastering *The Art of the Tale*!"

—ROWAN GIBSON,
bestselling author and award-winning keynote speaker

"*The Art of the Tale* combines the power of storytelling with traditional public speaking in a way that current generations can relate to. Communication is not simply the transfer of information. It is influence. *The Art of the Tale* recognizes that. I have been teaching speech at the university level for more than thirty years. This is the most practical and exciting book on speaking and storytelling that I have seen."

—K. BRUCE MONTGOMERY, PHD,
professor of communications, business consultant,
and storytelling instructor

"Steven and Tom have created an easy-to-understand reference book with great visuals and useful tips. More importantly, they deeply understand that we are all storytellers and work best when we are also active listeners. *The Art of the Tale* is a powerful collaboration between arts, literature, and communication."

—MARGOT LEITMAN,
award-winning storyteller and author of
Long Story Short: The Only Storytelling Guide You'll Ever Need

"If you want to touch hearts and minds, form bonds with listeners, and build that elusive quality known as 'brand,' a well-told story is the key, and this is the book that helps you find that key."

—MEG CROFTON,
president (retired) of Disney Parks Operations, USA and France

"As a storyteller who has performed onstage for more than a decade and the author of my own book on storytelling, I've read every book on the subject. Most are philosophical, esoteric, and leave the reader with some interesting thoughts and theories but no actual tools for telling great stories. *The Art of the Tale* is not one of these books. Chock-full of specific strategies and lots of practical examples, it is a book that can objectively make you a better storyteller page by page."

—MATTHEW DICKS,
author of *Storyworthy: Engage, Teach, Persuade, and Change Your Life Through the Power of Storytelling*

"*The Art of the Tale* is a powerful guide reminding us to listen to experts when it comes to telling stories. Thankfully, we have experienced practitioners in Steven and Tom to lead us on the path. This cowritten and friendly text examines the practical and purposeful route to using storytelling in the boardroom and beyond. After teaching storytelling for years, I will be sure that this resource is close at hand for future lessons. This book demonstrates how a story needs to be built for our listeners out of curiosity and shares how we can pivot the tales as we create and tell them. Most of all, this is a powerful book that reminds us that serving the audience of the stories is the goal. The practical lessons are echoed by tips, testimonies, and even cautions that will steer us toward using storytelling to meet our successes."

—KEVIN D. CORDI, PHD,
author, podcaster, and national storytelling consultant

"I have walked many paths: coach, consultant, speaker, entertainer, writer, mother. This book applies to each of them. I don't care what title you carry beside your name, *The Art of the Tale* will be a solid tool in your box. An enjoyable read with many stop, think, underline it moments."

—KIM WEITKAMP,
storyteller, author, and creator of ProfitableStory.com

THE ART OF
THE TALE

THE ART OF
THE TALE

Engage Your Audience, Elevate Your Organization,
and Share Your Message Through Storytelling

STEVEN JAMES
TOM MORRISEY

HarperCollins
Leadership

An Imprint of HarperCollins

Published by HarperCollins Leadership, an imprint of HarperCollins Focus LLC.

Any internet addresses, phone numbers, or company or product information printed in this book are offered as a resource and are not intended in any way to be or to imply an endorsement by HarperCollins Leadership, nor does HarperCollins Leadership vouch for the existence, content, or services of these sites, phone numbers, companies, or products beyond the life of this book.

Book design by Aubrey Khan, Neuwirth & Associates, Inc.

ISBN 978-1-4002-3312-0 (eBook)
ISBN 978-1-4002-3311-3 (TP)

Library of Congress Control Number: 2022936277

Printed in the United States of America
22 23 24 25 26 LSC 10 9 8 7 6 5 4 3 2 1

To Safaia and Emmaya:
I look forward to sharing my stories with you,
and being a part of the stories you'll carry on.

—Steven

To Linda, my lifetime collaborator,
Carly, our magnum opus,
and every heart that has ever opened
to receive a story.

—Tom

CONTENTS

PART IV ■ THE STORYTELLER

INTRODUCTION

We're fortunate folks.

Over the years, Steven and I have gotten to meet and, in many cases, become closely acquainted with some of the most highly regarded people in the corporate and literary worlds. We've heard about their accomplishments and their regrets, and we've detected a pattern: the writers valued their ability to craft *stories* and nearly all of the executives we interviewed and worked with wished that they were better communicators. And the one communication skill virtually every one of them wanted to become better at was *storytelling*.

That's not surprising. The essence of leadership is communication, and the essence of charisma—the charm that convinces stakeholders to follow a leader—is the bonding experience that can be achieved through the art of a well-told narrative.

Stories connect with people in deep and powerful ways that can inspire, motivate, and impact them forever. Despite this, many business executives don't see themselves as storytellers—or they think that telling stories is for other people. In truth, all of us are storytellers in our own unique ways (as you'll learn more about throughout this book).

Steven and I have been honored to spend decades of our lives filling that need and helping leaders and professional communicators add the gift of storytelling to their repertoire. For the last twenty-five years, we've taught presentation skills and storytelling techniques to thousands of speakers, teachers, writers, and executives around the world.

Does that mean this book is intended only for corporate leaders?

Not at all. Educators of all types, civic leaders, pastors, teachers, camp counselors, scoutmasters, parents, and middle managers—who may hope to someday become corporate leaders—will all profit from reading this book. Whether you're preparing a business pitch, a conference presentation, a high school history lesson, or a Sunday morning sermon, you can benefit by telling stories more succinctly and impactfully.

With the unique perspective of a speechwriter and a professional storyteller, this book will help you understand the dynamics of an effective presentation and give you tools to elevate your storytelling to a new level. My chapters will take a deep dive into the intricacies of giving speeches that transform audiences. Steven's chapters will focus more on the nuts and bolts of telling stories that truly connect with listeners.

Without getting too obtuse or technical, we'll explore the social dynamics that affect how a story needs to be told in different settings.

We'll also guide you toward finding and identifying the stories that are hiding within the constant, jumbled data stream of your life. You'll learn to compose them in a compelling way, tell them in an engaging manner that actually makes people like you more (honest—we have the science to prove it), and make a point in the most palatable manner possible.

After all, the difference between charismatic leadership and a failure to connect often boils down to one thing: the ability to share ideas through story.

Research over the last twenty-five years continues to confirm what the greatest teachers in history have always known: stories reach the heart, change perspectives, inform listeners on a deep level, and have the ability to transform lives.

Storytelling is mouth-to-heart resuscitation.

In this book you'll learn why practice doesn't make perfect, why you should never tell the same story the same way twice, why there are countless ways to tell a story, and why good stories are absorbed, not memorized. You'll also discover how to pretend less and believe more, recite less and respond more, explain less and evoke more.

We believe that the best stories speak the truth about human nature and allow us to glimpse it, discover it, and better understand it. A good story is an escape that leads you home.

This is a book about how to engage in the oldest social moment of all, invented in a forgotten age when entire villages gathered around fires to share the stories they dreamt in the flames.

This book is for you, as you share the warmth of your organization and yourself in the stories you tell.

—Tom Morrisey

The personal stories in this book are true. All the people you'll meet are real people. In some cases, names and details have been altered to protect the privacy of the people involved.

THE ART OF
THE TALE

PART I
THE STORY
Tapping into the Tale

I t seems a little self-evident, but when shaping the delivery of your story, the first ingredient you'll take into account is the story itself. Whether it's humorous or serious, silly or soul-searching, understanding your story and the power it possesses to connect with listeners will help you craft more meaningful and memorable messages.

But what is a story? What elements does it contain? How does it differ—if at all—from an anecdote? This section answers these questions and many more. Read on to find out what lies at the heart of all great stories.

CHAPTER 1

THE UNPARALLELED POWER OF STORY

—STEVEN

"Stories are the most powerful form of human communication."
—Peg C. Neuhauser, author of *Corporate Legends and Lore*

When I was a college senior, I spent my final semester interning as a wilderness instructor in a program for at-risk teenagers. Many of the young men would have been sent to juvenile prison if they hadn't been court-ordered to participate in our program.

The goals of the twenty-eight-day course included helping the students learn responsibility and self-reliance in a challenging outdoor environment. The problem was, our backgrounds and upbringings were vastly different. I had no idea how to talk to these teenagers who'd been arrested for beating up police officers, dealing drugs, and planning drive-by shootings.

But now, there I was, seated with a dozen of them around a campfire. We had the next four weeks together in the woods. And no one was saying a word.

In front of us, restless campfire flames flickered and licked at the darkness.

Crickets *chirruped* from nowhere and everywhere.

Twelve students. Three staff.

Silence.

Finally, unsure what else to say, and figuring we were around a campfire—the perfect place for a scary tale or two—I said, "Have you ever heard the story about the babysitter?"

For a long moment they were quiet.

"Which one's that?" someone said at last.

"The one with the phone call about, 'Go and check the children.'"

And some of them had heard it, but still, that night, all of them wanted to hear it again.

So, beginning with that story, there in the firelight, I started telling them urban legends: the one about the man with the hook who comes after the couple in the car up on Lovers Lane, and the one about the guy who wakes up in a Las Vegas bathtub without his kidney, and the one about the giant alligators lurking in the sewers of New York City.

One after another I retold the stories I'd heard when I was a teenager myself, back when I was trying to sort out who I was and how to find my place in the world (just as these young men were doing), and I'd sat and listened to my friends tell stories around campfires that were distant cousins of this one.

Finally, when I finished, one of the teens said, "Do you know any more stories?"

"No," I said, somewhat reluctantly, but someone else said, "Yes," and began to tell the stories he'd heard.

It went on for hours and, in the end, we were no longer students and staff. We were no longer separated by age or ethnicity or demographics beyond our control. We were just a bunch of guys sitting around a campfire sharing stories. Our ages and our backgrounds weren't able to hold us apart as those stories drew us together.

The stories built bridges within us and between us, and the first chapter in our story together began.

FINDING YOURSELF IN A STORY

You may not get paid to write novels, perform plays, or direct movies—and you may have never thought about it this way before—but as a member of the human race you are already a storyteller.

We communicate and think in stories. We try to make sense of our lives by finding the way our choices and mistakes and dreams connect with the choices, mistakes, and dreams of others in our quest to find hope and meaning in the inexplicable and mysterious stories of our lives. We remember and make sense of our past through stories. Skilled teachers and communicators throughout the ages have known this: that's why they pepper their messages with stories to illustrate and illuminate their points.

As motivational speaker Bob Lenz says, "You can lose yourself or find yourself in a story."

In our fast-paced, hyper driven, cyberspace world, people are hungry for deep human connection. Stories offer that and help build relationships between us. They can explain heritage and history and help people better understand and apply their beliefs. For untold millennia, humans have used stories to pass on values, morals, and culture.

And you are part of that tradition—we all are.

We're surrounded by countless stories every day. We listen to the news on the way to work; we witness little tragedies and humorous incidents throughout the day; we read about our friends on their social media posts; and then, at night, we entertain ourselves by reading books, watching movies, and going to the theater. We're like fish who don't notice the water. We're so immersed in the stories that swirl around us that most of the time we aren't even aware of how they influence our thoughts, our hearts, our lives.

Every time you tell your spouse about your day, pass along a joke, reminisce about the "good old days," or rehash the game, you're telling a story.

Try this. Try to remember a place you've lived, a person you've worked for, a vacation you've been on, or the loss of something you cared about without remembering a story. It's tough, if not impossible. Over the last thirty years, researchers who study intelligence have been discovering what most of us already intuitively know: we don't remember events very well unless they're connected to other instances within the construct of—you guessed it—a story.

Still, despite all of that, many people don't think of themselves as storytellers.

And I get it.

Different social settings have different expectations about who's supposed to speak, who's supposed to listen, and when (and if) you should reply to the other person. And sometimes we step over the line—or don't even realize that it's there.

AN ICE CREAM SUNDAE REVELATION

When I was twenty years old, I took a college classmate of mine out for ice cream. We'd been friends for a year or so, but I'd become infatuated with her and was hoping our relationship might blossom into something a little less platonic and a little more romantic. However, I've never exactly been an expert in the romance department, and that night I was so nervous that I didn't know what to say.

After we'd ordered our ice cream sundaes and taken a seat, I started to do what I thought made the most sense—talking about myself, trying to impress her. (You're about to see how well that turned out . . .)

There, with the sweet smells of peppermint ice cream and honey roasted nuts permeating the air around us, I told her all about playing basketball in high school. It seemed like safe territory, since our team had won two state championships. I found myself really getting into the story. Certainly she would like me more when she heard about my high school sports success.

I must've gone on for a while, because finally she held up her hand and said, "Steve, can I tell you something?"

"What's that?" I was hoping she might take the opportunity to point out what an amazing time she was having.

She looked me straight in the eyes. "I feel more like your audience than your friend."

Ouch.

Not *quite* the response I was hoping for.

You can see what happened, can't you? Since I tend to feel more comfortable onstage, I'd started *performing my life story* for her rather than *sharing a conversation* with her.

Imagine this: You go out for coffee with a friend, and she pauses in the middle of the conversation. You might be wondering what's going through her mind, but you probably wouldn't be thinking, *Huh, she forgot her lines.*

However, if you go to a one-person play and the actor stops in the middle of the show and stares off into space, you might be justified in wondering if he forgot what he was planning to say next.

If you and I were sitting in that coffee shop having a conversation, it would seem natural for us to interrupt each other, move seamlessly between a variety of topics, talk in short sentences, riff about things that annoy us, go on tangents, and pause to reflect on what we're going to discuss next.

On the other hand, if we went to that play, we would expect to sit quietly (perhaps for an hour or more) as the performer spoke to us. We wouldn't interrupt, change the subject, or expect a turn to talk.

Clearly, different social encounters bring with them different expectations. Every told story lies somewhere on a continuum between conversation and performance. In a conversation, people talk with spontaneity and listen with the intent of being able to respond to what's being said. In a performance, on the other hand, one person (or a small group of people) prepares something to say and everyone else is expected to listen without interrupting.

THE COMMUNICATION CONTINUUM

Conversation   Performance

Now, think back to my ice cream parlor debacle. Without realizing it, I'd been telling my story to my friend at a completely different place on the continuum than what was appropriate for our situation. I was performing, not conversing. And she was courageous enough and honest enough to let me know that.

(By the way, that date didn't blossom into anything lasting—or even a second date—but at least that night she taught me a lasting lesson about myself and the way I communicate with women when I'm nervous! And don't worry, I did find the right someone further down the line—but that's a story for another time.)

To become an effective communicator, whether you think of yourself as a storyteller or not, it's important to understand your listeners and match the level of informality with the expectations they have. As you read this book, you'll learn specific ways to take their needs into account as you consider the social context and adapt to it in your style of communication.

Knowing yourself is as important as knowing your audience. Once you realize where on the communication continuum you're most comfortable, you can begin to look for places to tell stories within your comfort zone. Many people are more at ease sitting around chatting with friends than going onstage in front of a few hundred people. If that's you, you'll probably do well telling stories

to a small number of people in a boardroom or a classroom setting...
at least, at first.

Some of us, on the other hand, are more comfortable on the performance end of the spectrum. We're intimidated by small groups. Personally, I'm much more at ease being onstage in front of a thousand people than speaking to a group of ten. (Cocktail parties and game nights terrify me.)

But whether you're more comfortable in a conversation sharing stories off the cuff, or spending time beforehand preparing them for a performance, stories are a core part of how we communicate and relate to each other.

A lot of freedom can come when you acknowledge—and embrace—the fact that you are already a storyteller.

In conversations, most people put more effort into composing responses than they do in simply listening to the person speaking. Historically, this has been a benefit to performance settings such as lecture halls, churches, conference rooms, ballrooms, and auditoriums; the listeners are freed of the pressure to respond, and can devote their entire attention to simply listening. But in the contemporary world, there is a new hurdle to consider: personal mobile devices now make it possible to share a conversation with virtual companions without making a sound. As a speaker, I know that even if I'm not being interrupted, I may not have my listeners' full attention. Whenever I speak, I'm aware that easily half the audience probably has a device open to a text messaging or social media app, and I'm also aware that an extra effort is necessary to keep my listeners there in the moment with me—in my performance—rather than in cyberspace, where they can direct their comments toward others.

—TOM

Of course, no one wants to appear unprepared in front of others, look silly, or make a fool of themselves. Because of that, many people are afraid of public speaking. But no matter who you are, you can develop more confidence and improve your innate storytelling abilities.

Storytelling is a natural way to teach and to lead. It immediately captures the attention of your listeners, helps them remember the lesson, and allows them the chance to more easily apply truth to their lives.

In his quest to understand the impact stories have, storyteller and author Kendall Haven read more than 100,000 pages, including poring over 350 books and research studies from 15 separate scientific and sociological fields covering over 70 articles that reviewed and evaluated more than 1,500 additional studies and articles. He concluded, "Results from a dozen prominent cognitive scientists and developmental psychologists have confirmed that human minds *do* rely on stories and on story architecture as the primary roadmap for understanding, making sense of, remembering, and planning our lives."

One challenge communicators face is shaping our messages in such a way that they reach our audiences. To do that, we need to speak in the language our listeners understand best—and the language of the heart is the language of story and emotion, rather than dry logic and reason.

That doesn't mean you can't use logic, but it does mean you'll want to fill your messages and teaching with imagery that appeals to imagination, not just facts that appeal to intellect.

Neuroscientist Antonio Damasio discovered that "although we *think* we make decisions based purely on logic, it's *emotions* that actually play a key role at *go time*." Very often, people *feel* their way into commitments and *think* their way out of them. Emotion is the fastest pathway toward change, so it's often wise to lead with that and follow it with logic. Don't discard the truth, just search for fresh ways to serve it up. Rather than presenting a progression of premises to be argued, present a progression of emotionally infused images to be believed.

In other words, tell a story.

Stories appeal to our sense of wonder, to our curiosity, and to our imagination. They connect people, shatter societal barriers, and build community, just as they did on that wilderness course the night those teens and I told stories to each other and the walls between us came down.

TENSION: THE BEATING HEART OF EVERY STORY

You've probably seen it happen.

The presenter gets to the point in his message where he's about to share a personal experience with his listeners, and he says those six simple words: "Let me tell you a story . . ."

And everything changes.

Folks look up, set their phones aside, and lean forward.

At a recent conference, after I finished presenting, a business leader named David told me that in their meetings, the execs use the same fifty words all the time: *vision, lead, brand, mission, customer, client, employee, opportunity*, and so on, and that he and his team would inevitably find themselves tuning out. "But if somebody actually tells a story," he said, "that's the thing we remember."

There's nothing like a well-told story to grab people's attention. People love stories and would rather you tell them a story than give them a lecture any day.

But let's explore this for a minute. What is a story, exactly? Is it more than a list of events that occur?

For instance, is this a story?

> Yesterday I went to the beach, then I came home, then I ate a
> hamburger, then I watched TV, then I went to bed, then I woke
> up, then I got dressed . . .

Some people might say that it is a story (albeit not a very good one!), but in truth it's really more of a report. After all, nothing goes wrong, there's no tension, no struggle, no transformation, and no insight into the character's life.

A story isn't simply a series of events; it's the account of someone who wants something and can't get it. When you discover who has the struggle, you'll know who the story is primarily about. As Pulitzer Prize–winning author Robert Olen Butler put it, "Story is a yearning meeting an obstacle."

Without the tension that results from a character pursuing something she desires that's out of reach, you might very well end up saying, "Well, you had to be there."

So, yes, a story is more than a list of things that happen.

Stories contain four crucial elements: character, setting, struggle, and pursuit. If you lack any one of these four, you don't have a story. (Great stories have two additional elements that set them apart from the rest, but we'll get to those in a moment.)

With no *character* to cheer for, you'll end up with just the description of an event.

With no *setting* in time and place, listeners won't be able to picture what's happening.

Without a *struggle*, you'll only have a description of a character existing in bliss somewhere.

And without an active *pursuit*, your narrative won't go anywhere.

Think of these four aspects of story as sides of a square: If you remove any one of them, it ceases to be a square. If you remove any one of those four essential elements of story, it ceases to be a story.

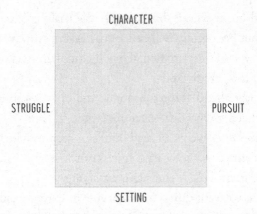

When people talk about "plot," they're simply referring to the journey that the *character* takes through the *setting* to overcome her *struggle* during her *pursuit*.

If your story isn't working, it may very well be because your listeners don't understand who it's primarily about, can't see it happening, nothing is going wrong, or the character is just being acted upon instead of making meaningful, goal-directed choices (that is, pursuing something that matters to her).

So, can you tell a story with just those four elements—character, setting, struggle, and pursuit? Certainly—but you can do better. You can add dimensionality to your story. You can make it more memorable, poignant, and meaningful to your listeners—if you add the two final elements.

THE TWO UNSUNG HEROES OF GREAT STORIES

If stories are too straightforward—for instance, a character simply struggles her way toward a resolution—many listeners will be left unsatisfied. Yes, they certainly want the story to move forward logically (to "make sense"), but not to be *too* straightforward. If they can figure out how things will end, or the exact pathway to the conclusion, they won't be satisfied. They'll complain that the story is "boring" or too "predictable."

On the other hand, if the solution to the story's problem "comes out of nowhere," they won't be happy, either.

Think about it. We've all read books or seen movies where the ending was either way too easy to guess or too outlandish to be believable. Neither of those endings is satisfying.

In essence, we want things to make sense in a way we didn't expect and twist toward a believable ending we didn't see coming.

No surprise = Boredom

No logic = Frustration

No resolution = Dissatisfaction

Here's the first unsung hero of story: the *pivot*.

A pivot is a powerful story element because it allows you to avoid all three of those unfavorable outcomes (boredom, frustration, and dissatisfaction) because it contains surprise, logic, and resolution.

If everything in your story is as it appears to be and everyone is who we think they are and everything goes where we assume it's going to go, there's very little room for surprise left. Instead, look for a way to pivot the story forward. As Peter Guber, former Hollywood exec and author of *Tell to Win: Connect, Persuade, and Triumph with the Hidden Power of Story*, puts it, "A story that fails to deliver surprise is dead on arrival."

To find the pivot in your story, look for moments when (1) you were taken by surprise, (2) an insight came from an unexpected place, (3) things didn't go as planned, or (4) life caught you unaware.

Search your story for a "gasp-worthy" moment. It might be a twist that tugs the rug out from under the listeners and leaves them with their mouths agape or their hearts in their throats, or it might be a clever but unforeseen choice that the character makes. How did the events twist toward an unexpected ending that, in retrospect, makes perfect sense? That's where your pivot is found.

You want listeners to be thinking, *I never saw that coming, but I'm glad it did!*

So, if a pivot is the first unsung hero, what's the final ingredient to great stories?

The *payoff.*

Payoff is why the story matters. What can we take away from it? What's the point? Does the story mean more than it says? Is it thought-provoking even if it doesn't have a happy ending? Is action imbued with deeper meaning in such a way that it reveals that the story has something significant to impart?

The payoff might be the theme, the application, or the deeper meaning. It might also contain an ingenious or elegant intersection of multiple, apparently disparate, story lines. It's what sets the incident apart and makes the story worth telling and worth listening to.

The payoff can happen in the same moment as the pivot. (For instance, in a short story with a twist ending.) Payoff will look different depending on the story's shape and its genre: the payoff for a cozy mystery is much different from that of a rom-com or a horror story.

Depending on your story, you might end with a call to action, an image that reinforces your key concept, or a revelation that shows what the story's characters learned.

I like to think of stories as six-sided cubes that contain those first four elements of every story (character, setting, struggle, and pursuit), as well as these two additional components of great stories—the pivot and the payoff. Taken all together, you get a full,

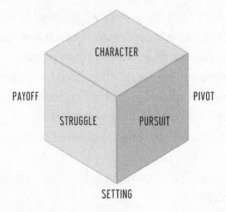

three-dimensional story. Without them, not so much. Without all six sides, the story will ring hollow.

This is why case studies don't necessarily make great stories. For instance: "A customer was having a difficult time until he tried our product. Now he's happy and fulfilled!" Why doesn't that narrative work? After all, it has a character with a struggle, and it even contains a beginning, a middle, and an end—three acts! Just like a summer blockbuster!

It doesn't work because everyone who's listening can guess how it's going to end. It's too predictable. Also, there's no payoff—no insights or deeper meaning.

Instead, look for accounts of underdogs who solve things in unexpected ways or stories that share deep truths without stating outright what they are. (See Tom's example of this on pages 285–286.)

For instance, including the pivot and the payoff often means looking for moments of dissonance or resonance in the stories you tell. What part of the story deeply affects or impacts you? What moment couldn't the story live without? What aspect of this story is desperate to be told or impossible to ignore?

Remember, every story is driven by tension: a character is hindered in some way from reaching a goal. Struggles should be intriguing and surprising. Listeners are most satisfied when they can't guess the ending, but will appreciate it in retrospect. Some people conceptualize the struggle at the heart of the story by asking the following questions:

- What is the problem/solution?
- What is the goal/conclusion?
- What is the desire/fulfillment?
- What is the tension/release?
- What is the complication/resolution?
- What is the journey/destination?

Any of those questions can be helpful, as long as there's a pivot and a payoff included in the story as well.

When establishing your story's main character, ask, "What does she want?" "What is at stake?" "Why should my listeners care?"

THE CAUTIONARY TALE OF BRYAN THE BARBER

Often, stories are about transformations or revelations. Keeping that in mind helps me find my place in the story, because the characters who struggle—not the ones who have all the answers—are the ones listeners will be able to identify with most closely.

If it's a personal story, that struggle might reveal something *to* you or something *about* you—both can be valuable and worthwhile stories to tell. Before you worry about polishing your story, make sure it has the framework to stand on its own. Is there a relatable character? A specific setting? A moment of discovery? A changed life or perspective?

Sometimes the change is subtle. Sometimes it's just hinted at.

And sometimes it happens to someone other than who you might expect.

The man who used to be my barber had been working in the same corner barbershop all of his adult life. Nearly forty years. Whenever I'd go in for a trim, Bryan would complain to me about having to stand up all day, six days a week, ten hours a day. Or he'd lament the lack of benefits, or how he never got enough time off. Honestly, I got tired of it and sometimes I just wished the moment was over and the haircut was done. "But," he told me one day, "I'm only three years from retiring. Then I'll finally be able to enjoy myself."

"Sounds nice."

From then on, he counted down the years, then the months, then the weeks to me.

As he snipped away at my hair, he would tell me about all the stuff he wanted to do when he finally retired—bass fishing and deer hunting and playing golf.

Just two weeks before his retirement, I went to get a haircut, and there was a sign on the locked door: Bryan was in the hospital. Heart attack. "Thoughts and prayers appreciated," the note said.

Tragically, he never came home again.

Bryan never got the chance to go fishing or hunting or golfing. He'd put all those things off. For forty years. Standing up all day, six days a week, ten hours a day. Dreaming about the future and letting the present slip away. Thinking all those someday thoughts.

I catch myself, sometimes, doing it too. *One day, one day, one day* . . . Thinking those things just like Bryan did. Now, when I go to my new barber to get my hair cut I remember that sign. That locked door. Someday thoughts. And I don't wish the moment was over.

In fact, I'm glad it's not.

If I had to drive home the point of this story, I could add that all of us face a daily choice: We can long for a future that might never arrive, dwell on a past that can never change, or celebrate and embrace the possibilities that only today offers. (But I'm not convinced I need to explain any of that. I think the message comes through just fine in the story itself, without elaboration.)

Could I tell the story simply about Bryan dying? Sure. But it wouldn't have quite the same poignancy. "Once there was a barber who died," isn't much of a story. "Once there was a man who learned to embrace life," is more on track. The pivot comes when you realize the story isn't ultimately about Bryan; it's about me. The payoff is the change in my attitude at the end of the story.

Whether they comfort you or trouble you, whether you love them or hate them, find stories that you can connect with on an emotional level. Those are the ones that will touch your listeners' hearts even if you can't succinctly summarize what the stories *mean*. As novelist Kurt Vonnegut Jr. wrote, "Find a subject you care about and which you in your heart feel others should care about. It is this genuine caring, and not your games with language, which will be the most compelling and seductive element in your style."

That's the payoff in a story.

WHEN TELLING YOUR STORY, REMEMBER:

- Character—Give us someone to cheer for.
- Setting—Help us see what's happening.
- Struggle—Introduce a difficulty that needs to be overcome.
- Pursuit—Track the character's progress.
- Pivot—Include a satisfying surprise.
- Payoff—Make sure the story is worthwhile.

▪ ▪ ▪

A few years ago, I was teaching writers in Switzerland, and one of the women was from Uganda. I mentioned that I'd heard a saying from Africa: "Something happens and then a story comes along and finds it." She corrected me, "That's close! It's, 'When an event occurs, a story discovers itself.'"

I like it.

(Actually, I like both sayings!)

Sometimes, events occur in our lives and, in a strange sort of way, stories discover themselves in our hearts. They grab hold of us and won't let us go. Whether they make us smile, weep, shiver, or pound the table, they affect us. The image or memory resonates with who we are and fits the shape of our souls. That's natural. Each of us has certain holes inside of us that will be filled by differently shaped stories.

How can you tell when a story is filling the hole Steven talks about? Not long ago, I met a man who, driving home after work late one night, saw a vehicle ahead lose control, flip, and land upside down in a pond. This man called 911 and then leapt into the dark, cold water. He was able to get everyone out of the car except one small passenger—a four-year-old trapped in his car seat. This man stayed in the car, holding the little boy's head out of the water for close to an hour until help arrived and an emergency team was able to free the child from the wreckage.

Every time I share that story, listeners gasp. That is the sound of the hole being filled.

—TOM

"WOW. LOOK AT THE WORLD."

Our lives are rich with stories. Once we begin to open our eyes, we'll start to see stories emerging from everywhere. But that's the secret: opening our eyes.

I spent the summer after my freshman year in college working as a camp counselor for a YMCA camp in northern Wisconsin. (I know, outdoor education again!) That year, we hosted a session for children with special needs. Each cabin was limited to five children, ages five to eight, with two adult counselors and a full-time therapist assigned to it.

That gives you an idea of the individualized attention required for each of the campers.

One boy thought he was an airplane and would fly off everywhere—typically in the opposite direction from where we were supposed to be going. Another boy didn't use the toilet because he'd seen a television commercial with a toilet that had teeth, so he was terrified of them. (That created its own set of unique challenges for all of us.)

But it's Philip who I remember the most. He'd just finished second grade.

Six months earlier, he'd stopped talking.

No one knew what the problem was, but he was obviously having a difficult time fitting in and adjusting to his class at school.

"He won't talk," his mom told us when she dropped him off. "But he'll listen."

And she was right. For the first three days of camp, as we played games, went swimming, made craft projects out of popsicle sticks, and the rest of us sang camp songs, he did listen.

But he didn't speak.

Well, it was the fourth day of camp and it'd been raining all morning, putting a crimp on our activities. Being cooped up in the cabin had made us all a little stir crazy. The other counselor was zoned out, strumming absently on his guitar; the therapist was speaking in hushed tones with the boy who liked to fly away into his own world; and I was on the porch, desperately trying to come up with something we could do in the cabin to pass the time.

As I was reviewing my notebook of indoor game ideas, the rain broke, and a few minutes later Philip joined me on the porch. When he did, I glanced up from my notebook and noticed a double rainbow cresting the sky, but I was so focused on my work that I quickly went back to my brainstorming without giving it another thought.

But when Philip looked up, he didn't turn away. He just stood there stock-still beside me on the porch and stared at the heavens, at those twin rainbows, at the sunlight streaming through the narrow gaps in the gray, anvil-shaped storm clouds. And then Philip held his arms out as if he were trying to embrace the day, and he said the only words I ever heard him speak. The first words that, as far as we knew, anyone had heard him utter in half a year.

As he stood there, arms outstretched, Philip said in a bright, astonished voice, "Wow. Look at the world."

And then he glanced back at me, lowered his arms, and was quiet again, disappearing into whatever place he'd retreated to six months earlier.

But I did look. I opened my eyes and I looked at the world—at the rainbows and the clouds and the illuminating sunlight finding its way toward me. Something deep inside of me stirred and I marveled at the beauty before me and the child who'd managed to get me to open my eyes and notice it.

I never heard Philip speak again. But he taught me more in that one sentence than some people ever learn in a lifetime.

On the porch that day, next to the list of activities I was hoping to do, I wrote in my notebook, "Look at the world. Be amazed."

Maybe Philip had something to do with my journey toward becoming a storyteller, something to do with my goal of trying to help other people open their eyes and glimpse, even for just a moment, the wonder of the world that we so often miss.

Wow.

Look at the world.

Yes, Philip. I will.

I am.

▪ ▪ ▪

What stories have found you? Tell the ones that matter to you—that whisper and scream and rattle against the cage of your heart and beg to be told. As preaching professor Richard L. Thulin noted, "Any event that evokes an emotional response from us is a personal story in embryo. It is worth retelling and exploring."

The event doesn't need to be something extraordinary. It isn't the unusual that will necessarily draw people in, but the unexpected accentuation of the familiar. Open your eyes, speak from your heart, and direct our attention to what we all see but don't always notice. That's where the poignancy of your story will lie. Start with what is normal, end with what is new.

Maybe it's the emotions of the story or the poetry of the language or the message or the images or the humor that draws you in. Maybe you don't even know what it is, but the story has grabbed you and won't let you go.

That's a story that has discovered its place in your life. That's a story to hold onto. To tell.

This book will help you do precisely that.

SUMMARY

As you develop your storytelling skills, you'll be able to make your stories more engaging, interesting, and humorous, but for now remind yourself, "My listeners are on my side. They're not out to get me, or to laugh at me, or to embarrass me. They want to hear an entertaining story. They want me to succeed. I am a storyteller. My stories matter and I can tell them well."

Introduce us to a memorable and irresistible character who faces a pressing and intimate struggle. Give her choices and sacrifices that matter. Invite us to see the pursuit unfold in an evocative setting. Then, lead us to gasp at the pivot, and nod at the unstated, yet unforgettable, payoff.

Stories have the ability to underwhelm people. To sneak past their radar. To climb in through the window while your listeners are busy boarding up the front door. They slip past our natural defenses, take up residence in the important parts of our hearts, and impact us with the truth. A story doesn't just touch heads, it touches—and changes—lives.

Key Points to Remember

- Embrace the fact that stories build bridges within us and between us. They help us learn and make discoveries of our own.
- Adapt your storytelling to the event. Different social settings have different expectations as far as who speaks, when they do, and for how long.
- Focus on including all six sides of the Story Cube in your stories: character, setting, struggle, pursuit, pivot, and payoff.
- Since stories are about unmet desires, think of them in terms of *pursuit* rather than *plot*. To track a story's progress, don't ask, "What happens?" but rather, "What's pursued?"
- Look at the world with open eyes. Stories are searching for you. Let them find you. And let them discover themselves in your life.

CHAPTER 2

STORIES ARE GREAT . . . FOR OTHER PEOPLE?

—TOM

"The moment you doubt whether you can fly,
you cease for ever to be able to do it."
—J. M. Barrie, novelist and playwright, in his play *Peter Pan*

We'll call him Howard.

Howard was vice chairman of a world-renowned Fortune 500 company, responsible for expanding its business to developing nations. He spoke on his company's behalf frequently—sometimes several times a week—and I was responsible for helping him develop those talks.

Howard was wise, astute, and a warm and engaging person . . . once you got to know him. But it took a while to get to know him.

Quite a while.

Howard bore an uncanny resemblance to the farmer in the Grant Wood painting *American Gothic*. Unfortunately, when he stepped up to the lectern, he projected a personality to match. You could almost feel the frost creeping into the room.

This was something I noted the first time I attended one of his speaking engagements. I came away certain that we needed to warm

Howard up. He was the ambassador for his brand—the man who needed to convince trade ministers, presidents, prime ministers, and media representatives that their countries and his company had a future together. He wasn't advancing that mission by coming off as dour and distancing at the microphone.

So, one evening, as we flew home to the Midwest on the corporate jet from a conference in New York City, I waited until the flight attendant had retired to the gallery. It was just Howard and me in the cabin, in seats facing one another, and I mentioned an upcoming event in Detroit. I suggested that he open his remarks there with a story.

"No," he replied, not even looking up from his *Financial Times*.

For better or worse, if you slam a door in my face, I'm the sort of person who usually knocks on it. It's gotten me in trouble more than once, but in this case, I decided to risk it.

"Howard, I don't understand. I work with the chairman of your company as well, and he uses stories all the time. They work really well for him."

Howard lowered the newspaper.

"That's the chairman," he said. "He's wonderful at things like that. He's a natural performer, and that's his style."

He raised the newspaper again.

"So, what are you telling me?" I asked. "That you don't like stories?"

> Notice Tom's approach here. Of course Howard liked stories— the secret was finding a way to help him admit to himself that he could also be a storyteller. This is a good example of a communicator knowing his audience!
>
> **—STEVEN**

This time, the newspaper came down just far enough for me to see the Grant Wood spectacles.

"Of course, I like them. A good story, well told? Very effective. But . . ." He raised the newspaper again. "I'm not a storyteller."

The flight attendant brought us moist towels, and we set our reading materials aside as she arranged the tray table between us and served a light dinner.

"My wife and another couple and I went to a comedy club last weekend," I said as I dipped a bite of salad in dressing. I mentioned who we had seen: an extremely well-known comedian.

"He was at a club?" Howard asked. "He's very good. I didn't know he did clubs anymore. I saw him on HBO just last year."

"Yes. The club only sells general admission, so I tipped the host twenty dollars, and he put us at a table that butted right up against the center of the stage."

Howard smiled. "Pretty good, for a five-buck-a-head tip."

"No kidding. When the comedian came out to do his act, his mic cord actually landed on our table a few times. He wound up doing much of his act directly to the four of us."

"Sounds like a memorable evening."

"It was." I showed Howard my phone, with a photo of my wife and me with the comedian after the show.

"You met him!"

"It's a small club," I said, "so he invited the audience to stay after the show if they wanted pictures. And when he met my wife and me, he thanked us."

"Thanked you? For what?"

"He said that he was getting ready for his next television special, which was why he was touring the country and playing small clubs. I think his exact words were, 'When I come up with a new gag, I *suspect* that it's funny, but I don't *know* that it's funny until I've tried it out on people, and you can tell how funny it is by the way people react.' He pointed to my wife, and said, 'I had you laughing so hard that you were crying a couple times, and that's gold! Those are bits that I'm definitely going to use.' So, he was genuinely grateful for our reactions. We helped him validate his material."

Howard chewed a sliver of salmon and nodded.

"That's smart," he said. "Using small venues to try out new material."

I finished my salmon before mentioning, in what I hoped was an offhanded way, "You know, Howard, you can do the same thing with stories."

He removed his spectacles and sat back in his seat.

"Okay, Tom," he said. "What are you trying to sell me?"

PLAY THE SMALL VENUES

What I sold Howard was this: I told him a story—one that he agreed segued well into his main topic for the Detroit event. Then I got out a notebook and wrote the story down. I tore the pages out and handed them to him.

"This is *not* a script," I explained. "I don't want you to read it aloud. This is just to refresh your memory so the story will come back to you easily. Do you eat breakfast with your family most mornings?"

Howard nodded. "With my wife, usually, but our son's home from grad school right now, so it's the three of us."

"Good. Tell them this story at breakfast tomorrow. Use the pages as a prompt if you need to, but, again, don't read it. Tell it. And try not to share that you're testing it on them. Just work it into the conversation."

Howard squinted at the pages. Then he nodded at me. "All right. I'll give it a shot."

The next morning, as soon as Howard got to the office, I called and asked him how breakfast had gone.

"They laughed at the funny part," he said, with just a little bit of wonder in his voice.

"Great. Who are you having lunch with today?"

"My steering committee."

"Perfect. I'm sending you the same story, but broken down into bullet points. Ask your assistant to print them out for you on note cards—take them with you to lunch. Tell the story to your steering committee, and try not to look at the notes unless you need to."

We did that for a couple of days. Every time Howard had a meal with people who hadn't heard the story, he told it to them, and every time, his list of bullet points grew smaller and smaller.

One morning he called me and asked, "You know that part in the story where the traffic stops because there's a flock of sheep on the road? I'm finding that I get a better reaction if I call it a herd of goats. Can it be goats? Is that okay?"

"You're fine-tuning, and that's exactly what I want you to do. If goats work better, then goats they are."

After a week of telling his story at meals and meetings, adjusting the elements for better reactions and tailoring the details, twists, and turns to his immediate audience, Howard had become very comfortable with the story. He no longer used notes of any kind. In fact, when we used it at the Detroit event, all the teleprompter displayed when we came to that part was: "[TELL STORY]."

Detroit was a watershed moment. The audience reaction was noticeably warmer, there was laughter in the room, and the train of people waiting to speak with Howard after the event had concluded was much longer than usual.

When we met to discuss his next speaking engagement, Howard's first question for me was, "What story do we want to use?"

A BREAK FROM THE SPEECH

Although a sizable number of people know me from my novels, I have enjoyed a considerably longer career in the corporate world.

I worked in publishing and advertising for a while, and was a vice president at firms that did both of those things, but really found my stride when I moved into public relations and public affairs.

My business card for my current corporate role says that I work in public affairs and that I handle executive communications. Nowhere does it say that I am a speechwriter. In fact, I have never had a business card that identifies me as a speechwriter.

Yet speechwriting is a principal part of my job.

I write speeches and, in many cases, senior executives rehearse and deliver what I have written for them, word for word. There are specific reasons for this.

Litigation is a fact of life for most sizable corporations, and public statements made by executives can be used during lawsuits as implied guarantees, statements of policy, or evidence of slander. I know this and write accordingly. It has kept me on a cordial first-name basis with the legal teams at the companies for which I've worked.

In addition, almost all of the companies I've worked with in this capacity have been publicly traded. That's important: the Securities and Exchange Commission sets strict limits on what an executive can say without venturing into the murky waters of "forward-looking statements" or other material that could be construed as swaying current or potential shareholders.

When a company is in the midst of a public relations campaign, consistency of message is also extremely important. If everyone is trying to find their own way of communicating something, the message can be reduced to a blur of gray noise. So, particularly in the bits of key messages that are apt to wind up on the evening news—those brief clips known as "sound bites"—it's often imperative that executives say the same things in the same way, preferably using the same words.

A key goal, of course, is to have senior executives do this without reducing them to "talking heads"—puppets delivering the company line.

It helps in this regard to carefully examine scripts and ensure that every paragraph, every sentence, every phrase, and every word sounds like something a person would say in everyday conversation.

It's vital to tell stories in a way that draws listeners in. Author and storyteller Donald Davis once taught me that it's sometimes helpful to shift your perspective from telling someone *the story* of an experience, to simply telling them *about* it. That simple change in framing can take the pressure off and help you recount the events in an authentic, comfortable, and engaging way. So, mentally reframe things: "Let me tell you about what happened when I got cut from the soccer team when I was in eighth grade . . ." And then, in your own words, take your listeners through the story.

—STEVEN

One of the first things I tell new people in my department is, "Avoid corporate mumbo-jumbo. If you see a phrase that sounds like the company talking, get rid of it. If a phrase is trending on LinkedIn, avoid the temptation to jump on that bandwagon, because that phrase will just be another piece of buzz by the time the year's up. Make sure what you're writing sounds like something your particular speaker would actually say."

A logical question at this point is: If we are striving so hard to make a script sound natural when it comes from a particular executive, why isn't that executive writing the speech? Why are we doing it for them?

Usually, that question comes in this form, "Can't they write their own speeches?"

The answer, in almost every case, is, "Yes. Absolutely, they can."

Most of the executives I've been fortunate enough to work with are extremely well-spoken people. But the fact is that by the time I have consulted with subject-matter experts, written the speech, and vetted it with the many people who have a fiduciary responsibility to review it, I've used up every bit of a forty-hour workweek, and then some. If an executive did all that, no one would be running the company. Essentially, I write the speeches, not because I do it better, but to provide those leaders with a bit of breathing room.

So, I often write the vast majority of what a speaker is going to say, and I work hard to make sure that what I'm writing flows naturally—that it uses the phrasing, inflections, and pet words particular to that speaker.

But the icing on that personalization cake—the part that makes it obvious that what you're hearing is Jane Smith, and not Cogswell Cogs or whatever company it is that Jane works for—is when Jane steps away from the script for a moment to tell a story in her own way, unfettered and unfiltered.

When a script is being used, no matter how polished the presenter, the audience is usually conscious that they are being read to. A story, known well by the speaker, is an opportunity for the speaker's personality to shine more brightly, because the script can be set aside, removing that subtle barrier between speaker and audience.

Moreover, once they've become familiar with the stories they're sharing, executives have told me that they consider the stories to be the most comfortable parts of their presentations—a chance to "speak from the heart" and truly interact with the audience. The story, if second nature, becomes a welcome break from the script.

THE SILENT REACTION

My wife has Cherokee lineage in her family tree, so every once in a while I find myself attending a powwow or visiting a reservation.

According to the federal government, there are 574 tribes, nations, bands, pueblos, communities, and native villages in the United States. Because all of these groups are recognized as American Indian, many people assume that they are all essentially the same, especially since most powwows welcome participants from any federally recognized tribe.

Jumping to that conclusion is a mistake. Chinook people and Navajo people are as different from Creek people as Irish and Danes are from Italians. The various tribes and nations have their own languages, customs, and standards of etiquette. In some settings, for instance, it is a grave insult to smell food before tasting it, while in others, smelling food is just part of dinnertime ambience.

I have, however, noticed two taboos that seem to transcend tribal boundaries.

One has to do with pointing with the fingers or the hands. To most native people, this is considered coarse and rude (although it is generally tolerated without comment when outsiders point). The accepted way of indicating direction is to lift the head and point with the chin.

The other seemingly universal American Indian taboo is against speaking while someone else is already talking. Listeners are expected to wait until they are certain a speaker has finished before voicing their own opinions.

This means that native conversations tend to be punctuated with pauses—but it certainly does not mean that no conversation ensues.

From what I've seen, even though native listeners won't speak while someone else is talking, that doesn't stop them from reacting. They'll smile slightly, raise an eyebrow, nod gently, grunt in assent, possibly even chuckle, or—if they want to register profound disagreement—listen without any visible reaction whatsoever.

Only one person is speaking, but an entire roomful of opinions is being shared. Sometimes a speaker will even alter course mid-sentence based on the reactions being displayed (but not voiced) by the audience.

Unless your venue is a nightclub, complete with hecklers, story-telling to a group is very much like that. You may be the only one speaking, but you are leading a conversation, nonetheless.

> This interplay of a storyteller with his listeners and the impor-tance of responsiveness in storytelling is something we'll ex-plore in more depth later in the book. No matter your culture or the venue, being willing and able to adapt to the circum-stances and alter your story on the fly is important.
>
> **—STEVEN**

You can tell if you are engaging the audience by gauging the laughter and murmurs throughout the room, and you can tell if you are losing your audience by the number of heads down, looking at screens (although this is not necessarily the kiss of death—some of them may merely be sharing your latest sound bite on social media).

Naturally, you want your audience to be engaged during your story. The best way to do that is to try it out with a succession of small groups, beginning with your most empathic listeners (family and friends) and gradually moving to listeners who are less emotion-ally involved (business colleagues).

With stories, you can simply work your material into everyday group conversations. Or, if you want, you can do formal run-throughs.

One executive I worked with—the chief financial officer for a major corporation—would move the tables out of a large conference room, set up the chairs theater-style, bring in a lectern, fill the room with his staff, and rehearse both his scripts and his stories this way. While he always asked the audience what they thought of the material, he didn't place a lot of credence in the feedback (they did, after all, work for him). Instead, I would watch the group from the side of the room, he would note reactions from the lectern, and the two of us would compare notes after the audience had dispersed. We'd tweak the script and its accompanying story based on that, and a few days later we'd invite a new group in and rehearse again. By the time he got to his speaking engagement, this particular executive was prepared to tell his story.

THE EXCEPTION (THAT DOES SOMETHING OR OTHER) TO THE RULE

In roughly three decades of working with executives on their engagement strategies, I can think of only one time that I advised a leader against rehearsing his story in front of others. In fact, it is the one and only situation in which I recommended that an executive refrain from rehearsing at all.

His company was about to have a global safety conference, shared via video across five sites in Asia, Europe, and North America. We were preparing four hours of content based around two primary themes—"24/7 safe" and "prevent the irretrievable moment"—and, as part of the conference theme, I was asking each participating executive to share a brief, three-to-five-minute personal story that would reflect one or both of those themes.

I always looked forward to meeting with this one executive—we'll call him Dave—because he always had great, and frequently hilarious, stories. But on this occasion, when I asked Dave if any story came to mind for the safety conference, the smile melted from his face.

"Yes," he said. "But it's . . . difficult."

"Try me."

Dave told me a story about his daughter's best friend in high school. Both girls were on the soccer team, and while his daughter was a talented and competitive player, her friend was an absolute cut above: recruited by several major universities and considered a strong candidate for a future Olympic team.

"She's my daughter's best friend, but to our family she's been like a second daughter for years," Dave said. "Friday and Saturday nights, we just got in the habit of setting an extra place at the dinner table because we knew she'd be joining us."

Then, on a Saturday morning in her senior year, everything changed in an instant. She and some classmates were conducting a charity car wash, and she walked behind a car at the same moment that one of the boys was jumping in to move it. He mistakenly put the car in reverse, there was a cinder-block wall behind the car, and the girl was knocked down and pinned between the wall and the car. Her spinal cord was injured and the accident resulted in paraplegia: paralysis from the waist down.

"She's a great kid," Dave said, his voice cracking. "Even today, she inspires everyone she meets with her positive outlook on life. But still . . . when I think of what she lost, in the blink of an eye . . . I'd give everything I have if I could just go back in time and . . ."

Dave stopped talking. Tears were rolling down his face.

"Don't worry," he told me, turning away to blow his nose. "I know the drill. I'll practice the story in front of people until I can keep it together all the way through it."

I considered this.

"Actually," I said. "I don't think you should practice. Use the story, but don't tell it again until the conference."

Dave straightened up.

"Tom, it's a global teleconference. If I don't practice, I'm going to lose it in front of the better part of a thousand people."

"And if you lose it, you may inspire someone in your audience to exercise that extra bit of vigilance that spares someone else from another terrible injury like this."

Dave looked down at his desk and then up at me.

"You're right," he said. "I'll do it."

Dave's a brave guy. He kept his word and kept his story close to the vest. On the day of the conference, he was speaking on camera from the West Coast. I was in the audience, watching the screen on the East Coast, and even from more than two thousand miles away, I saw the glisten of tears in his eyes and heard his voice quaver and then stop. It was the turning point in the conference—the moment when we stopped viewing the statistics in terms of numbers and started to think of them in terms of valuable and vulnerable human beings.

That conference was eleven years ago, and people still talk about that moment and the impact it had on them.

Now—and Steven and I are in complete accord on this—ninety-nine times out of a hundred, tears during a story are a bad idea. They make everyone, storyteller and listeners alike, uncomfortable. Plus, if the storyteller is clearly using tears to milk the audience for empathy, it's simply embarrassing for all concerned—nobody can get out of the auditorium fast enough.

The same is true of uncontrolled laughter. If you think what you have to say is so hilarious that you can't spit a complete sentence out without doubling up and slapping your knees, then you haven't thought your story through to the point where it is ready for an audience.

When pain is an observation and not a "poor, poor, pitiful me" reflection, or when laughter is in appreciation of someone else's comic genius, then maybe—just maybe—it might be what the moment calls for.

But in all of my years of coaching speakers, I've only encountered one such moment. Most stories need to be rehearsed—and it's best to do so in front of listeners.

THE PUPPY AND THE FACE-PLANT

After the same safety conference, the president of our company (we'll call her Mary) wanted to stress one point—that safety could not concern our people only while they were on the clock. We knew that the people who consistently made good decisions around safety were those who thought about the safe way to do things literally every waking hour. The safest people at work tended to be the people who went above and beyond to stay safe *everywhere*—during their commute, while mowing their own lawns, while walking across the parking lot at the shopping mall.

The subject was so important to Mary that she decided to have a face-to-face conversation on the topic with every salaried leader in the company—about eight thousand people.

We combined and divided department rosters to come up with a series of eighty-three meetings spaced out over a little less than half a year, with attendance at each capped at one hundred participants. We'd begin with no more than ten minutes of comments by Mary and then open the floor for questions and discussion.

Mary and I had worked together for years, so it went without saying that her comments would include a story. We came up with a short narrative about how, rather than beelining straight to her car when she left our headquarters building, she took care to walk to the crosswalk, conscious of the scores of windows at her back and the probability that someone was watching to see if she, too, followed the rules.

It was a pretty good story, but—unluckily—we soon had a better one tossed into our laps.

It was the first week that we were conducting our safety-conference conversations, and I had just checked the venue for that morning's meeting when my cell phone rang. It was Mary.

"Can you find some antibiotic cream and a Band-Aid or two?" she asked. "I had a bit of a mishap."

Just to be sure, I met Mary at her car with a registered nurse and two EMTs (a fact of which she reminds me to this day). As we walked to the first-aid station, she explained what had happened.

"I was going upstairs, stepped on the hem of my robe, and tripped," she said. "I'm okay, but I've got a rug burn from the stair runner on my knee."

Then, when she was sitting on the exam table in the first-aid station, she added that her husband—a commercial airline captain—was long accustomed to seeing the world through a safety lens and had frequently implored her to use the handrail when going up and down the stairs.

As the nurse finished wrapping her knee with gauze, Mary said, "You'd think that today of all days, when we have this event scheduled, safety should have been the first thing on my mind."

As soon as she said that, we looked at each other and said, "We've got to use this as our story!"

We went to the ballroom where the meeting was being held, and she used the new story, generating nice measures of concern and restrained chuckles from the crowd. Still, as I walked her to the car, Mary said, "It's an ironic story, so it should be funny, but people weren't sure if they should laugh. We need to make it obvious that they can."

In unfamiliar settings or events where you're the guest speaker, clarifying expectations is huge. Even if they don't realize it, the people in the audience want to be cued in on what reactions are appropriate for them. Often, composure and a warm demeanor will do wonders to set an audience at ease.

Also, see how Tom worked with Mary to edit and craft the story? They wisely let the audience's reaction affect the story's development. They didn't start with a finished product, so to speak. The story morphed with each retelling—and Mary was wise enough to let it do so.

—STEVEN

The next morning, we met, and I asked, "How long is your robe, anyhow?"

Mary laughed. "Ankle length. I always think the house is too cold and my husband says it's too warm, so he bought me the robe for Christmas as a compromise."

"We should add that in." I made a note. "And why weren't you holding the handrail?"

"Both of my hands were full."

I nodded. "What was in your right hand?"

"A glass."

"Iced tea?" As I asked, Mary sighed and then nodded. Around work, the joke was that her blood type was "Lipton."

I made another note and then asked, "And what was in your left hand?"

"Sylvie; she's afraid to go up and down the stairs. But if I say that, I'll have to explain. Maybe I should just say, 'My dog.'"

I shook my head. "If you do, half the audience pictures you carrying a Yorkie and the other half has you lugging a Saint Bernard."

"So, I should say, 'miniature dachshund'?"

"All we want is to convey that it's a small dog. A puppy is a small dog, and I like the word 'puppy.' It has that 'ooh' factor. We'll say you were carrying a puppy."

The next safety meeting we had, Mary tried the story with those changes, and the people in the audience visibly cringed when she mentioned tripping, so Mary—reading their reaction correctly—blurted out, "The puppy was fine! No puppies were injured in the making of this safety story!"

It worked so well that we used these exclamations in every further telling of the story.

There were additional tweaks. We changed the trip to a "face-plant" on the stairs. The sound of the phrase earned the nervous laughter we were looking for. Mary even worked me into the story, describing how a simple request for a bandage resulted in me mobilizing a makeshift emergency room. By the time we were on our tenth meeting, the story had evolved to a great self-deprecating piece of humor—the president of the company confessing that even she had lapses that she needed to mend, as she humbly asked the audience to join her on the journey.

Over the remaining seventy or so meetings, Mary's timing evolved. She inserted an onomatopoeic "whap!" before the phrase "face-plant," and we learned to pause for thirty seconds after telling the story, so the laughter could die down.

Today, Mary is retired but still touring on the lecture circuit, and when the subject is safety she trots that story out like the trooper that she is. It never fails to get a great reaction, and that's hardly surprising—she's rehearsed it eighty-three times in front of live audiences.

SUMMARY

There are many reasons why people shy away from storytelling when they speak. Some of this is tied to ego; they are afraid they will look silly when telling a story to other adults. Some of this is based on insecurity; they are worried that the "softness" of narrative could hamper their careers. Still others are concerned that they don't have the skills to share a story.

But a major reason for story shyness is fear. Many people fear the way that a story draws the focus away from the subject and places it on them. Stage fright is a common phobia, but is fairly easy to overcome once you realize that the audience wants you to deliver a great talk.

Your audience came to hear you—not only for your content, but also because they want to know you better and they want to be entertained. A story opens the window that your audience desires. It forms a connection. And the wonderful thing about a story is that the more you tell it, the better you hone it and the easier it becomes to tell.

Key Points to Remember

- Don't read your story; *tell* it. Use cheat sheets the first few times you do so, but try to wean yourself from them as soon as possible. Trust the fact that a story is the sort of narrative that human beings are born to tell.
- Try out your story on friends and family at first, and then rehearse in front of colleagues and acquaintances.
- Once you're freed from reading a script, you have the luxury of looking at your listeners and reading their reactions. Use this as a tool to adjust your timing and phrasing.
- Be extremely cautious about excessive emotional displays such as tears and laughter. In the vast majority of instances, they tend to embarrass listeners and make them feel uncomfortable.
- A presentation is nothing more than another rehearsal, but on steroids. Use every presentation as an opportunity to further hone the story.

CHAPTER 3

THE THREE QUESTIONS THAT WILL CHANGE EVERYTHING

—STEVEN

"Men . . . hardly stir except when jolted by imagination."
—Blaise Pascal, seventeenth-century philosopher and mathematician

Once, about a decade ago, I was listening to a professional speaker explain how important self-control is. Yes, that was it. His entire point was, "Self-control is good." Of course, this was something I already knew. And by the looks on the faces of the four hundred other people in the auditorium, I wasn't the only one who was finding his talk dull. Folks all around me were surreptitiously checking their phones, glancing at their watches, and trying unsuccessfully to hide their yawns. Not good signs for a presenter.

However, if he noticed any of that, it didn't affect his speech. He just continued plowing forward, explaining to us what we already knew.

I found myself doodling and then absentmindedly scribbling down a sentence that, at the time, I had no idea would alter the entire trajectory of my teaching and storytelling from that day forward.

Here's what I jotted down: "Never tell people what they already know in a way they already expect."

I drew a few more curlicues on the side of the page (I'm not a very gifted doodler), then my gaze settled on those words again and suddenly, as the man at the lectern droned on, the impact of that sentence hit me full force. It was all I could think about.

As I stared at the words, I realized that if I truly put them into practice, it would result in a tectonic shift in the foundational questions I asked when preparing a presentation. It would affect how I thought about my listeners and their readiness to learn what I was teaching; their expectations, desires, and understanding would all necessarily come into play.

It would change everything.

And it has.

Never tell people what they already know in a way they already expect.

Now, I should mention that if you're telling people something they *don't* know, some explanation will probably be necessary. Many people don't have the faintest idea how trigonometry works, and so some explaining would likely be needed in a lecture about it. However, if you're telling your listeners something that they *do* know—such as how important self-control is—you'll need to find another, unexpected pathway past their defenses and into their attention spans.

Imagine that you're at a marriage conference and the presenter says, "It's important for you to listen to your spouse." No one is sitting there in the audience thinking, *Listen to your spouse?! I had no idea! That's life-changing advice! No one ever told me any of this before! This stuff is amazing!*

Of course not. The listeners already know what they're being told, and the information will have little or no impact on their lives. So, evaluate what you're trying to teach. Is it information that people have heard before? Then present it in a new way. Is it information they already know ("You should be honest," "You should work hard," etc.)? Then ask how you can share the truths in a way they don't expect.

Stories work wonderfully for doing that. (Remember the pivot? It turns expectations on their head. Often, the best stories are ultimately about something that they don't initially seem to be about.)

What you're saying has probably been said before. Why should these people here listen to you say it now—especially if you're telling it to them in a way that's predictable and, therefore, boring?

Many presenters start their preparation with the assumption that information dissemination is the best way to teach or inspire others. (I know I used to.) People who adhere to this paradigm start by asking three questions:

1. "How can I explain this?"
2. "How can I clarify this?"
3. "How can I help people understand this?"

Now, there's nothing *wrong* with these questions. It's just that they're not the best place to start. This whole approach is built on the assumption that the more people know, the more they will change. But is that true?

TEARS THAT TRULY MATTER

Sometimes I cry when I watch movies. Not often or anything. It's not a huge issue, and I usually hide it when I do, but sometimes, yes, I cry.

Yet the weird thing is, I almost never cry in real life. When I jam my finger playing basketball, I act tough. When one of my books gets a miserable review, I go and build something with a hammer and lots and lots of helpless nails. But I don't weep. Even when I find out someone I know has died, I don't usually cry. I get really quiet. I feel sad about it. I don't know what to say. But I don't typically cry. At least not right away.

On December 26, 2004, an earthquake that measured between 9.1 and 9.3 on the Richter scale rocked Southeast Asia near the island of Sumatra, sending out a series of tsunami waves traveling at 500 miles per hour. At first the reports said 12,000 people were killed. A few days later they thought it was 45,000. Then 76,000. Then 155,000. Every day, the total rose; on January 25, 2005, it was up to 288,000 people. Later, I heard it might be half a million. In the weeks that followed the tragedy, I found myself turning on the news to see what the new number was. But I didn't cry.

I was talking with my friend Jason about it at the time, and I shook my head and mentioned that I hadn't cried yet. "What's wrong with me?" I said.

He was quiet for a moment and then he said, "Whatever's wrong with you is wrong with me too."

We didn't anguish over those deaths. We just went on with life, flipping the channel at night to catch the next episode of *CSI*. Or maybe popping in a movie and breaking out the tissues.

■ ■ ■

Let me put it this way: Imagine that your pet dog, the one you love, the one you've had for ten years, gets hit by a truck in front of your house. You rush out to try to save him, but find that, sadly, it's too late. Would you cry then? Many people (I'd say most of us) would. But when hundreds of thousands of people die in a tragedy on the other side of the world, we don't.

Why not?

Certainly, we *know* that the loss of more than a quarter of a million human lives is a greater tragedy than the loss of one dog. We *know* this. This issue has nothing to do with lack of knowledge.

So, would more education help?

I doubt it.

A teacher might *explain* to me that I should mourn when I hear about the tragedies like the ones I've listed. She might help *clarify* when to cry and when not to. She might do all she can to help me *understand* the value of human life, but even with all of those additional facts and all of that added information, I doubt my reaction would change. Why?

Because, while it's true that information dissemination can lead to increased knowledge, it doesn't necessarily lead to personal *transformation*.

Think of that dog. You have a history with him, a connection with him, and an emotional investment in his life. That affects you more than knowledge does. If you lost him, you are experiencing loss personally, not just thinking about it in a general sense.

> If you're like me, you might feel a little relief when you hear Steven's "no tears" observation. It makes me think of how, when a Nobel Prize–winning medical researcher passes away, the only one who appears sad is the anchorman delivering the news. Yet when a rock star dies, the TV features legions of weeping fans placing flowers and teddy bears at the gates of the celebrity's home. The work of the researcher may have saved millions of lives, but the rock star gets the tears because people feel that they *knew* that person. The former makes an abstract connection; the latter is profoundly direct.
>
> —TOM

It's very difficult to explain your way into someone's heart. In a way, explanations allow for emotional disengagement. In *Stories for the Journey*, William R. White observes, "Few love affairs have begun by reading a resume."

Often, information that only touches our intellect and not our emotions or imagination merely informs us, but doesn't transform us all that much.

Something else is at play in teaching and speaking that makes a lasting difference.

What does change us, then? If it isn't facts and knowledge, what is it?

LOGIC OF THE HEAD—AND THE HEART

I used to teach eighth-grade logic. Yes. Logic. To eighth graders. When I told my friends about the job, it wasn't uncommon for them to say something along the lines of, "Eighth graders and logic? Isn't that a contradiction in terms?"

And, honestly, the first year was rough. By the second year, though, I'd gotten to know more about how eighth graders think, and I tried a different approach than simply blithely sharing facts. I started the first class by telling the students, "This year you're going to learn how to win arguments." Believe me, those kids were all about learning logic.

So, yes, understanding my audience's needs helped me to better connect with them, but there's something else that I also took away from teaching that class, and it had to do with the way I prepared my lessons.

As I planned them, I found that the more time I spent in preparation, the less I ended up lecturing—but the more the students learned. In contrast, the less time I spent in preparation, the more I ended up lecturing, and the less they learned. I also discovered that the less I had to say, the more I would talk, but when I'd finally mastered the material, I spoke less—but taught more.

Why? Because when I spent more time preparing, I developed learning activities that were more engaging and tapped into a wider array of creative teaching methods that better appealed to the various ways the students learned.

My explanations were never as impactful as my stories—even when teaching logic.

One day it struck me that an artist who is painting a picture of a landscape doesn't ask, "How can I best explain this?" but rather, "How can I capture the essence of what I see?" A novelist doesn't ask, "How can I best explain forgiveness?" but rather, "How can I explore or expose the essence of forgiveness in an honest way through my story?"

Their art forms aren't evaluated by how clearly they present a message, but by how powerfully they draw their audiences toward the truth.

When I noticed that, I couldn't help but think that I was onto something important here, something that would reshape the way I thought about teaching, leading, and inspiring others.

I remembered a professor in college who created an atmosphere in which curiosity was encouraged, wonder was facilitated, and meaning was discovered rather than explained.

She was one of the best teachers I ever had.

Slowly, as I took all of this into consideration, I found that both my students and I learned best when we discovered truth for ourselves, experienced things firsthand, and then taught what we'd learned to others.

Over the last thirty years, as I've taught thousands of leaders and educators around the world, I've found that when I start talking about discovery, personal experience, and the importance of teaching to others, I see heads nodding all around the room. Those in the audience already know that these are foundational principles of transformative teaching—and yet they rarely change the fundamental questions they ask to refocus their lessons in the direction people learn most effectively. I'm not sure why that is, but it doesn't need to be that way. We can start today, each of us, teaching and leading in more dynamic and productive ways.

When we can guide people to discover truth on their own, it'll do more than inform them; it'll enlighten them. One day I realized that, for the most part, whatever I can explain, I can lead people to discover—and they'll probably learn it better, remember it longer, and apply it more readily to their lives.

If you believe your main job is disseminating information, you'll prepare one way. But if you believe people learn best through discovery, experience, and by teaching to others, you'll ask an entirely different set of questions. In essence, data can lead to knowledge, but curiosity-based learning leads to deeper understanding and choices that transform lives.

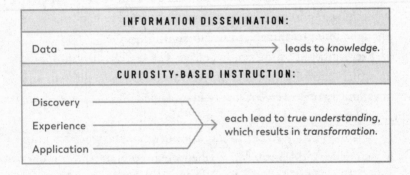

As Tom indicated in the last chapter, statistics rarely affect people as much as stories do. They're good for informing folks, but not great for affecting them. Curiosity drives us to learn more, while information dumping stops us dead in our tracks. In her book *Story or Die*, story consultant Lisa Cron puts it this way: "Throw facts at us, we duck. Personify those same facts in a story, we lean in."

Statistics can be a starting place, but don't rely on them alone to impact your audience. Rather than overwhelming listeners with facts, data, and information, allow your audience to learn inductively by identifying with someone else's struggles, discoveries, or moments of illumination—all of which stories naturally do.

The truth moves people most when it tugs at their heartstrings and isn't just poured into their heads.

▪ ▪ ▪

Socrates is legendary for his wisdom, but rather than lecturing his students, he used questioning to lead them to discover truth for themselves. In essence, he wasn't the one with the answers, but the one with the *questions*. He wasn't trying to make a point, but raise an issue. He would prod. Unsettle. Provoke. Rather than being an answer-giver, he was a question-igniter.

Questions lead us to discovery.

And so do stories.

By reframing the way we look at our role from that of the person with all the answers to the person guiding others toward discovery, we can more effectively reach them, teach them, inspire them, and transform them.

Indeed, your listeners' curiosity is one of the most valuable assets you have as a presenter. You can appeal to it . . .

- by having an unusual object with you onstage: *I wonder what's in that trunk she just dragged up there?*
- by starting your presentation by saying something listeners aren't expecting: *Where is she going with this?*
- by moving from one topic to another, seemingly unrelated, topic: *What does that story have to do with anything?*

Once I realized how vital curiosity is, I changed the guiding questions I ask from "How can I explain this?" to "How can I help my listeners discover this?" from "How can I clarify this?" to "How can

I help them experience this?" and from "How can I help them understand this?" to "How can I equip them to teach this to others?"

INFORMATION DISSEMINATION QUESTIONS	CURIOSITY-BASED QUESTIONS
• "How can I explain this?"	• "How can I help my listeners discover this?"
• "How can I clarify this?"	• "How can I help them experience this?"
• "How can I help them understand this?"	• "How can I equip them to teach this to others?"

And, as we'll see, stories can help us do all three.

QUESTION #1—"HOW CAN I HELP MY LISTENERS DISCOVER THIS?"

One afternoon nearly twenty years ago, I swung by the local Target department store to buy some coffee cup coasters for my office. I got into line, and the cashier glanced up at the woman in front of me who had a whole cart full of towels, dresses, and children's puzzles. The cashier mumbled, "So, how are you."

It wasn't really a question.

And the woman said, "Fine."

And it wasn't really an answer.

Then she wordlessly unloaded her items one by one, and the cashier dutifully scanned them. At last, without another word, the customer walked away and it was my turn to check out.

"So," the cashier said, "how are you."

When I replied, I wasn't trying to be clever or provocative; it was just one of those things that you say and then wonder if you should've maybe just kept your mouth shut: "Actually," I said, "I'm tired."

She looked at me then, for the first time.

"I'm tired too," she said. "I've been working here since seven."

It was 5:30 p.m.

I nodded. "It's been a long day for me too. I just want to get home and spend some time with my kids. Do you have kids?"

"No, just a couple of cats—but I hope to someday." Then she added, "Most people just say, 'I'm fine,' or, 'I'm good.'"

She still hadn't scanned my coasters. We were looking right at each other. It was one of those moments.

She asked me about my kids and I asked her about her cats and we talked for a minute—maybe less—while she rang up the coasters. And then she was done taking care of me and it was the next person's turn, so I retrieved my coasters and headed for the door.

I hadn't made it ten feet before I heard her say to the next person, "So, how are you."

And from behind me I heard someone say, "Oh, I'm fine."

I couldn't help but smile. I turned and glanced at the cashier. And she had turned, too, and was looking at me.

Smiling.

Yeah.

It was one of those moments.

■ ■ ■

If I tried to summarize what I learned that day at Target, it would have to do with making room in our lives to really connect with people, or that it doesn't take a lot of effort to lift someone's spirits (in that case, both of us left the encounter with a smile). Or maybe, that we're all enriched when something human passes between us. All of these life lessons from a brief encounter all those years ago.

But I probably don't need to point this out to you. You probably discovered all of that for yourself, just by reading the story.

When Steven says you don't need to explain a story, I have to restrain myself from saying, "Amen." When writing, one mistake people often make is that they begin their article, but then they write another paragraph that would also function as a beginning. When I work with new writers, I point this out and say, "Pick one."

And after telling a story, many people try to explain it because they think it clarifies the point, but what they are actually doing is dulling its impact.

Steven is right. A story stands on its own.

—TOM

Rather than stating and then arguing that something is true, stories from your life will disarm your listeners and allow your truths to be heard without objection. People can take issue with your propositions, but not with your discoveries. So, if you want to start an argument, tell folks *what to believe.* If you want them to listen to you, share with them *what you've learned.*

Stories work well in teaching through discovery, especially when listeners can identify with the unmet desire or pursuit of the characters in the story. Teaching through discovery can come from activities that the listeners do, or from the stories that the teacher tells. Often, it's as simple as highlighting four things: "Here's what I struggled with . . . Here's what I noticed . . . Here's what I learned . . . Here's how I changed . . ."

(By the way, here's another powerful teaching technique that appeals to curiosity: telling people what they think they know about, and then revealing to them that they don't know the full story after all. Radio personality and author Paul Harvey was famous for sharing "the rest of the story" in a way that engaged millions of listeners for decades.)

Listeners will remember your illustrations longer than they'll remember your outline, so to get your point across, make sure that the story *is* the point and doesn't just dress up your message. Stop thinking in terms of explaining your point and focus instead on conveying it through a dilemma or a discovery. Ask yourself:

- How does this memory connect with a central idea, issue, image, or incident?
- What do I hope to teach about this topic?
- What specific details do I need to weave into my story to bring out this concept?
- How is this lesson similar to something I have experienced?
- What is a real-world example of this concept?
- How can I relate this message in an interesting way?
- Is there a parallel (or metaphor or analogy) to this idea?

Take that last question, for instance.

Sometimes stories can be metaphorical, giving us insight into another realm of life. I remember a time when my middle daughter was learning to ride her bike and she ended up veering off the road downhill toward a tree. As she was angling across the grass toward it, she held on tightly rather than choosing to tip off the bike.

And she saw that tree coming. We all did.

She knew it was coming closer—clearly, she was headed toward a crash.

And what did she do?

She gripped those handlebars even tighter than before.

My daughter clung with white-knuckle tenacity to the very thing that was taking her toward calamity.

(Thankfully she was okay in the end. No children were harmed in the making of this story!)

If you told a story like this, you could then ask your listeners, "I wonder if that's ever happened to you . . . ? Can you think of attitudes you've been clinging to that are leading you off the path? What has our company been holding on to that's taking us in the direction of a crash? What would it look like to tip off the bike and avoid the tree?"

Rather than telling people that they need to change, if you share how you struggled and grew, they'll be able to draw truth from that experience and apply it to their own situation.

Ask yourself, "What's a story I can share that will help my learners discover how important this idea is?" Or, "How can I help them discover how to apply this principle in their own lives?"

As I was thinking about how we learn through discovery, it occurred to me that if you asked me to look back over my life and identify the most important lessons I've learned, the insights that have shaped and impacted me the most, and then followed up by saying, "Now, Steven, how did you learn those lessons?" rarely would the answer be, "Someone told me how to live a better life, I simply put their advice into practice, and look at me now!"

No. Sometimes it would be a discovery I made by watching other people. Often, it would come from firsthand experience, but rarely have I been transformed all that much by someone simply telling me, "This is important. You need to live this way."

I tend to learn best the hard way, or vicariously, by hearing stories of others learning the hard way.

The transformative moments at the heart of personal stories don't need to be huge life-altering events. Sometimes they're simply moments of insight that were learned the hard way. If the lesson was learned the easy way, it won't seem as valuable to listeners. For instance, "I used to be selfish but then I thought about it a lot and decided not to act that way anymore. Since then, I've been a changed person." What external event caused that change? That's the hinge your story depends on.

Whether you're a corporate executive, a spiritual advisor, an educator, a speechwriter, or a life coach, stories will help your listeners discover poignant truths for themselves. Teaching through curiosity can offer insights, capitalizes on novelty, and incorporates surprise. Leading people toward discovery can be a powerful way of guiding them toward life-transforming insights and personal epiphanies.

QUESTION #2—"HOW CAN I HELP THEM EXPERIENCE THIS?"

As I mentioned in the first chapter, I spent time during college working as a wilderness instructor. We would teach outdoor skills such as rock climbing, caving, canoeing, and backpacking. Additionally, we would provide meaningful choices and clarify the consequences to the students regarding the decision. So, rather than saying, "You have to cook dinner now," we would say, "If you don't cook dinner tonight, you're going to be hungry tomorrow for our ten-mile hike. You decide."

By tying a choice to a consequence, we strove to help the students understand that their decisions mattered and that taking responsibility for them was important.

Experiential learning can be a powerful way to teach.

In his book *Talk Like TED*, author Carmine Gallo points to the research of Princeton Neuroscience Institute researcher Uri Hasson, who found, through fMRI studies, that the brain waves of listeners mirror those of storytellers. Through stories, we can vicariously experience struggles and identify with the characters' discoveries.

As strange as this may sound, there are things that we know but don't believe. For instance, we all know that we're going to die—and that it could happen at any moment—but we rarely think about that fact, and, by the way we live, we show that we don't really *believe* it.

After all, if we really believed that we might die today, would we be so worried about the things that are right now making us so anxious? Would we reprioritize our lives? Would it affect the way we spent our day? I'm guessing that it would.

Stories help us to start believing the things we already know.

Take a second and let that sentence sink in: *Stories help us to start believing the things we already know.*

That's why we leave the movie theater breathing the air more deeply, noticing the stars that glisten above us, valuing the soft touch of our lover's hand as we walk to the car. Even though we know that those stories in the theater weren't necessarily real—the truths of life and death and love and hope and romance that they touch on *are* real. They resonate with our souls.

So, track with me here: when we "suspend our disbelief" during a story, we actually open ourselves up to finally *stop* suspending our *disbelief* in reality and—if only for a moment—begin to actually *believe* the truths we already know.

TO HELP PEOPLE LEARN THROUGH EXPERIENCE:

- Encourage them to question their assumptions.
- Guide them to notice truths that are all around them.
- Teach them to reason clearly.
- Assist them in visualizing the abstract.
- Let them feel deeply by making the universal more specific.
- Surprise them.
- Lead them to believe what they already know.

Oddly enough, the more specific you are in portraying a universal desire, the more intimately people will identify with it, even if they haven't experienced that specific event themselves. For instance, if you're trying to highlight your company's emphasis on honesty, more people will identify with a story of how someone was dishonest by stealing pens and thinking that it was no big deal than if you just talk about the importance of honesty in a vague or general way.

When we identify with a story's characters, we vicariously experience emotion, tension, discovery, and transformation through the story.

All of these outcomes can result from the empathy our listeners feel when they hear powerful, emotionally resonant stories. The audience members might not have actually experienced the story's events for themselves, but through the stories, they can naturally and organically apply the moral lessons to their own lives.

QUESTION #3—"HOW CAN I EQUIP THEM TO TEACH THIS TO OTHERS?"

My friend Shawn used to teach outdoor enthusiasts how to do a kayak roll. This technique involves flipping your kayak to one side and using your paddle to rotate it around while you're underwater, leading you to pop up on the other side of the boat. It can be tricky to learn, but it's super cool when you master it.

To teach the roll to a class, Shawn would have the first student show up at the pool or lake at five o'clock. He would spend an hour teaching her the roll. Then, at six o'clock, two people would come. He'd teach one of them the roll and his first student would teach the other person. At seven o'clock four students would arrive. Everyone who'd learned the roll so far would immediately teach it to others. And so on.

By the end of the night, some of the students had already been teaching the kayak roll for four hours. Guess who knew the roll the best by the end of the evening? You got it—the teachers became the greatest learners. My friend had discovered that one of the best ways for people to learn something is by teaching it to others. As author and folklorist Jack Zipes put it, "The role of the storyteller is to awaken the storyteller in others."

> I love the Jack Zipes quote. It echoes Stephen King's observation, "If you don't have time to read, you don't have the time (or the tools) to write." For storytellers, listening to stories is great training, and recorded TED Talks abound with remarkable examples of people opening new worlds through narrative.
>
> —TOM

When you're preparing your talk, ask yourself how you can tap into this powerful educational principle. Rather than trying to figure out a way to get your learners to simply understand something, search for ways to help them (1) apply the principle, (2) practice it, (3) share it.

Ask yourself:

- Will my listeners be able to identify with this because of shared experiences?
- How can I evoke emotion as well as engage intellect?
- What stories will help personalize this for these listeners?
- How can I share this lesson in a way that will equip people to teach this concept to others?

Give your listeners the opportunities to put the principles into practice, and provide them the chance to share their insights and skills with others—and often, the best way to do that is giving them an opportunity to share their discoveries with others through the stories they themselves tell.

SUMMARY

Stories and storytelling fit hand in glove with teaching toward curiosity and appealing to imagination.

When you're telling your listeners something that they already know, do so in a way they don't expect. Rather than looking for ways to explain your lesson, look for ways to help your listeners discover it. Rather than asking how you might clarify it, ask how you might lead them to experience it. And finally, rather than simply trying to help your listeners understand something, equip them to share it with others, perhaps by telling stories of their own.

Key Points to Remember

- Avoid telling people what they already know in a way they already expect.
- Remember that your listeners' natural curiosity is one of the greatest assets you have.
- Let listeners connect the dots, but show them where the dots are.
- Instead of viewing yourself as the one with the answers, look at yourself as the one guiding people through the questions.
- As you teach, tap into storytelling, since stories allow us to vicariously experience tension and resolution on an intimate level, personalizing the lesson in a way that lecturing alone won't do.

CHAPTER 4

STORY? OR ANECDOTE?

(How to Tell the Difference and Why It Matters)

—TOM

"I haven't got many anecdotes.
Maybe I should do something scandalous."
—Cate Blanchett, actor

A few years ago, I began to see a lot of business cards, LinkedIn profiles, and résumés that listed "storyteller" as a job title.

The funny thing was that virtually none of these people told stories for a living. Some wrote advertising copy. Others wrote marketing pitches. Many were publicists.

This is not to say that stories cannot be used to advertise, or to market products or services, or to publicize an individual or an organization. They can, and to great effect. But a bombardment of images or information does not a story make.

And even among people who genuinely believe that they are telling stories as part of their day-to-day work, what the vast majority are sharing is not a story at all, but its conversational cousin: the anecdote.

So . . . what's the difference? And, more importantly, why does it matter?

IS IT LENGTH?

This is a reasonable assumption, as most anecdotes are notable for their brevity. Yet there is a type of story—known, reasonably enough, as a *short-short story*—that is likewise quite brief.

In most English translations, "An Imperial Message," by Franz Kafka, is fewer than four hundred words in length, yet it is certainly a story. Mark Twain and Saki both forged connections with readers through stories that could be read aloud in fewer than five minutes.

If you are thinking of the mythic Ernest Hemingway six-word super-short-short story ("For sale: baby shoes, never worn."), I regret to say that it *is* mythic. There's no concrete evidence that Hemingway ever published, wrote, or said anything of the kind (darn you, internet!).

On the other hand, it is feasible (although not common) for an anecdote to ramble well past the five-minute mark. The one that accompanies this chapter certainly comes close to knocking on that door.

So . . . no. Length is not necessarily the characteristic that distinguishes the two.

IS IT TONE?

Oh, yes . . . I can practically see the heads nodding. Tone is so widely associated with anecdotes that the phrase "amusing anecdote" is practically redundant. If someone tells you that they are going to share an anecdote with you, you even might find yourself smiling in anticipation. (Okay, maybe only writers talk this way, but I think you get the point!)

That said, it is entirely possible for an anecdote to come to a conclusion that is negative, snarky, or even downright depressing.

Originally, anecdotes were almost uniformly *all three* of those things. The word "anecdote" comes from the Greek roots *an* (not) and *ekdotos* (to be published). So, *anekdotos* were "things not to be published"—presumably because they were scandalous or even potentially libelous. Think "damaging gossip" (or modern political campaign advertising), and you are on the right track.

Most modern, English-language anecdotes do tend to be humorous, but that's not an all-encompassing requirement. It's quite possible for an anecdote to be sobering—even profoundly so.

IS IT THAT IT IS TRUE?

Sort of. Yes, anecdotes are true, or at least they are presented as such.

But not every true narrative is an anecdote. From *Lawrence of Arabia* to *Seabiscuit*, many narrators have found full-blown stories in real life, and when they are made into feature films, there is usually a text card near the beginning of the film that states it is "based on a true story" or "based on true events." (This claim changes the audience's expectations and, honestly, often makes plot holes more acceptable to them.)

So, we find ourselves in an "all dogs are mammals, but not all mammals are dogs" situation. Simple veracity does not an anecdote make.

OKAY, THEN . . . WHAT IS IT?

I'll be frank. A perfectly valid argument can be made that an anecdote is one type of story. Many well-respected dictionaries begin their definition of "anecdote" with a phrase such as, "A short story that . . ." So, if you insist that an anecdote is actually a story, I'll defer to your opinion.

But if you declare that the terms are absolutely interchangeable, you'd better pack a lunch, because you and I are in for a long discussion.

Particularly when it comes to public speaking, I see a clear and obvious difference between the use of anecdotes and stories, and it all boils down to what students of marketing refer to as "brand."

In everyday use, "brand" is a nebulous term. When most people think of it, they think of things such as the Nike "swoosh" or the Starbucks mermaid (both are actually logos). Or they may think of the words of advertising jingles (properly described as "slogans" or "taglines").

People also frequently assume that a brand is something that can be built, created, or cooked up, but that's not entirely the case. If a company wants to be thought of as innovative, it can be, but first it must have a solid track record of innovation. If a leader wants to be thought of as intelligent, warm, and approachable, the first steps toward that brand are for that leader to make smart decisions, place the needs of others first, and actually *be* approachable.

The best way to become a leader that people want to follow is to become the kind of person that people will want to follow. Let your integrity establish your brand.

The hard truth is that a brand does not reside within an organization or its spokespeople—it originates in, and resides with, the people who are observing that organization and its leaders: customers, shareholders, congregants, students, industry observers, reporters, columnists, and other stakeholders.

Brand is what *other people* think of you, your organization, your product, or your cause.

Every time you or someone else in your organization speaks, it's an opportunity to help reinforce your organization's brand: to help shape what your listeners think about you and what you represent. You cannot "build" a brand, per se, but you can shape and guide the way your audience is building it in their minds.

That's where I draw the distinction between anecdote and story. It's in the brand impact made by the two: while an anecdote may awaken a glimmer of who you are and what you represent, a story has much more profound resonance—that great-movie afterglow that Steven mentioned in the last chapter—and this resonance lives at a deeper level within the psyche. It encourages your audience to adopt your brand.

Anecdotes are great entry points or summary points for discussions, whereas stories help cement a relationship through emotion (as we'll examine in chapter 6).

I remember visiting the Smithsonian for research for one of my novels. With all respect to the artists, I had no idea what some of the paintings or sculptures were supposed to mean. I was a bit exasperated and ready to bail when I noticed the signs at the bases of the artwork. Each placard contained a short description of what the artist or sculptor was trying to convey, what the colors stood for or represented, and so on.

I have to admit, as a novelist I didn't love it. My books need to work without an explanation at the end, without a line that says, "By the way, here's what that imagery meant, what you should be remembering, and what I was thinking when I wrote it." No. Instead, the story needs to stand on its own and do all the work.

Those pieces of artwork were like anecdotes—they needed context to be understood.

The greatest stories require no explanation.

And neither do the greatest works of art.

If you need to interpret a vignette or explain to your listeners what it means, you have an anecdote on your hands. In essence, an anecdote relies on context for its meaning; a story contains the meaning inside of it with no explanation necessary. For example, if you end your message by saying, "In the same way . . ." then you're bridging to the application that you're trying to make with your anecdote. If you say, "From then on . . ." you're showing the change in the character within that story.

—STEVEN

WHICH ONE SHOULD I USE?

If I'm sounding here as if an anecdote is a lesser form of narrative, that is certainly not my intention. In my speaking, I frequently use both anecdotes and stories. They are like hammers and screwdrivers—each is a tool with its own particular use.

Happily enough, it is rare that anecdotes or stories are an either/or proposition. Both are narrative forms—and human beings are wired from the inside out to absorb and digest narrative.

Add to this a proven psychological principle known as the "serial recall effect" (essentially, the idea that in anything we watch, read, or hear, we tend to most effectively recall the things that happen first and last), and you can make a talk memorable by beginning with one of the two narrative forms and concluding with the other.

So, you could begin your keynote address with a brief anecdote that makes your opening point and later conclude with a heartwarming story that invites the audience into your circle. Or you could open with a story that helps the audience start to genuinely like you, and conclude with the anecdote that will convey the point you want to resonate with them for days, weeks, or months to come.

	STORY	ANECDOTE
Does it stand on its own?	Yes. No explanation is necessary. No moralizing is needed.	No. Listeners might be confused unless you clarify what the "takeaway" or "point" is.
When should I use it?	Anytime, really! That said, since no explanation is needed, stories make especially strong closings to speeches.	Anecdotes serve well as openings to speeches and allow you to naturally introduce the talk's theme or topic. If you close with an anecdote, remember that you will probably have to explain it.
How will it affect our brand?	Stories can be powerful for connecting with people, no matter what services you're offering or what you might be selling—a vibe, a virtue, a lifestyle, a lesson, or a product.	An anecdote is a good brand-reinforcing "nudge." It can serve to establish a point ("People really love our company"). It can also depict a willingness to develop new initiatives by introducing an issue ("Most people overseas have never heard of our company").
How should I transition out of it to the rest of my talk?	While you don't need to explain a story, you can segue out of it by inviting your listeners to create a parallel between the story you just told and their own lives. Or you can close with the story and let that be your end.	An anecdote, by its very nature, needs to be followed by commentary. It has to be explained, but the explanation can be a very brief transition into the main point of your talk (see the anecdote at the end of this chapter for an example of this).

A presentation is an opportunity to connect with people on a variety of emotional and intellectual levels. The anecdote is a perfectly valid tool when you want to use narrative to make a resonant point that you can then expand upon. Just don't confuse it with the more fully developed story, which contains the point that it is making.

A hammer is, after all, not a screwdriver. And vice versa.

THE ROAD TO "AHA!"

This is an anecdote that I used several times years ago when I wrote for and frequently spoke to audiences in the automotive and technology industries. It is not especially brief, but it is an anecdote, nonetheless.

On Yap

I am not much for details when it comes to air travel itineraries. Three things are about all that I pay attention to: what time my flight leaves, what gate it leaves from, and when it gets to where I'm going. As long as I'm not changing planes, that's all I care about.

So, back in the mid-nineties, when I was freelancing for an adventure travel magazine and flying from Guam to the Republic of Palau, in the western Pacific, I did what I usually do on airplanes, particularly when flying over oceans: I fell asleep.

I was due to arrive in Palau's former capital, Koror, shortly after sundown, and I was surprised when I was awakened by a change in the pitch of the engines and saw that, rather than descending in twilight, we were shedding altitude in the bright sunlight of midafternoon.

That's about all the scene-setting this narrative needs. If I go into further depth and include why I was flying to Palau (I was going scuba diving), what airline I was flying (Continental Micronesia), or precisely what year this was, I start to clog up what needs to be a quick, simple, and straightforward entry into the narrative. When people hear narratives aloud, they can only remember, word for word, the last ten to thirty seconds, so I need to be conservative with that window.

> The captain solved the mystery when he announced on the intercom that we were descending for a scheduled stop at the international airport for Yap Island in the Federated States of Micronesia. He added that, as we would be on the ground for half an hour, passengers were welcome to deplane and stretch their legs, as long as we didn't stray too far from the passenger terminal.
>
> This intrigued me. I had never been to Yap before, but I'd read about it.
>
> Yap was one of the few islands in that part of Micronesia where visitors could come and go as they wished; every other place required a formal invitation from the island chieftain. Within their culture, Yapese citizens were divided into a number of different caste levels—if you were unlucky enough to be born in the wrong village, you were not allowed to fish on the reef. The principal industries were burning coral in kilns to make lime (used to prepare betel nuts for chewing), and tourism. People fished as well, but that was mostly subsistence for their families; commercial fishing had not yet been implemented on the island.
>
> And then there was the stone money. That was the thing I remembered most from what I'd read: the big disks of stone that were still used for significant transactions, such as transfers of land and wedding dowries.

We're getting into tricky territory here. I'm trying to present Yap as distant and exotic, without being judgmental. At the same time, I am presenting details that may cause the listener to leap to a judgment. If anyone does, they will receive a rude awakening as we get deeper into the narrative.

Rather than sit on the plane for thirty minutes, I decided to get off and get my passport stamped. Being a travel writer, I hung my camera around my neck. Then, rather than leave my brand-new laptop on an empty plane, I grabbed that as well and took it with me.

Remaining near the passenger terminal was going to be easy; you could fit the whole thing inside a typical high school gymnasium. Even though I wasn't staying, the immigrations officer understood I wanted a souvenir and, with the easygoing attitude typical of the western Pacific, gave me a stamp and a wink. Then I wandered outside, found a disk of stone money displayed on a lichen-stained pedestal, took a picture of it, and looked around for something else to capture with the camera.

I found it almost immediately: an entire family—a toddler, a boy about ten years old, a teenage girl, a man and his wife, and a grandfather in his eighties—standing outside the arrival door-way, evidently waiting for someone to clear customs and join them.

It was apparently a big event because the entire family was dressed in traditional attire. Everyone was barefoot, and the men wore knotted red-and-blue loincloths. The women were in layered grass skirts—plain on the married woman, but dyed a brilliant red, yellow, and green on her daughter—and both had belts of shells and beads. They all wore lanyard-like shell neck-laces and the elderly man's back, chest, and arms were covered in faded black tattoos: symbolic, no doubt, of his status within his community. When he caught me looking, he smiled, his teeth stained a startling reddish black from decades of chew-ing betel nuts.

Again, this is tricky territory in the anecdote. I would like my description to allow the listeners to leap to a conclusion here . . . without leaping to that same conclusion myself. Oftentimes, Westerners tend to demean primitive and tribal societies, yet whenever I hear someone leaning that way, I remember one evening in a South Pacific island, sitting with a group of people under the stars, stuffed with the wonderful fish we had caught earlier that day on the reef, when one of the men confided in me that they thought people from "developed" countries were crazy: "You go away from your families all day, do work you don't enjoy, live in debt, and give yourselves heart attacks so you can spend, what, one or two weeks a year doing the same things that we do every day of the year. How can we not think you're crazy?" The man had a point.

I'd visited enough other cultures to know better than to take a photo without asking. So, holding up my camera and speaking in that clipped, pronoun-free English that Americans use when addressing foreigners, I asked, "Take picture?"

The grandfather nodded, and—following my pantomimed instructions—everyone gathered between two gracefully arching palm trees.

I raised my camera to frame the shot, but my laptop—trapped between my elbow and my ribs—was getting in the way. So, I laid it on the ground in front of me and got back to taking my picture.

After the shutter had snapped, the patriarch of the group stepped forward in his calloused bare feet, leaned forward, and inspected my shiny new IBM ThinkPad from a distance.

Then he looked up at me.

"Is that," he asked, raising one eyebrow as he did, "a 486 or a Pentium?"

This is it. The anecdotal surprise. Still, we need a bit more, or listeners will just be confused.

> The entire family laughed at my reaction, and then the man explained that his granddaughter—the person they were waiting for—was a sophomore at a university in California. Mail being slow and undependable, the family could stay in touch through the use of a fax machine, but phone bills would add up quickly.
>
> There was a solution, though. The island would soon be wired for internet, so families with members overseas—which was just about everyone—were reading every computer magazine that they could get.
>
> Up until this time, the only computers on the island were in businesses and government offices. But families needed computers if they wanted to send email, and, if they were going to spend the money, they wanted to make certain that the computers they bought were the most up-to-date models that they could find.

That's it. That's the entire anecdote. If I wanted to, I could develop it from this point into a full-blown story—for instance, I got caught up in a conversation with a woman from the Yap tourism bureau and very nearly missed my flight; we wound up literally chasing the jet down the taxiway . . . but I digress. I don't need to take the narrative any further, because it is enough to introduce the point I want to convey—that, in terms of technology, there is no longer any such thing as "the third world." I've used this story countless times in speaking to automotive engineers, information-technology professionals, and marketing people. Every time, my listeners got the point.

SUMMARY

An anecdote—a snippet of narrative—and a full-blown story both have a place when you are speaking to a group. The difference between the two is that the story tends to be self-explanatory; there is no need to explain the point it makes to your listeners. For this reason, a great way to bring narrative into your presentation is to open with an anecdote, develop the point it makes through explanation, and then close with a story that echoes your overall message.

Both can help reinforce your company's image or values, but stories tend to be the stronger of the two for establishing brand.

Key Points to Remember

- You are born wired to share anecdotes and stories. You tell them routinely in everyday conversation. There is no reason *not* to use them when you speak.
- An anecdote is a type of narrative that illustrates a point while a story is a type of narrative that contains its own point.
- Keep your transitions after anecdotes brief and beware of over-explaining.
- It is permissible to use both an anecdote and a story in the same talk. In fact, it's recommended!
- When using both, a simple and proven approach is to open with the anecdote and close with the story.

PART II
THE LISTENERS
From One Heart to Another

W ho is your audience? Is it your board of directors? Your customers? Your clients? Your employees? Your students? Conference attendees? Knowing who you'll be telling your story to is as important as knowing what story you're going to tell. In this section, we'll examine how to best relate to your listeners—and why the act of storytelling itself will help draw you all closer together.

CHAPTER 5

SHRINKING THE SPACE BETWEEN US

—STEVEN

"The shortest distance between two people is a story."
—Unknown

One day in the lobby of a hotel in Ohio, I overheard a man in his late twenties talking on his cell phone. After a moment or two it became clear that he was a lawyer and was speaking with a client. He was articulate and composed, used complete and complex sentences, and sounded well versed in legal terminology.

A few moments after hanging up, he received a call that was obviously from an old college buddy. Suddenly, this man's entire demeanor changed. He was joking around and talking like a frat boy once again, not at all like a law school grad.

That man's history with those two people affected his tone, word choice, grammar, sentence structure, use of idioms, everything. Even his posture changed.

Here's the thing: he wasn't being disingenuous with either of the people he was speaking with. This is important. He was simply talking to different audiences with different goals in mind. Both the lawyer voice and the frat-boy voice were a part of him.

BE WARY OF OVERLY
ENTHUSIASTIC EMCEES

Think of how you talk to your friends—casually, informally, lightheartedly. Now, think of how you speak to someone when you're interviewing for a job, or getting (or giving) a formal reprimand, and compare that to how you talk to your lover. Each instance is unique, and your style of communication will differ accordingly. Even if you're not aware that you're doing it, you naturally adapt the way you speak to the person you're speaking to.

Good storytellers do the same.

Each storytelling event has its own expectations—a keynote address, a watercooler conversation, a neighborhood barbecue, a junior high school English class, a corporate board meeting, a comedy club performance. Each is a little different. Sometimes, listeners expect to be entertained; other times, they expect to be taught a lesson, to be motivated to act, to learn a set of moral principles, or simply to laugh.

In each case, however, understanding those expectations while respecting the relationship between the teller and the listeners is important.

An effective storyteller understands his audience, addresses their needs, and prepares his material with them in mind. As speaker and communication expert Ken Haemer puts it, "Designing a presentation without an audience in mind is like writing a love letter and addressing it: 'To Whom It May Concern.'"

Listeners are an integral part of the live storytelling experience. They're not just observers. In a very real sense, they're also participants, and the way the story is formed, told, and communicated results from the relationship of the storyteller to his listeners as it develops during the storytelling event.

Even though it might sound strange to put it this way, a storyteller listens to herself, her story, and her audience while she's performing. How does she listen to the audience? By observing their facial expressions, body language, and reaction, and then responding to them as she tells her story (as Tom pointed out in his description of the powwow conversations in chapter 2).

Clues from the setting, the social context, and the listeners themselves will help determine expectations.

For instance, have you ever been at an event and the person up front grabs the microphone and says, "Hello! Thanks for being here! How is everyone doing today?"

Some people might mutter a reply. A few might cheer. Others will remain quiet. Then the enthusiastic emcee, clearly wanting people to hoot and holler, says, "Oh, that was *terrible*! I said, HOW IS EVERYONE DOING TODAY?"

This goes on until the audience finally cheers the way he wants them to.

But he's also managed to insult ("that was terrible!"), belittle, and manipulate them in the process.

It wasn't that people were unexcited to be present when they were first asked the question; it's just that they didn't understand how, or if, they were supposed to reply. They were probably trying to figure out if it was their job to respond verbally, or nod, or whatever.

Without clear expectations about how we want our listeners to respond to a story, it can be confusing to them and undermine the relationship between the teller and the audience.

When you're addressing a group, make it clear to your listeners how they can best listen. This can be done contextually, through staging and lighting and the seating arrangement. It can also be accomplished through the way you communicate with them, warmly inviting a response or formally speaking in a way that indicates that you want them to remain quiet as you proceed.

When we tune into a television show or are settling in with our popcorn at the movie theater, we know what we're in for—an hour or two (or more!) of entertainment. But when you're giving a speech, the time frame isn't always so clear to the listeners. It can be hard for them to know what to expect (consequently making it tougher to pay attention). So, to help set expectations, sometimes it's a good idea to indicate how long you'll be talking:

- "In the next ten minutes, I'd like to . . ."
- "I have two stories for you today: one old, one new . . ."
- "Before our break at two o'clock, I'm going to share with you something close to my heart . . ."

If possible, get to know your audience. If you work with the same group each week, you'll soon learn their expectations about how long they think a talk should be, what types of stories they like, how much humor they expect, and how much exaggeration is acceptable.

On the other hand, you may find yourself speaking to a group you've never met before. If so, observe them closely. Are they leaning forward with anticipation as you begin, or leaning back with their arms folded as if to say, "I dare you to entertain me"? Take that into account as you share your story.

Help your listeners understand how you expect them to respond to you and your story. Do you want them to actively participate, or to sit quietly and listen? Is the primary goal of this story to teach, or to entertain? The way you relate to your audience members will communicate your expectations of how they should act during the storytelling event.

REHEARSE YOUR WAY TOWARD CONFIDENCE

One of the greatest compliments I ever received as a storyteller came from a hulking biker dressed in a black leather jacket who came up to me after I'd finished telling a children's story about two frogs. I'm 6'3" and I was dwarfed by this guy.

"Hey, storyteller," he barked. "C'mere! I wanna tell you something!"

"Yes?" I gulped as I tilted my head to look up at his rugged face. "What's that?"

"You know when you were telling that story? Well, I felt like that big fat frog. You kinda remind me of the skinny frog. Maybe I could tell that story with you. You could be the skinny one and I'll be the big one!"

Needless to say, his words took me by surprise. Any time you can make a 280-pound biker feel like a pudgy little amphibian, you know you've connected with your audience.

The thing was, I'd completely misjudged this guy. He was as excited as a little kid about the frog story when I'd assumed he would be tough to reach.

It taught me to be wary of my preconceptions. It also opened my eyes to how important it is to be ready to jettison them once I got to know my audience better.

The goals of the storyteller and the expectations of the listeners will affect the way a story is told. As corporate executive and story consultant Nancy Duarte put it, "Consider carefully what different audiences need to hear, and how they want to hear it. Whenever your audience changes, so should the language you use."

An experienced teller will take into account the context of the social encounter that the storytelling takes place in, not just as he's beginning the story, but also the whole time he's delivering it. Watch your listeners as you tell your story. Be prepared to change and adapt the story to fit their needs and responses.

Every audience has its own unique quirks and characteristics. Try to climb into the minds of your listeners, attend to the moment, and respond to the mood of the room as you strive to strike the best balance between preparation and responsiveness as you present.

Despite the amount of (or lack of) experience you might have in public speaking, you'll want to come across as someone who takes this role seriously, is prepared, and is here to serve your audience by putting their needs above your own. Even if your listeners work for you, when you're onstage you're there to serve them instead of yourself.

Develop trust and intimacy with your listeners. When the audience and the teller feel comfortable with each other, creativity can express itself without fear and a sense of community can be formed. Ask yourself where your listeners are at . . .

- Relationally—Do they trust me with this story and with their time? If not, what do I need to do to earn their trust?
- Mentally—Are they alert, or do they need a mental break?
- Physically—Are they hungry, tired, or uncomfortable; or are they ready to listen?
- Emotionally—Are they prepared for the content of this presentation? If not, how do I need to alter the story to connect with them?

A genuine and authentic speaker will be more impactful than a slick and polished one. An audience's response to you is a reflection of your composure, not so much your mastery of language. Usually, the only people who are impressed by eloquence are the ones who are trying to be eloquent. Be authentic. Be yourself. Don't try to be too literary or "put on a show."

Composure is simply the ability to be yourself in front of other people while putting them at ease. Poise is more important than polish.

After all, people are attracted to confidence. It sets us at ease. Think of a comedian who walks onstage and gazes at the audience without saying a word, and everyone claps. The guy just stands there and somehow gets people to laugh and applaud! How does that work? Just by his posture and composure, the confident comedian assures the listeners that they're in good hands and that their time isn't going to be wasted.

Though we laugh alongside confidence, when we sense a lack of confidence it makes us uncomfortable.

To develop confidence, rehearse your story. First, practice by exploring it by talking *about* it and retelling it in your own words. Then, as Tom emphasized when he recommended playing the small venues, tell your story whenever you can, over and over. By hearing your voice and moving your body through the story, you'll learn what needs to change to improve the way you tell it. Since stories are told with our bodies as well as our voices, when you practice, don't just practice the words, practice actually moving through the story.

Just thinking about how you might tell the story isn't the same as actually talking your way through it—ideally with some listeners present.

In track and field, when someone is learning to become a triple jumper, he doesn't just read books, study videos, or watch others jump. Those things might be helpful to some degree, but nothing teaches triple jumping quite like triple jumping. Trying to learn to tell stories by thinking about your story is kind of like trying to learn to become a triple jumper while sitting in the locker room watching a video. To become a better storyteller, you need to practice telling stories.

You need to jump.

Work on learning your story, not just the specific words that make it up. Get to know the story so well that you're comfortable changing, deleting, or emphasizing sections of it based on reactions from the audience.

Go through it in a variety of ways until you become comfortable with the way it sounds and feels. Take your time exploring the story. Discover what it's really about, and then think about how it applies to the lives of your listeners. It's more important to know the story well than to try to learn it word-perfect.

> Samuel Clemens—best known by his "Mark Twain" pen name— was a riverboat pilot before he became a writer. Once he became a writer, he made much of his money as a speaker and, while writing certainly influenced his speaking, I think the riverboat experience helped him immensely. In the days before radio, GPS, and constantly updated electronic maps, pilots on the Mississippi River navigated by always knowing what eddies, snags, sandbars, or bends were in the section of river they were about to enter. They did not commit each turn of the wheel and boiler setting to memory, but they always knew what came next in the journey. Storytelling is like that. As Steven says, the exact words needn't be memorized, but you always want to know what's coming up next.
>
> —TOM

If I asked you to tell me about a time when you were in an accident, or were hospitalized, or when you were scarred in some way, you would immediately be able to do so. You wouldn't need to practice or rehearse the story; you could tell it to me naturally.

So, once again, don't feel like you need to memorize stories. Just tell them in your own words, in a way that feels natural.

During rehearsal, practice walking up to an imaginary microphone, introducing yourself, and beginning your story. Stage presence is how well you carry yourself and present yourself to your listeners. Take things slowly, breathe, and deliver. Readiness means not only preparing your story but also being prepared to respond to the audience while you're telling the story.

Also, if you include learning activities or slides during your presentation, practice transitioning into and out of those as you prepare your story.

Care about the story you're learning. Find a personal connection to it. If you're not passionate about learning and telling the story, your lack of zeal will likely come through in your delivery and become evident to your listeners. If you don't care, why should they?

Think about the language you're choosing for retelling this story. Is it appropriate for your audience? Are the words or concepts too obscure? Are the ideas too complex (or too simplistic)? Are the topics too controversial or potentially offensive? Adapt as you tell, taking special care to be sensitive when addressing topics that are hot button issues.

Finally, relax before going onstage—and stop worrying about what people think. Your listeners want you to appear comfortable and at ease speaking to them. They don't want you to be nervous or embarrassed or afraid. So, face the audience, straighten your posture, and smile at them. If you're nervous, squeeze your thumb and forefinger together and then relax your hand. No one will even notice. Then take a few deep breaths to compose yourself. And begin.

PREPARE YOUR SPACE
(NO BIKINIS ALLOWED!)

The environment in which you tell stories affects the mood of your listeners, how they feel about the story, and how well they can listen. Many educators overlook the importance of the classroom space, the seating arrangement, lighting, sound, and the mood of the room when they plan their lessons and tell their stories.

Many conference speakers do as well.

Let's look at a few simple steps you can take to make sure your venue is best suited for your presentation.

First, unless there are health or safety restrictions in place that require physical distancing, do your best to keep everyone seated close together instead of scattered all over the room or auditorium. If people are sitting on the fringes, their attention and focus may be negatively impacted. Also, make sure structural barriers such as posts and pillars don't block anyone's view.

I was teaching a conference in San Diego some years ago, and when I arrived at the venue where the eight-hour-long seminar was scheduled to take place, I saw that the entire wall behind the podium was a mirror. That was bad enough—I could only imagine the listeners staring at themselves all day—but then I realized that the back of the room behind them was entirely glass, overlooking the pool! So, I was supposed to teach these educators all day while, every ten or fifteen seconds, the reflection of someone in a bikini was going to walk across the stage in front of them.

I knew there was no way I could compete with Southern California pool life on display.

Thankfully, I'd arrived early enough to reset the room before anyone else showed up. I turned all of the chairs toward a side wall. It only took a few minutes. No one else knew that I'd rearranged the room, and the seminar went fine, with no swimsuit-clad interruptions. That day, I learned to always arrive early enough to adjust a room if necessary to provide the best environment for my listeners.

Next, if possible, I try to match the number of seats to the number of participants. If there are thirty people coming, I don't want to be in a room that seats four hundred. After all, if you walk into a seminar and there are four hundred seats and only thirty people show up, what are you thinking? *Man, this seminar is going to be awesome!* Probably not. Something more along the lines of, *Huh. Looks like not too many people showed up. This is probably going to be pretty lame.*

Once, I was hired to emcee a conference in Gatlinburg, Tennessee. The conference center was set up with 4,400 chairs. Guess how many people showed up?

One hundred twenty.

Awkward!

At times, I've spent fifteen to twenty minutes taking chairs down. (That day, it would've taken hours!)

Ideally, I want people to think that there's standing room only for this event. Otherwise, simply because of the seating arrangement, I might have negative expectations to overcome right off the bat. I'd be sabotaging the program before I even said a word.

Various seating arrangements affect the mood of the storytelling event differently. Slanted rows (or "chevron-style" seating) will create a less formal feel than strict, straight lines. If the listeners are seated in a semicircle, it'll draw attention away from the storyteller, creating more of a feeling of equality between the presenter and the listeners. Use the seating arrangement that best creates the mood you're shooting for.

STAND IN THE LIGHT AND STAY ON THE STAGE

In a theatrical production, the background always serves to draw attention to the actors and the story, rather than divert attention away from them. The same is true for a good storytelling background.

Position yourself in front of a neutral background or a plain wall—not one mirroring back a bunch of people splashing around in a pool or sunbathing in Speedos.

When you set up your space to tell stories, make sure nothing is going on behind you. Remove anything that might distract you or your listeners. You want to draw as little attention past yourself as possible while keeping the focus of the group on you.

- What do you see that will help facilitate a good atmosphere for storytelling? What might detract from it?
- What distractions might present themselves at your venue? How will you handle them if they arise?

If people have difficulty seeing you, they'll have a tough time paying attention to the story. So, make sure you can be heard—and seen.

Regardless of the venue's layout, if you're onstage, find the spot with the best lighting and present from there. Before beginning to tell stories, look around and decide if you can move into better light.

Typically, you'll want to face the brightest lights in the room. For example, if you have a window in your boardroom, never stand in front of it while you speak because the light streaming into the room will be shining into the eyes of your listeners. As a result, they won't be able to watch you, and will look away from you to rest their eyes.

VENUE CHECKLIST

- Am I standing in a well-lit area of the room?
- Is the space behind me free of distractions?
- Are all background sounds turned off?
- Can the audience easily see me (and my visuals or slides)?

- Is the temperature comfortable—even a little on the cool side?
- Is the seating arrangement conducive to this storytelling event?
- Can the listeners easily hear me?

Even if there are spotlights available, you may not want to use them. Many storytellers like to be able to see the faces of the people in the audience so they can naturally respond to their reactions during the story.

The most light should be onstage, or in the performance space in which you'll be sharing your stories. If there's light in the back of the room (behind the audience), it'll disperse your listeners' attention.

Years ago, I met a popular speaker on the circuit named Michael Capps. Michael was a dynamic communicator, and as people arrived at his workshops, he always had activities for them to do the moment they came through the door. Michael told me one time, "The lesson begins when the first student arrives."

I'll never forget that.

If you're up front doing a sound check when there are people in the audience or if you're resetting the room when they walk in, they might think you're unprofessional or unprepared. Remember, no matter where you're speaking or teaching, the moment the first attendee arrives, the event has begun, and their impression of you will be shaped by how you present yourself.

Also, your appearance (clothes, posture, smile, and overall demeanor) will speak long before you do. Typically, you'll want to dress in a way that shows not only your professionalism, but also your approachability. The better you know your audience, the better you'll be able to choose an outfit that expresses your individuality without distracting from your presentation.

AVOID SQUIRRELS AND OTHER UNNECESSARY DISTRACTIONS

One time, I was speaking to a group of business leaders and there was a window off to my right overlooking a forest. A squirrel decided to play on a nearby branch just as I arrived at the climax of my story.

No one was looking at me.

All eyes were on the squirrel. (Furry little long-tailed distractor!)

It taught me to close the shades of nearby windows from then on.

Someone told me many years ago that "movement is an attention magnet," and it's true. You might be telling the most amazing, engaging, imaginative story ever, but if a latecomer walks up to the front of the room to find a chair, every eye in the room will follow their movement.

(By the way, to avoid this, if it's appropriate for the event, I invite people to sit toward the front before we begin. Sometimes I'll leave a few sticky notes on chairs in the back row of the seminar room: "Reserved for latecomers. Thank you." That simple step can do wonders to remove the awkward instances of a latecomer searching for a seat up front while you're presenting.)

MICROPHONE CHECKLIST

- Are the batteries properly installed and new?
- Can I move freely throughout the room without the speakers squealing?
- Have I practiced walking through the story to make sure that I don't get tangled in the microphone cords?

- Will this microphone pick up all the sounds (both loud and soft) that I make during the story?
- If the microphone has a power switch, is it turned to "on"?
- Is the volume set to a comfortable level?
- Is a sound technician ready to adjust the volume after I begin talking to make sure everyone can easily hear the story?

You've probably heard that people today have a "short attention span." While that may be true, I've found it more helpful to think in terms of people having a "large distraction span."

It's our job to keep their attention despite that fact.

Avoid speaking in venues while servers are busy clearing the tables. Typically, it's best to clarify when you're booked for the event that, in order for the listeners to get the most out of the presentation, you'll be waiting until the tables are cleared before speaking.

Also, it's very difficult to hold the attention of those whose backs are turned to you. Because of that, one of the most challenging venues to speak in is a conference hall filled with people seated at round tables. If you find yourself in that setting, you might ask the emcee to invite people to turn their chairs to face the stage for the presentation before she introduces you.

Before going onstage, check yourself over. Do you have keys in your pockets? Get rid of them. Are you wearing a name badge? Leave it at the table before going up front. Zippers zipped. Buttons buttoned. Shirt tucked in. Microphone on.

There. Done.

Deep breath.

And.

Go.

SUMMARY

Different factors affect the audience's expectations—past experiences in similar situations, familiarity with your material, how long they expect the presentation to be, and so on. So, make sure your listeners feel welcomed, valued, and that they're cued in on how best to listen.

When appropriate, acknowledge what people are thinking. For instance, at a conference that I attended about fifteen years ago, the third speaker of the evening started by inviting the audience to stand and stretch. "We've all been sitting for some time," he said. "Why don't you take a moment and shake the hands of three people who are dressed worse than you are? Go ahead . . ."

It brought a laugh, broke up the monotony, gave us a mental break, and allowed people to pay better attention to his presentation once they took a seat again. (He came across as a pro; see Appendix A for ten tips on how you can do so as well.)

If your listeners anticipate that your talk will be boring, you'll want to communicate to them early on that this story is exciting and worth paying attention to.

Key Points to Remember

- Arrange the seating to your and your listeners' advantage. Find a neutral background, stand in the light, and make sure you can be easily seen and heard.
- Remove distractions such as keys, pens, change, pudding, bowling balls, and your cell phone from your pockets.
- Movement is an attention magnet, so avoid standing in front of windows, squirrels, jugglers, or bungee jumpers. Any of them can draw attention away from you and your story.

- Match the level of formality or informality in your storytelling to the level expected by your listeners.
- Remember, poise is simply the ability to be yourself in front of other people while putting them at ease. The audience's response to your storytelling is a reflection of your composure—which is always more important than your eloquence.

CHAPTER 6

THE CHEMISTRY OF STORYTELLING

Hugging the Audience with Story

—TOM

"Dogs sniff each other. Human beings tell stories.
This is our native language."
—Stephen Denning, author and management consultant

I've taught storytelling for public speaking to thousands of people, and usually when I get to the subject we're going to cover in this chapter, I put these twelve words on the board or a screen and ask everyone to read them aloud with me:

Just because I know why it works

doesn't mean it isn't magic.

Okay. Maybe you're reading this in bed at two in the morning and your sleeping spouse—who is possibly not all that keen on your reading in bed at this hour—will not appreciate your choosing this moment to start talking. Or maybe you're on a subway or an airplane or sitting in a coffee shop and would rather not have strangers staring at you. In any of those cases, just read those words under your breath and we will consider the deed done.

But if you're alone—possibly on the patio with no one but the dog to see you acting weird—read those words out loud. Trust me; it will be better.

Because if you ever had the good fortune to fall in love at first sight, we are going to explore *why* you did that. We are going to look at why you sometimes make snap judgments and decide that someone is a good person. We are going to learn why your mother loved you from (and even before) the very first breath that you took. We are going to discover how to use that when we speak to people. And no, it's not charisma or magnetism.

It's biochemistry.

MAMMALS, EMOTIONS, AND MOLECULES

Most members of the animal kingdom raise their own young, but some species do not. The most famous examples of these are certain birds, such as cowbirds and cuckoos, that lay their eggs in the nests of other types of birds and let them become unwitting nannies, while the cowbirds and cuckoos go on doing whatever it is that cowbirds and cuckoos do.

It's not just birds that do this. Some fish lay their eggs in the clutches of other fish. There are wasps that place their larvae in the nests of other wasps, ants that invade and place their eggs in the nests of other ants, and even butterflies that trick ants into believing that butterfly larvae are ant larvae.

Biologists refer to such species as "brood parasites." But while there are birds that are brood parasites, and fish that are brood parasites, and even bugs that are brood parasites . . . there are no species of mammals that are, by nature, brood parasites.

Mammals are also the only animals on earth that produce a hormone known as "oxytocin."

It turns out that these factors are related.

In 1909, oxytocin was identified as a pituitary secretion that stimulated birth contractions. Indeed, *oxy* in Greek means "swift," and *tocin* means "birth." Within two years, physicians were using extracted oxytocin to assist in childbirth. It was later found to also be associated with the release of mother's milk, and that's how oxytocin came to be thought of through much of the twentieth century—as a maternal hormone that shows up throughout pregnancy and early child-rearing.

Oxytocin was recognized as a significant contributing factor to the bond between mothers and children. Yes, there is indeed such a thing as a mother's love, but oxytocin is the hormone that drives it. Babies likewise produce oxytocin; they begin to do so while still in the womb, and this helps cement the bond between mother and child.

MORE THAN MOMS

As the twentieth century progressed, endocrinologists—those bright and brainy people who study hormones—noticed something mysterious: women produce oxytocin even when they are not pregnant or raising toddlers. Even women who have never had children can produce oxytocin.

Even more perplexing: *men* produce oxytocin as well.

Studies of burrowing mammals and rodents shed some light on why this is. If you are, say, a prairie dog, you're going to be living in close quarters with others of your kind, and it was found that oxytocin has something to do with this; it helps you view your burrow-mates as family and accept their proximity.

In primates, this tendency, which is known as "tribalism," leads to close bonding with one's own familial group and suspicion of outsiders. Chimpanzees, for instance, interact with members of their own clan by grooming one another, holding one another's young, and sharing food. Life is, by and large, an oxytocin-fueled dream. But if a strange chimpanzee shows up—an outsider—the clan will rise up and drive it away.

Toward the end of the twentieth century, researchers in several fields began studying oxytocin. One was neither an endocrinologist nor a biologist—he was Paul Zak, an economist who was interested in discovering what, precisely, it was that caused prospective business partners to trust one another. He discovered that people given to trust and trustworthiness tend to easily produce oxytocin. On the other hand, distrustful and untrustworthy people are frequently deficient in or even incapable of secreting the hormone.

Zak summarized his findings in 2011 in a now-famous TED Talk called "Trust, Morality—and Oxytocin?" A year later, his book *The Moral Molecule* was published, and interest in the subject of oxytocin skyrocketed.

There were studies on how oxytocin affected first impressions (shallow as it may seem, we are given to like healthy, good-looking people with great facial symmetry). Researchers began drawing blood from people who were in love, and they found oxytocin levels to be particularly high during the first six months of a romantic relationship. Studies of adolescents showed that the oxytocin floods stimulated by the proximity of one's parents gradually gave way to similar floods stimulated by the company of a favored peer group. People who were huggers were virtual oxytocin tooth fairies; not only did they give themselves an oxytocin boost throughout the day, but they also provided the same to the people they hugged.

Consider that, look back on your life, and you can practically chart the rise and fall of your personal oxytocin levels.

And remember: just because you know why it works doesn't mean it isn't magic. It's endocrinology—yet every bit as enchanting as the Fairy Godmother's wand.

WHAT THIS HAS TO DO WITH STORY

Let's return for a moment to Paul Zak. Over the course of his research, he studied oxytocin levels in everyone from British graduate students to the indigenous Māori of Papua, New Guinea. This made Zak highly attuned to signs of oxytocin production in people—including himself. And he began to notice that certain movies and even certain commercials turned on his own, personal oxytocin waterworks.

The stories within these works affected Zak so strongly that it was as if he were experiencing the elements of the story himself, as if he were personally part of the narrative.

This stimulated further study, by Zak and others, into whether narrative can cause people to secrete oxytocin.

It turns out it can—so much so that the United States Department of Defense funded research into the use of narrative to escalate negotiation and de-escalate conflict.

Those studies established that stories that build to a climax and then resolve are the types of stories that do best at building oxytocin, and its related love/trust emotions, in their viewers or listeners.

The dramas of Shakespeare tend to follow that pattern, and they were the subject of close study by the nineteenth-century philosopher and novelist Gustav Freytag. He found that the most resonant of Shakespeare's works (and of the more popular fiction of Freytag's time) tended to contain five essential elements, in this order:

1. The work opens with what ancient Greek dramatists referred to as *protasis*, a word that translates loosely as "proposal." Today, this is most commonly referred to as "exposition": a literary device that provides background relating a character, a setting, or other essential elements of the narrative.

2. The narrative proceeds into an inciting incident that sets the main character or characters in motion. This starts the character's pursuit or, as some people refer to it, the "rising action" of the narrative.

3. The action then rises to *epistasis* (again, Greek—literally meaning "stopping" or "the highest standing"). In everyday language, we say this is where the story builds to a climax.

4. Dramatists refer to the next stage of the narrative as *catastrophe*. This is Greek for "the downward step." In literature classes today, this is usually called "falling action." It leads toward the resolution of the story.

5. The story concludes with a moment of *denouement*. A French word, "denouement" means "unknotting" and it is the point in a narrative where everything becomes clear.

Freytag's story structure is usually displayed in a chart (an example is coming up later in this chapter) in which "exposition" and "denouement" are on separate horizontal lines with an inverted "V"—indicating the placement of "rising action," "climax," and "falling action"—in between them.

> A few things to remember: (1) The climax of a story often does come at the very end and Freytag's Pyramid isn't meant to convey that the climax must occur at the very center of the story, (2) The tip of his pyramid (the highest point of tension) will occur at different places for different stories, and (3) It's

> more important to focus on the pace of your particular story
> than to try and cram it into any particular plot template. Story
> always trumps structure.
>
> —STEVEN

The illustration of this particular narrative structure is known as "Freytag's Pyramid." It is so clear and intuitive, even to people who are not students of drama or literature, that it was adopted by several teams studying how stories could cause readers, watchers, or listeners to experience a rise in oxytocin levels. Stories that followed Freytag's Pyramid tended to perform remarkably well—particularly if the denouement was also a moment of poetic justice.

USING STORY TO CREATE TRUST

I know what you're thinking right now: *Cool! I can find Freytag's Pyramid on the internet! I'll just use it as my "formula," create a story with it, drop it into my next talk, and*—voila!—*everyone who hears it will think I'm amazing.*

Not so fast. You're not only getting ahead of me—you're also getting ahead of yourself.

First of all, while it's true that the stories that best stimulate oxytocin production are those that follow Freytag's Pyramid, many stories that tick every box of Freytag's Pyramid have virtually no emotional effect whatsoever on their audiences. In fact, some audiences find those follow-the-dots stories to be exceptionally boring. If we're hearing a story that we already know by heart or that's too predictable, we are not apt to be moved by it. Also, if we don't have a reason to care about the central character, we don't have a reason to listen. (See chapter 1—especially the info on pivots and payoff—for more on all of this.)

There are numerous other factors that have to be taken into consideration: how the characters of the story are developed, the relationship of those characters to the storyteller, whether the challenges faced are those the audience can identify with, how satisfying the climactic elements and resolution are to the audience, and whether the lingering final sentiment resonates with listeners.

In other words: storytelling matters. Good structure might open a portal to the heartstrings, but it takes great craft and a skillful narrative to tug at them.

PUTTING IT TO WORK

I have been writing speeches and creating presentations for most of my adult life, and storytelling has always been part of this work. I intuitively knew that stories were a very natural and organic way of connecting with people. I knew that audiences warmed quickly to a speaker who told good stories. Practically every time that a story was included in one of my scripts, the audience's reaction was vocal and positive.

Over time I began to discover what sorts of stories I needed to use if I wanted to make that heartstring connection.

The speaker needed to have a personal, direct relationship to the subject of the story. So, it might be a member of a company talking about its historic and popular founder; a longtime member of an organization remembering a turning point in its history; a parent talking about a child; or a child talking about a parent—that sort of thing.

There also needed to be an element of jeopardy in the story. There is no story unless something is at risk, and this peril creates tension—the thing that keeps listeners hanging on every word.

Plus, the story needed to be simple enough that it could be easily digested and repeated, because a story told is almost always preferable to a story that is read. It also had to move swiftly to its climax, because I knew that audience attention spans were notoriously fickle (even before smartphones became ubiquitous). A tightly told story helps keep eyes and ears fixed on the speaker.

I understood that if I added a bit of poetic justice to the end of my story, it would help place the audience on the side of the storyteller, which was critically important.

While most people think of public speaking as a form of communication, it is actually far more than that. Speakers don't just share ideas; they also project personality, and that impression helps shape how the audience perceives the speaker, as well as the organization or cause that the speaker represents. In other words, the act of speaking helps shape what in marketing is referred to as the "brand," and, as we covered in chapter 4, stories can be immensely powerful tools in shaping brand.

The beauty of the research regarding narrative and oxytocin is that it lends the weight of credible science to what storytelling speakers have strongly suspected all along. We now know scientifically that a well-told story does more than illustrate a point to the audience; it also provides a palpable emotional connection and further cements the bond between the storyteller and the listener. It makes a likable person even more likable.

Those same bodies of research also confirm that the oxytocin generated by hearing a good story can help people feel more strongly allied with the storyteller's brand, organization, or cause: that "Sign me up!" feeling we're all familiar with.

I've often said that if you want to clearly communicate a body of information to people, you should put it in writing, but if you want to motivate people to stand with you and act on that information, you should get in front of them and speak. Story helps immensely in reaching that goal. You are not here to simply convey information. You're here to build connections.

So, now you know why it works. And, yes, it's still magic.

TUGGING THE HEARTSTRINGS

"The Telegram Story" is a true story I composed as an illustration in 2015, when I was asked to deliver the closing keynote to the annual conference of the UK Speechwriters' Guild (absolutely no pressure there!), at Cambridge University. The story contains essential elements that various researchers have identified as elevating oxytocin levels in listeners.

I should note that, in this story, we have strong evidence for several of its key, concrete elements, and little or no evidence for many of the smaller details that give it the "you were there" flair.

Insofar as we know, no photographer was present, and no reporter was there to take notes. So, when I could do so without changing the key story elements, I exercised a storyteller's artistic license: inferring, embellishing, and inventing the details necessary to move the story along.

The Telegram Story

Like most modern stories, this begins "in the middle of things," but the opening also sets the stage.

SETTING

Let's travel back in time to March 13, 1928: a cold, damp, winter's evening on America's East Coast.

We are in a train station and, in the late 1920s, years before diesel-powered "streamliners" would become common on transcontinental rail journeys, steam trains are the rule of the day. The scent of coal, cinders, and grease—the muscle and blood of steam locomotives—lingers faintly in the air. Beyond the lighted platforms, steel tracks lead off into darkness.

SETTING

Like other train stations serving New York City, this one would bustle by day, with commuters and intercity passengers making their way to the cars. But now the hour is late. The platforms are mostly dark and only a few passengers wait to board a night train.

My setting has been established. It's time to introduce my main character: Walt Disney. I'm lucky that he remains well known even now, better than half a century after his death. I don't have to do much to make listeners sympathetic to him, other than to indicate that this story takes place relatively early in his career, before he became a Hollywood icon.

There are no known photographs of Walt on this particular evening but, in 1928, people usually did not dress casually for travel. Plus, we have other photos from this general era to give us a hint as to how Walt would travel. I plug those in to give us a sense of this well-known figure during this relatively early stage of his life.

CHARACTER

Walt Disney is there, dressed with his usual deliberate flare: fedora cocked at a rakish angle and topcoat worn open, to avoid crushing the carnation in his lapel.

He is sporting a well-groomed moustache. It's something originally cultivated as a lark, during a studio contest, but he has kept it because he feels it makes him look older than his twenty-six years. He has expressive eyes and—usually—a ready smile.

STRUGGLE FORESHADOWED

But in this moment, we can imagine him as somber.

With him is Lillian, his wife of two years, and, in all probability, she—like he—is uncharacteristically silent.

Those last two sentences are deliberately slanted to lead listeners to believe that something isn't right. That dissonance will create intrigue and concern—both of which will keep listeners tuned in and wanting to learn more as we begin a rise in action.

> Here's what has happened.
>
> The Walt Disney Studios has created its first hit cartoon character, a likable little fellow named Oswald the Lucky Rabbit.
>
> Since April of the preceding year, Disney has produced twenty-three Oswald cartoons. But—following the convention of the time—even though Walt Disney is the creator of Oswald, he produces his cartoons under contract for his distributor, a New Yorker named Charles Mintz. And Mintz, in turn, has contracted the Oswald films and character rights to Universal Pictures, who ultimately promote and release the films to theaters.
>
> Now, with only three cartoons left under the original agreement, Walt has traveled cross-country from Hollywood to New York to negotiate a new contract
>
> Oswald the Lucky Rabbit is popular. He has even inspired his own merchandise.
>
> The contract rate for the initial Oswald cartoons has been $2,250 per film, but everyone agrees that the character is a hit. So, after a week of socializing in the Big Apple, Walt has, earlier on this cold, damp winter's day, asked for an increase to $2,500 per installment.

PURSUIT

And . . . here comes the conflict. This is the part that gets the audience emotionally involved.

The request is reasonable—a mere 10 percent bump. But Charles Mintz has both refused it and countered with a cut: to a mere $1,800 a picture.

Walt is stunned. His company is still making the payments on its new animation studio in Los Angeles. They have staff to pay, the cost of materials; accepting a mere $1,800 per installment means that the Disney studio will lose money on each cartoon.

Then Mintz drops a bombshell; he has already spoken to many of Disney's principal animators. If Walt fails to sign the new contract, these key personnel have agreed to leave his studio and create the Oswald cartoons directly for Mintz.

That prospect shakes Walt Disney even further. If he agrees to Mintz's terms, he will bankrupt his company. So, Walt decides that he has no choice; he walks away.

This is what has brought him to the train station.

Often stories have a moment at which all seems lost. This typically comes right before the climax, when listeners are thinking, *How on earth is the character going to get out of this?* It also gives listeners an indication that a twist is coming. The story needs to cross this hurdle and get to its "downward action" on Freytag's Pyramid.

Walt Disney, who had arrived in New York just a week or so earlier, riding a wave of optimism . . . is now leaving in defeat.

The character that he created is gone.

Virtually his entire skilled workforce is leaving.

He has no contract, no product, no continued income stream, and—for all intents and purposes—no company.

It will soon be time to board the train and begin the long, cross-country trip back to Los Angeles, where Walt will have to break the news to his brother and business partner Roy.

Put yourself in Walt's shoes. What would you do? What would anyone do?

Here is what Walt does. Before boarding his train, he stops into the station's Western Union office to send a telegram to Roy.

It reads:

> LEAVING TONIGHT, STOPPING OVER KC.
> ARRIVE HOME SUNDAY MORNING SEVEN-THIRTY.
> DON'T WORRY. EVERYTHING OKAY.
> WILL GIVE DETALS WHEN ARRIVE.

"DON'T WORRY. *EVERYTHING OKAY.*"

That line sounds like bravado. It sounds like a bluff.

For most people, it would be.

But while Mintz may have walked away with Walt Disney's creation, his finances, and most of his workforce, Walt knows that the principal asset of his studio remains entirely intact.

That asset is Walt Disney's imagination.

PIVOT

Now, Walt rescues himself by creating the world's most beloved cartoon character.

So, as the train pulls out of the station, Walt settles down with a sketch pad and a pencil.

Perhaps he retires to the club car to let Lillian rest. That detail is lost to history.

What we do know, from Walt's later accounts, is that by the time his train arrives in Los Angeles, he has a brand-new character.

This character has the slapstick humor of Buster Keaton, combined with the natural curiosity of a twelve-year-old boy. And this character is not a rabbit.

PAYOFF

PAYOFF

He is a mouse.

In telling the story later, Walt will add a charming detail: he is thinking of calling his new creation "Mortimer." But when he shares this idea with Lillian, she thinks it sounds too old-fashioned, so she suggests an alternative . . .

. . . Mickey Mouse.

With the creation of Mickey Mouse, the story is resolved.

PAYOFF

You know the rest of this story.

Within eight months, the Disney studio releases *Steamboat Willie*, the first Mickey Mouse cartoon.

Less than a year later, Mickey is one of the most popular cartoon characters in the world.

Now the denouement adds a touch of poetic justice. Walt may not have been treated ethically, but in the end he wins.

And around the same time, the scheming Charles Mintz gets his just deserts. He loses the production contract on Oswald the Lucky Rabbit, when Universal decides to move the work in-house.

I've told this story numerous times over the years, and to help audience members remember it, I often end with a small surprise.

"Look under your seats," I'll say. "There's something there that I want you to have." Taped beneath their seats is an envelope with a copy of the telegram from Walt to Roy.

This helps end with an "Aha!" moment and inspires the listeners to dream big, too, and believe in themselves as Walt did that day, all those years ago.

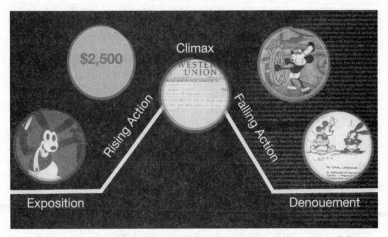

© Disney.

Major elements of "The Telegram Story" overlaid onto Freytag's Pyramid—a commonly used method of representing the rising-action and falling-action elements of story. To the far left is Oswald the Lucky Rabbit, as depicted on the title frames of several 1927 Disney-created cartoons. Next is the amount Walt Disney hoped to receive under a new contract. Depicted in the center is a portion of the actual "DON'T WORRY. EVERY-THING OKAY" telegram sent by Walt to his brother Roy. The fourth image is a still shot from *Steamboat Willie*, the film in which Mickey Mouse made his cinematic debut. And to the far right is a piece of artwork created years after that debut, depicting Mickey Mouse and Oswald the Lucky Rabbit, and inscribed by Walt Disney to Carl Laemmle, owner of Universal from its inception until 1934.

SUMMARY

While you may have a very specific reason for speaking to a group—convincing them to support an initiative that your organization favors, urging them to prefer your product or service, or encouraging them to get involved with your organization—an underlying goal of speaking is almost always to encourage the group to bond with you and, by extension, your brand. The outcome you're after is, to quote Sally Field, "You like me!"

When you speak, story is the best way to encourage people to like you. A well-told story—particularly one with which the audience is not familiar—can actually excite the production of a number of hormones, such as endorphins and dopamine, in your listeners. But the hormone that has the greatest effect is oxytocin; narratives that focus on triumph over adversity and that bask the audience in the afterglow of that triumph can stimulate production of that hormone in your listeners.

Key Points to Remember

- A hormonal response to a story is not a trick. It is simply the automatic response that great stories induce within their listeners.
- Constructing stories by using Freytag's Pyramid is not the only way to get a warm response from your listeners, but it is a reliable method that has been scientifically tested.
- Listeners won't respond warmly to a story they are already familiar with; it has to be novel enough (or told in a sufficiently novel fashion) to convince them to engage emotionally.
- If you are telling a story designed to build a closer relationship with your listeners, be someone they want to be nearer to. Smile. Nod your head at key points of agreement. Make eye contact.
- Remember that, although a certain sort of plot-path often helps, it isn't a formula. Let your guiding light be, "Does this pluck the heartstrings?"

CHAPTER 7

THE SIX MOST COMMON MISTAKES SPEAKERS MAKE

(and How to Avoid Them)

—STEVEN

"All of us are born with a set of instinctive fears—of falling, of the dark, of lobsters, of falling on lobsters in the dark, or speaking before the Rotary Club, or the words 'some assembly required.'"
—Dave Barry, author and humorist

Back in the late nineties, after I finished speaking at an event in Dover, Delaware, the program's organizer pulled me aside, visibly upset.

"You know that story you told about going rock climbing?" he said icily.

"Yes." I'd shared a detailed account of how once, when I was climbing at a bluff called Backbone Rock, in southwest Virginia, a man from another group had been rappelling Australian-style (headfirst rather than backing off the cliff). He lost his grip on the rope and fell about eighty feet. He survived, but, needless to say, it was a harrowing day for everyone at the crag that day.

"Well." The event organizer crossed his arms. "Last week, I heard another storyteller tell that exact same story at another conference and she claimed it happened to her."

"What?"

He told me the details. I recognized the storyteller's name. She was someone on the circuit.

I assured him that I was telling the truth, and even offered to give him the names and phone numbers of the other people who were present in my climbing party at Backbone Rock that day, so he could confirm my story.

He shook his head. "Man. She told it word for word—even describing how the guy's leg was broken and twisted back behind him."

That night as I was trying to figure out how this woman could have recounted the story so closely to my version, I remembered that I'd written up the account for a magazine a few months earlier. Since it was in a magazine she might very well have subscribed to, I guessed that she likely read the story and decided to retell it as if it had happened to her. Consequently, when I shared it, this man who'd invited me to speak thought I'd stolen it from her. I can't blame him—anyone who heard the two stories might have thought the same thing.

Initially, it caused him to lose trust in me. I'm just glad he spoke to me and not to someone else about it.

The woman was on tour around the country sharing my story. If she would have simply contacted me and asked if she could tell it, I would have said, "Sure, just say that it happened to this guy you met named Steven." The story would have had the same effect.

She was making one of the six cardinal mistakes that public speakers make.

MISTAKE #1—STEALING OTHER PEOPLE'S ILLUSTRATIONS

Perhaps the woman who was telling my story had no idea that what she was doing wasn't ethical.

So, what's the rule? If you hear a good story, can you retell it? Can you claim it as your own? It's possible to plagiarize written work—what about orally told stories? Is it possible to plagiarize those?

A pastor once told me that taking a sermon you heard someone else preach and then preaching it yourself was like eating someone else's food and then throwing it up on your congregation. Good intentions don't excuse dishonesty. Whenever you personalize someone else's illustration and claim the event happened to you, you're undermining your own authority. Most public speakers today view this as unethical.

As author and speaker Mike Yaconelli noted, "Life is lived with interruptions, boring trivia, details that don't fit together. It's not unethical to remove all these factors when you tell a story. That's the art and heart of storytelling. What is unethical is when I make somebody else's story mine, when I speak as though an event happened to me—when it actually didn't. Or when I knowingly take a story that ends *this* way and I deliberately distort it to end *that* way because it makes a better story."

Here are five principles to remember:

1. People's personal stories belong to them. You shouldn't take someone else's experience and claim it as your own.
2. If you want to tell a story that's not your own, get permission. Even if you're not being paid to tell it, it's still your responsibility to clear your telling of the story with the person who wrote it.
3. It's not your job or your right to expose someone's personal life without their permission. Don't tell stories

that would offend or embarrass others—or obtain their permission first, before telling those stories.

4. If you hear a folktale or an urban legend, those are in the public domain. However, a storyteller's unique take on it or specific approach to retelling it remains their property. Don't copy that.

5. If you hear a story told as part of a sacred or religious ceremony from a culture not your own, it's wise to ask the teller for permission to tell it—and be respectful and understanding if the answer is no. (For more tips on telling multicultural stories, see chapter 8.)

Key thought: Your own life is bizarre

enough. Use it. Be honest.

MISTAKE #2— FAILING TO PROPERLY PREPARE

The best storytellers prepare with their listeners in mind and also remain flexible to respond to the audience's nonverbal feedback as they tell. Storytelling combines both preparation and alertness. Read the room. For instance: *This isn't making sense to them. I need to slow down, regroup, and help them picture what's going on.*

Listen to the way the story sounds as you practice it. Some storytellers string every sentence together with the word "and." This is common when a story is in early development, but can be annoying in live delivery. Listen for words that you repeat over and over such as "um," "uh," or "well," and repeated phrases such as "This is interesting." Weed those out.

Listen—really listen—to inspirational speakers, actors, comedians, storytellers, and other gifted communicators. Listen to the way they use sounds to shape mental images. Notice the good habits they have—the delicate pause, the rapport with the audience, the natural flow of movement and gestures. Also, take note of the bad habits—the distracting mannerisms, the way they sway when they speak, the annoying verbal tics, the awkward transitions. Learn from those as well.

Avoid letting your narrative wander all over the place. Typically, it'll be clear to listeners when you haven't put in the time in your preparation.

Focus your story, think it through, and practice it aloud.

A lack of spontaneity and response to the listeners will also come across as evidence of poor preparation. The audience can usually tell when a presenter is just going through their schtick, the exact same way they did at the last conference or event. Sure, the speaker has organized and clearly rehearsed his material, but he isn't being responsive to how it's going today. That will turn listeners off.

Responsiveness is just as important as preparation. Listening is as important as speaking. Take the time to really learn your material, and then appropriately respond to your audience.

Key thought: Practice your story.
Prepare, but also be ready to improvise if
the circumstances dictate doing so.

Often, when you're asked to speak at an event, those who have invited you will want you to do a Q&A. They certainly have the best intentions, but Q&A sessions have several drawbacks. Often, the questions might not apply to the whole group and so some people end up feeling left out (that's when the phones come out and folks start checking their texts).

Second, some attendees just like to hear themselves talk and never actually get to a pertinent question, wasting everyone's time. Other times, audience members might be argumenta-tive. And finally, during a Q&A, you're no longer the one in charge of the pace, flow, or energy of the presentation—people who may not have the best interests of others in mind are call-ing the shots instead. We want to save the best for last, and Q&A sessions often undermine that.

So, if a Q&A is essential, tell attendees, "I'll be addressing some of your questions in a few minutes and then I'll share some closing thoughts." Then, after the Q&A, end with a pow-erful closing story and leave the listeners wanting more—that you can deliver the next time they invite you to speak.

MISTAKE #3—INADVERTENTLY BECOMING THE HERO

Years ago, when I was writing personal stories for magazines, my editor, Eddy Hall, told me, "Steven, whenever you write a story about your life, be the mistake-maker. No one wants to hear about how great you are—or think you are."

So, I started brainstorming and listing memories of the most em-barrassing, boneheaded, and idiotic things I'd done over the years. I realized I had plenty of material after all. (If you know me at all, you know how true this is!) It helped me sell more than a dozen stories to different publications.

Once, around that time, I was speaking at a Valentine's Day ban-quet for teens. I was there to provide some comedy, but before I went onstage, the local youth pastor took the mic to, as he put it, "say a few words."

I knew that was not a good sign.

He began his few words by saying, "I'm not trying to brag, but . . ."

I remember thinking, *Oh, this is going to be brutal.* (Any time you find yourself tempted to say, "I'm not trying to brag, but . . ." avoid the temptation. No matter how well you try to hide it, it'll come across as if you are bragging.)

He went on, "When I was in high school there was this girl who wanted to have sex with me, but I told her, 'No! How could I do such a wicked thing and sin against God?'"

Then the youth pastor went on to explain how often she came onto him and how he had "stood up for purity and for abstinence." A year after they broke up, she became pregnant while in a different relationship. The youth pastor helped her get through the situation. Maybe adopted her baby for her . . . before moving overseas to solve world hunger on his way to a Nobel Prize . . . during spring break.

This was in the days before the popularity of cell phones, but by then nearly all the teens at the banquet were slumped in their chairs—bored—or whispering and snickering to each other.

Finally, twenty-five minutes after announcing that he was going to say a few words, the pastor introduced me: "Okay! It's time for Steven James!"

Not the greatest "warm-up act" I'd ever had.

It was a rough night for all of us.

Tell stories about your struggles and discoveries rather than times when you were the hero. If I were that youth pastor trying to get his abstinence message across, I would've started in the back seat of the car:

> The windows were steamed up and I knew we'd been kissing too long. I heard a voice in my head: *Go ahead, unbutton her shirt. You know you want to . . .*
>
> And another voice: *No, get out now! Step away!*
>
> Two voices pulling me in different directions . . .

Teens have heard those voices. The choices, consequences, or mistakes that the minister might have included in his story would be an example for them. By being vulnerable and authentic, he could've emphasized how difficult it was to do what he believed was right. No matter who your listeners are, they'll identify far more readily with your struggles than with your successes. We don't typically identify with story characters who have no difficulties or who are just there to give advice.

So, whenever you're looking for personal stories to share, think about your temptations, questions, wounds, and regrets. Mull over the lessons you learned. Focus on the challenge, not the accomplishment.

As Eddy taught me, be the mistake-maker, not the answer-giver. You're the one who learns, not the one who teaches. You're crediting the hero, not claiming to be him. Hollywood script consultant Michael Hauge puts it this way: "Talk about the mentors who guided you, or the loved ones who stood by you or the words of wisdom and inspiration that kept you going."

This aspect of being the mistake-maker is such an important aspect of telling personal stories that it's worth examining more in depth. How does it actually play out in the stories you share?

For good material, look for memories of times when you were underprepared (naïve) or overconfident (proud).

Your listeners don't want to hear about your successes; they want to hear about your missteps and mistakes, how you took your knocks and learned something important that shaped your view of life. So, emphasize not how you triumphed, but how you floundered. Those are the stories people want to hear, not the ones about the times when you did everything right.

For practice, look at the list of story starters below and choose the five that would *not* be good to use since they focus on accomplishments rather than struggles. (Hint: Some stories deal with discoveries, so don't be tricked. If it seems like you'd end up looking like the hero, stay clear of that story.)

Okay, give it a shot:

- Things didn't go as planned . . .
- You learned a lesson the hard way . . .
- You tried to impress someone and it backfired . . .
- You consistently did the right thing and were finally appreciated for it . . .
- You wondered if maybe you'd finally gone too far in a relationship . . .
- You had a hard time letting go of something or someone . . .
- You worked hard to earn a second chance and it paid off . . .
- You faced a tough decision . . .
- You were stuck between a rock and a hard place . . .
- You decided to take life by the horns and embark on a new chapter in your life . . .
- You overcame great hardship to make something of yourself . . .
- You stepped out on a limb and it broke off . . . but you learned about the benefits of taking a risk . . .
- You sacrificed something for the one you loved . . .
- You didn't heed a warning and paid the price . . . but discovered something useful in the process . . .
- You thought you could do something but failed . . . and learned about the importance of humility . . .

Let's focus on the five examples that wouldn't be such effective stories to tell. Can you see that in each of these stories you would come across as the hero rather than the mistake-maker or the struggler?

- You consistently did the right thing and were finally appreciated for it . . .
- You worked hard to earn a second chance and it paid off . . .
- You decided to take life by the horns and embark on a new chapter in your life . . .
- You overcame great hardship to make something of yourself . . .
- You sacrificed something for the one you loved . . .

But wait, what about that last one? It can certainly be difficult to sacrifice for someone else, right? Yes; emphasizing the difficulty of that decision could make a good story, but if the story comes across as *Look at how much I sacrificed for so and so!* then it wouldn't be a great one to share.

Once again, focusing on recounting incidents of naïveté or over-confidence will steer you in the right direction as you consider which stories to tell.

Key thought: Your story is not about your victories, but about what you learned, how you changed, or how you grew through a struggle.

Often, when people start telling stories from their lives, the question comes up, "How much can I change my story and still claim it's true?" Some of the answer depends on the context—a campfire setting or comedy club has entirely different expectations than a courtroom or pulpit. For most story sharing, you'll want to stick to the core truths of the event. (Storytellers make changes to reveal the truth, not to conceal it.) In casual social settings, feel free to:

- Add dialogue that represents what might have been said.
- Include realistic details to create memorable images of the setting.
- Edit out or condense superfluous incidents when necessary.
- Conflate characters if there are too many people in your story.

MISTAKE #4— PORTRAYING YOURSELF AS THE VICTIM

This happens at the other end of the spectrum from the last mistake. Here, rather than telling the audience how great you are, you tell them how hurt you are. This might make you feel better by getting something off your chest, but it doesn't put your listeners' needs first.

You're not onstage for therapy. Your listeners are not your counselors. They're listening to you for their benefit, not yours. Resolve your issues before you're onstage, not while you are. Evaluate if you're plying for sympathy or perhaps venting to people you don't need to be venting to.

If you have unresolved conflict or issues, deal with them before you get up in front of the group. If you're still working through your divorce, don't tell your listeners stories about how miserable you are or how terrible your ex is. That might be more of a conversation to have with your best friend over a beer at the local pub rather than onstage or in a boardroom. Don't use the audience as a means of trying to resolve personal or psychological problems. They will feel used, and that's never what you want.

I've seen some speakers break into tears as they relate details about difficult times they're going through—inadvertently inviting pity from their listeners. Avoid this. Storytelling may be therapeutic, but not on your listeners' time. Clearly, those tellers hadn't yet worked through their feelings related to those incidents. A situation like that makes the listeners feel uncomfortable and they don't know what role they're supposed to play. If a memory is still so tender that you can't talk about it without tearing up, it might be too soon to start telling that story. (Apart from the exception to this that Tom mentioned in chapter 2.)

Also, don't start your talk by apologizing to your listeners: "I get nervous in front of people, so you'll have to forgive me," or "I'm sorry—I didn't know I'd have to go on without my slides." See how these types of comments don't serve the audience?

Stay in control of your emotions—it'll help your audience feel comfortable. You're not here for yourself. You're here for the benefit of the listeners, not the other way around.

Key thought: Storytelling isn't therapy. Deal with your issues before you get onstage.

MISTAKE #5—GOING TOO LONG

I remember speaking at a conference that was on a very tight schedule. I had eighteen minutes to speak. Period. There were 4,500 people in attendance and the organizers were doing all they could to stay on track with their schedule. So, when I went onstage, there was a digital clock positioned at the base of the stage and it started ticking down the moment I stepped up to the mic.

Eighteen minutes. When the timer had ticked off to three minutes remaining, a message flashed: "Wrap it up." When it hit one minute, the message read, "End now." That day I managed to get offstage in time, but I found out later that there was a third message that came up if you went over your time that read, "Get off the stage!"

Steven is right to emphasize this. Running over your allotted time is like sitting down at a table, eating all your dinner, and then—without asking permission—eating half your neighbor's food as well. It's rude, and it might rightly be described as passive aggression. Don't let a lack of preparation turn you into your conference organizer's nightmare. Be considerate and stay within your allotted time so that the rest of the program can get its full share of time as well.

—TOM

Speakers who go too long sometimes think that they're "giving the audience their money's worth," or something to that effect. But overstaying your onstage welcome makes you look selfish. So, be sure to find out before you accept the speaking invitation how much time you're being asked to speak for. You don't want to prepare for fifteen minutes and then be told right before you walk onstage that you have five (or vice versa!).

Also, as a general rule, don't tell a group that you're going to be brief or that you're not going to be long-winded. That's a promise that people will take in different ways, and there'll always be someone who thinks you didn't keep your word. (Also, never say, "To make a long story short . . ." By the time you say that, it's already too late.)

For the most part, people won't complain that your talk was shorter than they expected. However, if you go over your time—or go longer than they anticipated—you'll lose them.

This happens often with graduation speeches. The audience doesn't want a long litany of advice on how to live their lives. A short talk, a few salient points, a powerful story or two, and that's enough.

Make it a habit to respect your time limit. It's a way of being considerate to those who've invited you, any other speakers who are there, and your audience.

Key thought: Keep it short and concise.

Know when to end.

MISTAKE #6—BEING TOO PREDICTABLE

My college speech professor taught us that in our speeches we should "tell people what you're going to say, say it, then tell them what you said." The idea was that, through repetition, our listeners would remember the main point. (Tom mentioned to me that this saying has been variously attributed to Dale Carnegie or Aristotle—so, either way, it's been around for a while!)

When I started public speaking, I didn't know any better, so I went ahead and followed my professor's advice.

While my audiences were patient with me and put up with it, I had the sense that they were tuning out rather than tuning in after I told them where my talk was going. I was losing them right when I wanted them to pay closer attention.

Then one day when I was taking a break from work and catching an afternoon matinee, I realized why his approach wasn't working.

The film was a spy movie, one of my favorite genres. I love the action, surprises, twists, fight scenes, and glamorous locations.

Well, can you imagine a spy thriller that starts with this voice-over: "Against all odds, Secret Agent Carver will use the blowtorch in his wristwatch to cut through the handcuffs and escape at the climax!"

Then, as the climax arrives, the voice-over interrupts again: "See? Here at the climax, Agent Carver is using the blowtorch in his wristwatch to cut through the handcuffs and escape!" And then, as the movie comes to a close and the credits roll, the voice-over interjects one last time to remind us of what we saw: "As you noticed, against all odds, Agent Carver used the blowtorch in his wristwatch to cut through the handcuffs and escape at the climax!"

It doesn't work that way with movies. Instead, the filmmakers trust the audience's natural curiosity to keep them interested. Using the tools of a storyteller, they skillfully create a climax that both surprises and satisfies viewers—and is memorable. If they started by telling us the solution to the mystery or how the clever twist plays out at the end, we would lose interest. We might even become angry at them for ruining the movie.

My speech teacher's "tried and true" advice was like a spoiler for a movie—it gave too much away. His technique was a deductive approach rather than an inductive one. In other words, it was a way of telling people what *you* have concluded rather than inviting them to draw the conclusion *for themselves*. His formula focused on information dissemination but didn't foster discovery, as we covered in chapter 3.

I've found more success in approaching speeches like a movie director than like my speech professor. Audiences like to feel trusted, so give them the puzzle pieces and allow them to lock them together.

As people listen to your presentation, they're both processing what's being said and predicting what will happen next. The best speeches, jokes, and stories end in a way that is satisfying but isn't predictable. Just as with a great novel or movie, people want to guess how the story or speech will end, but they want to be wrong—yet still satisfied. The revelation that the conclusion brings should always be worth the time spent on the pathway toward it.

(Remember the pivot and the payoff from the Story Cube explanation in chapter 1? Keep those two unsung heroes in mind when you tell your stories.)

But how do you keep people's attention when you're telling them a story that they already know the ending to or teaching them a lesson they already know? Ask yourself, "What doesn't seem to fit?" "What surprises me?" "What have I never noticed in this story before?"

Even though it sounds paradoxical, you can use people's familiarity with a story to your advantage and leverage their assumptions to undermine their defenses.

When your listeners are familiar with a story or think they know where you are going with the lesson, pull the rug out. Add a twist. Add a surprise. Strive to give your listeners what they didn't know they wanted. Let the ending resonate with them in a way they weren't prepared for.

Key thought: Foster curiosity in your stories.

Don't give too much away too early.

SUMMARY

When telling personal stories, remain vulnerable. Walk the narrow line that separates vain self-indulgence and the off-putting uncomfortableness of true confessions. Honesty and vulnerability are vital ingredients in a personal story, although each appears in different stories to varying degrees, depending on the audience and the social context. So, be vulnerable, but not fragile.

In your personal stories, portray yourself truthfully and realistically, but not as the hero or the victim. Diligently prepare, but also be ready to adapt to the changing circumstances of the storytelling event as it occurs.

Be concise. Be brief. Get to the point. Tell your story the best you know how, then get off the stage.

Key Points to Remember

- Get permission before telling someone else's story.
- Make sure you're sharing your stories for your listeners' benefit, not just your own.
- Remember that in your personal stories you'll be the mistake-maker rather than the answer-giver.
- People are more interested in the lessons you've learned than in the accomplishments you've had, so focus on the challenges and setbacks, not the achievements.
- Give your listeners what they didn't know they wanted by adding a twist or surprise at the conclusion of your story.

CHAPTER 8

DIVERSITY AND INCLUSION

The Story of Each of Us, the Story of All of Us

—TOM

"Civilizations should be measured by the degree of diversity attained and the degree of unity retained."
—W. H. Auden, poet

In most businesses and many homes today, there is an elephant in the room. In the manner of elephants, it appears to be gray.

But, examined more closely, it is black. It is brown. It is white. It is all the colors that there are.

The sounds that it makes are every sound.

And the name of that elephant is "diversity."

WALKING CIRCUMSPECTLY

Of course, the "elephant in the room" is a common phrase, describing something that everyone knows is there, but no one is eager to mention.

That's one way to think about diversity. People seem, by and large, to be extremely wary of broaching the subject.

Part of the reason might be that a great many public figures have managed to alienate large segments of their audiences with comments on diversity. Some (possibly most) of these folks start out with the very best of intentions, but end up with the proverbial foot ankle-deep in their mouths.

Thinking about this brought me back to a university course I took on the Western storytelling tradition. To help us learn where the stories of Western civilization sprang from, my professor (whose background was theology) had us read Greek and Roman mythology, and he also asked us to read, in its entirety, the King James Bible (in fact, he even expected us to commit large chunks of it to memory—an arduous challenge, to say the least). In the course of doing that, I found several Bible passages that often make their ways back to the surface as I consider current events. One such passage is in the fifth chapter of the Book of Ephesians:

> See then that ye walk circumspectly, not as fools, but as wise, redeeming the time, because the days are evil.

That phrase "walk circumspectly" might not be familiar to every modern reader, so let's explain it this way: if you leave an unhousebroken puppy in a room with a tile floor, and you need to cross that room three hours later to answer the door . . . you'll probably need to walk circumspectly.

Foresight and caution are necessary when you discuss any subject that people are passionate about. Diversity is one of those subjects and, when I talk about diversity, I often find that—as I strive to walk circumspectly—a story is my friend.

UNPACKING DIVERSITY

To some people, "diversity" might seem like a relatively new term (as might its close cousins "inclusion" and "equity"). When it comes to the concepts of fairness and integration, these terms are not new;

diversity education has been around for more than half a century. But the reason they *seem* new is legislation.

The Civil Rights Act of 1964 outlawed discrimination on the basis of race, color, religion, sex, national origin, and (in later legislation and interpretations) age, sexual orientation, and gender identity. On the world stage, the International Convention on the Elimination of All Forms of Racial Discrimination was adopted by the United Nations General Assembly the following year, in 1965. So, today, most people in the Western world have lived most or all of their years in an environment mandating equality in terms of employment, voting rights, education, and other areas of access.

Because the first thing most organizations and workplaces wanted to do was put themselves in compliance with the law, the phrase used most commonly when discussing fairness was, for many years, "equal opportunity." You've heard it and you've seen it. For years, most businesses have displayed government posters espousing equal opportunity, so that's the value that first comes to mind when we discuss fairness, race, and difference; most people think first about *equality*.

Say "We are all equal" today, and—on principle, at least, regarding our human worth—most people will agree with you. Say "We are all the same," and most people will *still* agree with you.

The only problem is, in the second case, they would all be wrong.

That is because there is a world of difference between "equal" and "identical."

Yet we think they are the same because, however well intentioned, we've been taught that this is the goal of a free society.

This is particularly true in America, where one idea, almost as old as the country itself, is that—metaphorically—the nation is a "great melting pot." The phrase first appeared in the eighteenth century and has persisted to this day. The idea is that myriad cultures come to the United States and then are assimilated into a single new, homogenous, and distinctly American culture.

I once had a librarian from Illinois ask me what culture I told stories from. "Oh. American," I said.

"But what culture?" she said.

"American," I repeated.

"No, no. What *culture*?"

"American." I wondered if I was missing something. Was it a trick question?

"But where are your stories *from*?"

"Well, America. I'm from America. My parents are from America. My grandparents are from America. All of my family lives here. This is my country. I tell American stories."

She stared at me, bewildered. It was as if she'd never considered the fact that the United States of America had a culture of its own worth preserving. It was eye-opening for me. Stories aren't inherently better just because they're from far away or long ago. The stories we tell today are just as vital and worth sharing as the classic folk and fairy tales of the past.

—STEVEN

That does happen, to a degree, but some cultures melt more thoroughly than others.

Then there is the fact that—particularly in the first several generations as Americans—identity and family tradition all come into play when one group becomes part of another. This is to be expected: the past is known and familiar to us, and we are usually hesitant to let go of it entirely.

Case in point: My mother was Slovak, a head-scratcher of an ethnicity for most people. There is a country today known as "Slovakia" or "the Slovak Republic," but it did not exist prior to 1993. At the time my maternal great-grandparents immigrated to America, Slovaks were an ethnic minority within the Kingdom of Hungary.

Like many Slovak families, Mom's family settled near the end of the nineteenth century in the small northern Illinois town of Streator, not far from the site of the very first Lincoln-Douglas debate. On the surface, the family assimilated (my maternal grandfather was a deputy sheriff in his county) but, at their homes and in their neat and well-tended neighborhoods, Streator's Slovak community retained its Old World culture for several decades. They formed a Catholic parish dedicated to their members, complete with a parochial school that taught its students to speak and sing in Slovak, and I remember large family gatherings where my mother and aunts made *lokše* and other traditional recipes.

My father's family was Irish, but had been in the New World a generation longer than my mother's. His only language was English (it being the dominant Irish tongue at the time his family crossed the Atlantic), but we knew a smattering of Irish ballads and laments, and Dad had a green necktie that he wore only on St. Patrick's Day. So, since "Slovak" as an ethnicity was more than a bit obtuse, I grew up considering myself to be Irish (the "American" part of "Irish American" would not enter my vocabulary until my second or third year of college).

You can look at me and think that I am white. To a certain degree, the conclusion would be accurate. But, to me, this is a generalization that doesn't even begin to describe my roots.

And my case is just the very tip of the iceberg. Our society is extremely complicated.

So, when we interpret "We are all equal" to mean "We are all the same" . . . really, we're not. By using the term "diversity," we acknowledge that. The word "diverse" implies "many different kinds." It pretty much guarantees an assortment.

AND THE OTHER TWO TERMS . . .

To use a sports analogy (we're discussing business; we have to do that at least once): diversity gets you on the roster, inclusion adds you to the team, and equity guarantees that everyone gets to start within reach of the goal line—you don't get penalized for looking different, sounding different, or having your own values and beliefs.

"Equity" differs from "equality" in that equity eliminates potential barriers and makes participation possible for a much broader spectrum of people. Equity acknowledges structural imbalances (such as the biases that have traditionally made science, technology, engineering, and mathematics male-dominated fields) and takes steps to correct those imbalances.

In a diverse, inclusive, and equitable business, everyone is welcome and everybody gets a chance, even though they all have different and distinct identities.

It's not "equality" in the sense that not everyone gets the raise, the promotion, or the bonus—but those who do will achieve those things through talent and dedication, and not simply because they conform to a mainstream identity.

So, now that we have the groundwork laid, how do we talk about this?

In most diversity discussions today, there are three goals:

1. Educating your organization on the advantages of welcoming people from all backgrounds and all walks of life (in addition to doing the right thing socially, diverse organizations, by their very nature, address a broader population and therefore access a wider talent pool and a deeper customer base).

2. Assuring people from underrepresented groups that they are welcome, included, and needed in your

organization, and demonstrating that this is a fact, not a catchphrase.

3. Explaining that "diversity" means that everyone is sincerely encouraged to be themselves; no need to alter accents, appearances, attitudes, or beliefs in order to blend in. "Authentic" is a word commonly used in this context.

But before you discuss any of this, it is first necessary to break the ice and introduce the subject.

I've already said that I advocate story as a means of talking about diversity and inclusion. The best way for me to explain why . . . is to share a few stories.

WELCOME TO THE CLUB

Many years ago, my very first speechwriting job was for . . . well, there is a tradition among speechwriters that, unless we are encouraged to do so by the people for whom we write, we do not reveal their names. So, I will not. But allow me to say that my first speechwriting client was a household name at the time: the now-deceased chairman of a major automaker and a person frequently quoted in the news.

I wrote for him because, years before, I had done a favor for a fellow who was the chairman's director of communications and personal speechwriter. So, when my friend was about to go on vacation and needed someone to stand in for him, he asked if I was available, and I said, "Sure."

What he didn't ask is if I had ever written a corporate speech before.

I had not.

Newspaper articles? Scores. Magazine features? Dozens. Press releases and short stories? A few.

But other than rhetoric assignments in college, I'd never written a speech.

Still, I'd heard a bunch of them. I'd seen the chairman himself speaking on TV. So, flush with the confidence of unbruised youth, I felt I had a pretty good grasp of his style. Furthermore, even though I'd not educated myself at all on the mechanics of writing a speech, I had quickly checked to see what freelance speechwriters were charging in major markets, and planted my fee right in the upper third of that range.

I suppose I appeared to know what I was doing.

Amazingly, it all worked out—but not because I was such an accomplished rhetorician.

The chairman was one of those old-school public speakers who liked to open every speech with a joke; not a humorous story or anecdote, but a plain, minute-long, complete-with-punchline, best-told-while-gesturing-with-an-unlit-cigar joke. This is not a tactic I advise, as virtually every joke is likely to be offensive to *someone*, but it was what the chairman preferred, so I went with it.

Now, if I had bothered to research how professional speechwriters worked in those pre-internet times, I would have learned that most had handy, five- or six-book libraries of joke books.

I had no such library. I didn't even know such books existed. So, for that first speech, I researched the speech, wrote it, subjected it to an extensive review by the automaker's public affairs and legal departments, made their edits, and then, armed with the knowledge of where the speech was going and who the audience would be, I wrote an *original* joke with which to open the speech.

Then the chairman did what I would later learn was what he did *most* of the time when he gave a speech. He delivered my joke, verbatim—he understood that, in comedy, timing is everything— the audience laughed uproariously, and then he spoke . . . on whatever happened to be on his mind that morning.

He didn't read the rest of the script at all: not because he didn't like it, but simply because, unless the subject was highly strategic, he preferred to speak extemporaneously.

He loved the reaction to the joke, though, and he'd heard enough speeches to understand that what he'd read was original.

So, I was requested for another speech.

In all, I did five speaker's scripts for the chairman while my colleague was on vacation. In the meantime, I got as smart as I could, as fast as I could, on speechwriting. I found a mentor, an experienced speechwriter who advised me, critiqued my scripts, and—eventually, after I'd finished my temporary assignment with the chairman—took me on as an associate and regularly farmed out speeches to me.

I continued to do freelance speechwriting as I did other writing, even after I'd become an editor at an advertising agency, and even after I'd taken a publications editing job with another automaker.

I'd been in that role for about a year when I was summoned to that automaker's headquarters to meet with the head of the corporate speechwriting team.

Learning in advance that they were looking for a new full-time speechwriter for their corporate chairman, I spent several nights pulling together samples of my best corporate scripts, drilling myself on the names of my favorite rhetorical devices, and generally getting ready for as intense an interview as the department might wish to conduct.

Then I arrived downtown, and the interview began something like this:

DEPARTMENT HEAD (*in a thick, faux-Irish brogue*): "Thomas
    Morrisey . . ."
ME: "Nice to meet you."
DEPARTMENT HEAD: "And what would your confirmation
    name be?"

ME: "My middle name is 'George,' sir; I generally don't use my confirmation name."

DEPARTMENT HEAD: "But, still . . ."

ME: "Michael."

DEPARTMENT HEAD (*again with the brogue*): "Thomas George Michael Morrisey . . . as in Michael, the archangel."

ME (*hesitantly*): "Yes."

DEPARTMENT HEAD: "You came up here in Detroit, at Most Holy Trinity?"

ME: "No, sir. A small church in rural Illinois: St. Patrick's."

DEPARTMENT HEAD: "Ah! St. Patrick's! Of course! Let's go meet the team."

I met the team and we all headed out to lunch together. I cannot remember if there was a Houlihan, a McNamara, or an O'Neill in the bunch, but, of the seven or eight men at the table (and they were all men), red hair and freckles predominated, several were Notre Dame alumni, and the thing they all seemed happiest about was my Irish surname.

After lunch, I asked the department head if he would like to go through my samples.

"Oh, no," he said. "We hear you are very talented, and we have plenty of folks who can tutor you on the fine points, if need be. We think you'll fit in just fine; HR will be calling you."

I kept my composure, bid him adieu . . . and seethed through the long elevator ride down to the lobby, thinking about and dissecting what had just happened.

My surname had identified me as Irish American. The question about my confirmation name had been meant to ferret out my faith: Roman Catholics take an additional name at confirmation, while the practice is rare among Protestant faiths. Especially in that long-ago time, when the Troubles plagued Northern Ireland,

Irish Catholics and Irish Protestants had between them a gulf so deep and so wide that the two considered one another to be separate nationalities.

It was apparent to me that my experience and my talent were not what had placed me in the running for a role with the speechwriting department. True, having a modicum of experience was essential, but what had actually opened the door was my superficial ability to qualify as a member of the club.

I had worked hard at my craft. I thought I was being considered because the company felt I had talent. It disgusted me that I was being considered a *type*.

I did not want a role earned by my altar-boy upbringing or my potential to father redheaded children. I wanted to be recognized for my abilities, and I considered it providential when my former ad agency phoned me two days later—before the automaker's HR department had the chance to make their call—and hired me back as a vice president.

Yet I still bristle when I think of that interview.

And although the thought would not dawn on me until many years later, I often wonder today how many people of equal (or greater) talent had applied for the role at that speechwriting department and been denied an interview because of their heritage, their faith, their gender, the color of their skin, or some other superficial—and, in terms of qualifications, totally irrelevant—difference.

> I once had a renowned literary agent send me an email telling me flat out that she wouldn't work with me because I'm a white male. And she added an emoticon smiley face afterward! (I guess to make me feel better? Who knows?) At least she was honest . . .

Now, I realize that this experience is nothing compared to the discrimination some people face; however, it was at least a brief encounter with their world. It instilled in me a little more empathy toward those who experience more crushing forms of discrimination. And I've come to realize that every step in that direction is, in the end, a valuable one.

—STEVEN

PRIVILEGE

When we talk about equal opportunity, equal access, and inclusion, a word that often comes up is "discrimination"—almost always in a negative context. When someone is passed over or excluded because of a social, cultural, or ethnic difference, we say that person has been "discriminated against," and unfortunately the practice is so common that nearly everyone knows someone to whom it has happened.

Discrimination is, however, a two-way street. As my story about the Irish Catholic American speechwriting department clearly shows, it is possible to discriminate *toward* a person as well.

There is a word for such favorable discrimination. It is called "privilege."

Now, here's the thing about privilege: the mere mention of the term almost universally raises the hackles of the privileged.

It certainly did with me, the first time I heard it.

For most of my life, I had associated "privilege" with silver spoons in the mouths of babes, live-in housekeepers, trust funds, Ivy League colleges, and silk-stockinged professions—things as foreign to me as the far side of the moon. Like most people of my generation, I'd worked my way through college and grad school, didn't own anything even close to a new car until I was well into my twenties, and along the way did a lot of the menial work that I thought of as "paying dues."

I did not consider myself to be privileged. I was satisfied that I'd never had anything handed to me, and my family was so not "connected" that nepotism was not even a distant possibility.

The thing is, I had also never had anything *denied* to me because of my gender, sexual orientation, age, family background, beliefs, or skin color. When I applied for a role, I had every expectation of being considered for it, and when I went to meetings, I expected my opinions to be received and thoughtfully considered.

That is because my entire life, I have worked for organizations in which people who look like me, sound like me, and believe like me tend to constitute the overwhelming majority. While I believe I earned my way into every one of the roles I have played over the years, I never encountered a barrier based on any stereotype and would have been astounded if I did.

In other words, I was—and I am—privileged.

If, like me, you work for or lead organizations in which people, by and large, look like you, sound like you, and believe like you, a good way to open a conversation about diversity and inclusion is to acknowledge the privilege that you—consciously or unconsciously—have enjoyed for most of your career. It places your cards on the table; it makes it clear that you understand that the "ticket in"—elusive to half the world or better—has been in your pocket your entire life. And you cannot talk about equality without first acknowledging that for decades, centuries, and even longer, the scales have been heavily imbalanced.

That is a good way to start the conversation.

For the wrong way, let's share another story—a short one.

YOU DON'T KNOW ME

In economics and—by extension—in business, recessions are like sunspots. A new one shows up around every eleven years or so, and each affects its environment in its own way.

As a longtime speechwriter, I did not take more than casual notice of sunspots.

But recessions usually take a speechwriter's career and put it up on cinder blocks: idled until the time comes for leaders to make sense of it all as they lead their organizations back into the daylight. Since their roles appear to shareholders to be a dispensable extravagance, speechwriters tend to be among the first out when organizations are being streamlined due to a downturn.

But, because they are so essential to making sense of vision and of brand, they tend also to be some of the first ones back. So, after you have seen one of these cycles, the rest become simpler to weather.

"Simple" is not the same as "easy"; cinder blocks are a profoundly uncomfortable surface upon which to rest. Every time a person goes off contract, or on furlough, there is always the question of whether there will be an organization left to return to, or—assuming there is—how it will have changed.

On paper, I weathered one such twenty-first-century furlough relatively easily. I was on salary when I got the notice that my role was being placed on "pause." Thankfully, I had six weeks of vacation pay banked, so I drew from that and got a good start writing a book while I waited to be called back. The call finally came at the eight-week point, so I lost very little pay during the time off.

Still, I remember quite vividly a conversation I had with a senior executive at the company—one who had continued to work at full salary during the time I was away on furlough.

"I'm glad to see you back," she told me warmly. "I know how hard it was to be off."

Externally, I smiled and thanked her but—internally—I was annoyed.

You know? I thought to myself. *How on earth could you know? You weren't left flapping in the wind for nearly two months. You didn't have to burn all your vacation time, draw from your savings, and wonder whether there would come a time when you would be scraping to cover your car payment and the mortgage. You didn't have to face a spouse every morning, knowing that you were unemployed. You couldn't possibly know what my situation was like; how dare you say that you do!*

I got over that inner turmoil in short order, but it taught me an important lesson I hadn't even realized I needed.

It taught me not to presume.

I'm glad that's the case, because a few months later a colleague was telling me about how tough it was to be the sole Black candidate in his MBA cohort, and I began to say that I knew what a challenge that must have been for him. Then I stopped myself.

"I've never been in your shoes, so I can't imagine what that must have been like," I told him instead. "But it's obvious that you are a very strong person."

When considering our differences and similarities, it might be helpful to remember that, although cultures differ, human dreams and wounds are universal.

We all want to love and be loved, to find acceptance and belonging, to experience freedom and adventure, to discover truth and meaning and hope. We've all been wracked with guilt or filled with shame. We've all grieved and been insulted, demeaned, or bullied. We've all lost those we care about, and, at times, had our value and dignity as humans called into question. So, sometimes you can bridge the differences between us

> by sharing the similarity of the struggles within us, through the stories you tell.
>
> —STEVEN

COMPASSIONATE? OR DISMISSIVE?

This is one of those areas in which perspective is everything. The person saying "I know" is trying to express sympathy or empathy. Yet, to the person on the receiving end, the comment sounds tantamount to a dismissal. It feels condescending: a pat on the back before moving along to the next point in the conversation.

That is why, even when I am speaking with someone who has seemingly experienced something that I've gone through myself, I've learned to avoid responding with, "I know."

If a colleague has just lost a father and I lost my father years before, those two situations, while similar, cannot be identical. Perhaps the other person's father had left things unsaid, or perhaps they were closer than my father and I had ever been. Either way, they were not where my father and I were at our parting, and if I say, "I know," in actuality, I do not.

My colleague's situation is different and, if I say "I know," that comment—even if meant as a gesture of commiseration—is in fact an overreach and a slight.

I try to banish it from my conversations. That is especially true when I am speaking with someone whose background is profoundly different from my own.

▪ ▪ ▪

WHAT TO REMEMBER WHEN
SHARING MULTICULTURAL STORIES

The only way for stories to stay alive is for them to be heard, remembered, and shared. But what if you want to tell a story that's from another culture?

In recent years, there has been growing concern in the story-telling community about people appropriating stories from other cultures. This is a complex issue without a lot of simple answers, and speakers tend to have strong feelings about it one way or the other. Can a man tell a story from a woman's perspective? Why or why not? What defines culture? What about race? Ethnicity? Religion? Who's to say where one culture ends and another begins? How long do I need to be a member of a certain "culture" or geographic region before I can tell "their" stories? (For instance, do you need to be of European descent to tell Grimm's fairy tales? Why or why not?)

When considering telling multicultural stories, do your research. For instance, some stories are sacred to different religious groups or spiritual practices and are intended for use only in that context. Simply say to the teller, "That story really connected with me. I'd love to share it with others. Would I have your permission to do so?" Then, if the answer is "yes," when you share the story, mention its origins and that you received permission to tell it.

When transitioning to telling a story from another culture, you might connect the tale with your personal story. For instance: "I was on a business trip to Russia and when we were having dinner, the director of our branch there told me this really powerful story that he heard when he was growing up. I'd like to share it with you today." Then the story comes from your personal experience and not simply from another culture.

Or you might say, "We can all learn a lot from other cultures, and often the lessons in their stories stretch across cultural boundaries and teach universal truths. That's true of this story from Jamaica . . ."

If you're not sure where the story comes from, or if it has multiple variants from around the world (which is actually quite common), you may wish to say something like, "This is a story that's found in many different parts of the world and told in many different ways. This is my favorite version."

Through it all, be respectful of others, give credit where credit is due, and celebrate the stories that can span the divides between us.

—STEVEN

FINDING MIDDLE GROUND

So, especially in situations involving diversity and inclusion, how do you show empathy without overreaching?

One way is to share what I like to call "narratives of micro-insight."

If, like me, you are a middle-aged white American male, being pulled over by the police may be a cause for irritation, but it has probably never caused you to fear for your life. No one has ever mistaken you for your own administrative assistant. Unless (like me) you occasionally show up at places bearded, riding an obnoxiously loud Harley-Davidson, and wearing heavy boots, jeans, and a black leather jacket, people don't become frightened or uneasy in your presence (and I can easily change that perception with a change of clothes and transport, and a shave).

If you are a woman who has never worn a hijab, or if you've never shown up with a same-sex partner for a PTA meeting and suspected you heard whispers as you left the room, or been patronized because you use a wheelchair for mobility, or if you were never treated as a second-class citizen because of your accent, then you don't know what it's like to be disregarded or discriminated against in those situations.

Even so, you have almost certainly had, however briefly, episodes of exclusion in your life. Looking around my own circle of friends and colleagues, I can identify quite a few:

- There is the young woman who, after being told by her coach that she was too petite to make the varsity lacrosse team, tried out instead for the wrestling team, became the first female athlete in her high school to make the squad, and went through her seasons as a highly competitive part of the team. She was a team member, but she did not look or act like any of her teammates.
- There is the Baptist friend who went home with his college roommate for the weekend, attended Mass with his friend's family, and, wanting to show camaraderie with them, got up for Communion . . . at which point his roommate's mother caught him by his suit sleeve and whispered that the sacrament was reserved for absolved members of the faith.
- And then there's anyone who has ever learned a foreign language, spoken it overseas, and been greeted with the pained smile that says that—because of your accent—you are being tolerated, but not accepted as an equal.

These discomforts are moments. They are, in relationship to the greater breadth and span of our lives, little more than ticks of the clock. They are not necessarily something we have to experience every single day.

Still, they are glimpses into what daily experiences may be like for people who differ in some way from the mainstream world, yet must still find ways to navigate through it. They are places within which we can plant the seeds of a conversation.

And, in my mind, they are invitations—always—to share a story. You can:

- Talk about a time when you understood how simply being of a particular race, belief system, or identity gave you an advantage in being considered for a position—before anyone even peeked at your résumé.
- Remember a moment when you felt different and what you learned from that.
- Describe the journey you took with a colleague—how, in your mind, that individual evolved from a *type* to a *person*.
- Avoid stories that convey: "I know."
- Embrace stories that convey: "I feel."

And understand, always, that you are talking about the most interesting and fascinating beings in all creation: people . . . human beings. Speak of them accordingly.

SUMMARY

The purpose of diversity is to create an organization in which everyone belongs. The purpose of inclusion—always—is to recognize and respect the person within, and extend to them a "come as you are" invitation. The purpose of equity is to bring marginalized individuals to a point they would have already reached had they been provided the same opportunities as the privileged. Stories are a great way to talk about these subjects because, unlike memoranda or policies, storytelling is a person-to-person form of communication: one that brings the discussion to a profoundly human level. A well-told story can also express empathy and support without sounding condescending or patronizing. Stereotyping overlooks the soul, while storytelling seeks it out and touches it.

Key Points to Remember

- Understand that the point of diversity is not simply to allow equal opportunity; rather, it is to celebrate the uniqueness of each individual.
- Resist the temptation to say, "I know," or "I understand how you feel." Expressions such as these may feel like empathy, but they come across as a condescending overreach.
- If you are a leader considered diverse, be careful to recognize in your stories that the stigma or barriers you may have encountered in your career are not necessarily the hurdles others face; others may have completely different experiences.
- If you are a mainstream leader, a good way to talk about diversity is with a story that illustrates your understanding of the concept of "privilege."
- When talking with someone who has experienced exclusion firsthand, telling a story about when *you* experienced a feeling of exclusion can provide a portal into a deeper conversation.

PART III
THE CONTEXT
Where, When, and Why?

E very told story is experienced within a specific context—a social encounter that has certain inherent expectations. Taking the venue into consideration will go a long way toward helping you deliver your story effectively. In this section, we'll dive into the storytelling event's context and how it affects the way a story is best shaped and told.

CHAPTER 9

THE STORY THAT CHANGED AN INDUSTRY

—TOM

"Play always as if in the presence of a master."
—Robert Schumann, nineteenth-century composer and pianist

Here's a bit of motion-picture history for which no formal record exists: no film, no audio recording . . . not even a still photo. All we have are the memories of those who were present, from which—with a bit of artistic license—we can reconstruct an evening that altered an industry.

One autumn day in 1934, animators at the Walt Disney Studios found a surprise on their drawing boards. Each of them received an envelope containing fifty cents and instructions to go have dinner at the end of the regular workday, and then return to the studio for a special after-hours meeting.

Of course, in 1934, the country was still feeling the effects of the Great Depression; fifty cents could purchase a steak dinner with all the trimmings. The animators were well stuffed and happy as they made their way back to the studio.

In many industries at the time, a special meeting could only mean layoffs and trouble. But Hollywood was an exception; film studios actually thrived throughout the Depression. Cinema tickets averaged twenty-five cents, so, for a bit more than an hour's wage, a couple could go to the movies and get away from the cares of the world for a while.

So it was likely that it was curiosity, rather than dread, that the staff brought back with them from their dinners. No one knew why the boss had called the impromptu meeting.

Nor was its purpose any clearer when Walt asked everyone to gather in the company's sound stage.

According to Bob Thomas in his biography, *Walt Disney: An American Original*, the stage was bare, illuminated by a single naked light bulb.

The artists took their seats and, promptly, Walt Disney walked into the light. Then, without preface or explanation, he began to tell a story.

It was based partially on Tale 53 from *Grimm's Fairy Tales*, and partly on a silent film that Walt had seen when he was young—a special screening for newsboys, and a rare treat for a teenager whose working-class family had little or no money for entertainment.

That silent film was James Searle Dawley's 1916 production of *Snow White*, based in turn upon Dawley's 1912 Broadway play *Snow White and the Seven Dwarfs*.

Walt embellished as he told his tale, giving the dwarfs names and emphasizing not only the comic potential of the story but also the drama, the mystery, and—especially—the romance.

Moreover, Walt brought his story to life by acting it out. A Midwesterner who had originally traveled to Hollywood hoping not only to direct pictures but also to star in them, Walt Disney created distinctive voices for each character and turned from house left to house right and back again to simulate dialogue.

He used the stage light as a tool and a prop, placing it under his chin to cast deep shadows as he described how the Evil Queen transformed herself into the aged witch, and cupping it in his hands as he pantomimed the creation of the poisoned apple.

So realistic was his portrayal that animators who were in the audience that night remember gasps, sighs, and laughter. During Walt's description of Snow White in her glass coffin, surrounded by the dwarfs and mourning woodland creatures, grown men were reportedly pulling out handkerchiefs to wipe away tears.

Finally, Walt described the Prince's arrival, how he awakened Snow White with a kiss, placed her on his horse, and led her off into a glorious sunset.

Then, according to Thomas's account, Walt announced, "That's going to be our first feature."

RETHINKING THE WORLD OF CARTOONS

Walt Disney's evening of after-dinner storytelling was a dramatic departure from the way projects were usually initiated at the Disney studio.

The company's work until that point had been "shorts"—brief cartoons, designed to be shown in theaters in advance of a live-action feature film. For the past seven years, those cartoons had included fully synchronized sound, using a technique pioneered by Disney. Some were in the *Silly Symphony* series that Disney used to experiment with music and new animation techniques, but many featured the world's most popular cartoon character: Mickey Mouse, voiced by Walt himself.

Those cartoons were usually proposed and outlined in "gag sessions"—meetings in which Walt and his trusted artists would try out material and put together enough pratfall humor to fill a seven- or eight-minute cartoon.

The company had not gone beyond those time constraints for any number or reasons, beginning with the fact that animation, as

Disney did it, was prohibitively time-consuming. It took more than ten thousand individual, hand-colored drawings for the studio to produce a seven-minute cartoon; feature-length would require hundreds of thousands of individual illustrations, and using Disney's then-new multiplane technique—which was capable of capturing multiple illustrations painted on glass and stacked to convey a rich sense of depth on-screen—that number would be multiplied.

In Europe and South America, other studios had attempted the shortcuts of using stop-action puppets, movable silhouettes, and simple black-and-white line drawings to create feature-length animation. These shortcuts had not proved commercially viable. Partly because Disney had raised the bar in terms of cartoon quality, American studios balked at the thought of producing a feature film with nothing but animation. The costs were simply too high.

Nor did there appear to be a market for such a thing. As far as theatergoers were concerned, cartoons were good for a chuckle, and nothing more. The thought of sitting through more than an hour of simply drawn slapstick and burlesque humor didn't sound appealing to most people.

Then there were the so-called "experts" who said that, when viewed for more than a few minutes at a time, animation would cause headaches or nausea. Two years earlier, Disney had become the first major animation studio to adopt the recently perfected three-strip Technicolor process, and some neurologists were of the opinion that, when viewed for more than an hour, the brilliant colors in a Technicolor cartoon could cause convulsions.

It wasn't just industry observers who thought an animated feature film was a nonstarter. Many of the people in Walt Disney's own circle were troubled by the idea, and particularly by the budget that would be required to produce a more than hour-long animated film.

His brother, who was also Walt's business partner, was, according to Thomas, "alarmed by Walt's plan." Even Lillian Disney—Walt's wife—was concerned.

Faced with that level of opposition, Walt knew that a conventional meeting or gag session would never get past the debate over the viability of feature-length animation.

Yet, just as he'd thought of ways to bring sound to his Mickey Mouse cartoons in a manner so realistic that theatergoers accepted the concept of hand-drawn animals talking, Walt had already considered all of the opposition to feature-length animation.

His film would not aim itself specifically at heart and humor; it would spend most of its time unfolding drama and romance. The characters would appear much more realistic than the undulating "rubber-hose" animation of a decade earlier; in fact, one of Walt's ideas was to use human reference models for Snow White and some of the other central roles, to help guide the work of his animators.

He also had the common sense to dismiss the warnings of the so-called "experts." If conventional Technicolor movies did not produce adverse neurological reactions, there was no reason to assume that high-quality animation would do so.

So, to skip the debate, Walt decided to go straight to the story. And, to tell the story in a way that drew his audience in, and did not invite questions or interruptions, he elected to use simple stagecraft. Walt would not only tell his story; he would act it out, as well.

The technique worked so well that, overnight, the Disney studio became an island of believers, in stark contrast to the sea of skepticism that was the American film industry. Even when production schedules began to be measured in years and costs multiplied to six times the original budget, everyone at the studio believed in what they were doing. Hollywood gossip would call the film "Walt's folly," but his team knew better.

Their efforts would eventually be honored with a special Oscar—special because no category existed at the time for feature animation—and box-office results so resounding that the company's current studio lot in Burbank, California, would be purchased and built partially from the proceeds of *Snow White and the Seven Dwarfs* (1937). The film would not only set a decades-long box-office record for animated features—it would also outgross every other conventional non-silent movie, and it would hold that record for two years, until it was finally eclipsed by *Gone with the Wind* (1939).

And that—all of that—was ignited by one person, alone on a stage, telling a story.

Here are four questions your listeners are asking themselves while you tell a story (even if they're not aware of it):

- Why should I listen to this? (significance)
- Why should I care about it? (relevance)
- Does this make sense? (meaning)
- What can I take away from this? (application)

As you tell your story, be aware that your listeners will remain curious and engaged as long as they care about the characters, believe that the outcome matters, think that the story makes sense, and trust that it'll benefit them somehow to listen to it—even if that's simply to be entertained. If you keep them listening, caring, worrying, and wondering, you'll keep them engaged—and entertained.

—STEVEN

LET ME ENTERTAIN YOU

While not widely realized, the main reason people gather in an auditorium to sit through a presentation and listen to a speaker is *not* communication.

If you only want to communicate an idea or share data, presenting is actually a relatively inefficient method of doing so. A pamphlet is better—it's something people can flip back through, review, and absorb at their own pace. If it's sent electronically, links can be included: better-informed recipients can read right past them, while those not familiar with the material can click through to get the background material necessary to understand the information.

Plus, most people read much more quickly than the average person can speak.

So, why go through the trouble of presenting or speaking?

There are a number of reasons. When we see and hear someone speaking, we're getting clues about personality and energy. It's easier to develop sympathy for the arguments being made. By watching a presentation with others, we feel a sense of camaraderie—and this is true even if we're each sitting in our studies or offices and watching on a computer, tablet, or smartphone.

In other words, consciously or not, we watch for the entertainment value.

This means that when you speak to groups, and especially when you tell stories to groups, you are an actor.

There are two things you can do about that. You can either obey your first instincts and run and hide (pretty hard for your listeners to hear you that way), or you can embrace that reality. (We dive into a more detailed application of some of the acting tools in the last section of the book, where we'll focus on what you as an individual bring to the communication event.)

Connecting is obviously better than hiding. But how you use those acting tools will vary, depending on the situation.

CHOOSING WHICH "YOU" TO SHARE

We're all aware that when we step onto a stage or take our place at a lectern, we assume a *persona*, becoming what we want our audience to hear and see. We're also aware that this persona can shift, depending on the situation. This is good, because it *should* shift.

For instance, we know that Walt Disney's performance of the *Snow White* story did its job; the company knuckled down and produced the unprecedented animated feature. But imagine what it would have looked like if, rather than gathering his animators in the auditorium, he had taken the ghost lamp into each individual animator's office and performed the story one-on-one, face-to-face.

Walt's auditorium performance of the story line took two hours—thirty-two minutes longer than the completed movie—so one-on-one presentations would have been incredibly time-consuming.

But, setting that consideration aside, imagine that you are one of those animators and your boss, unannounced, marches into your office and starts acting and mimicking character voices. It would be uncomfortable, weird, contrived, and hokey.

What works well in a performance venue is going to smack of artifice in a more personal setting.

This is intuitive for most people—so much so that leaders frequently ask me when considering a speaking engagement, "What's the audience size?"

Yet, if you are asking that question to determine how intimate or sizable an event is going to feel, the question I prefer to consider is, "What's the throw?"

"Throw" is a stagecraft term for the distance from a light source to an object onstage. It's taken into consideration when determining how effectively the lighting illuminates its subject.

When I'm teaching people to tell stories to groups, I use "throw" as a metaphor for the distance from the storyteller's gestures and facial expressions to the average audience member. We use this term to help determine how effective those gestures and expressions will be.

In that sense, the throw is more important than the crowd size.

That's because it's possible to have a smaller audience in a larger venue.

When Walt Disney pitched the *Snow White* story to his key staff, he did so in a sound stage that, while not huge by Hollywood standards, would be larger than the rooms used for holding the studio's gag sessions. And it could be argued that the key personnel he needed to have on board with his idea could easily have fit into one of those smaller rooms.

Moreover, only one man would be performing that night, so Walt didn't select the sound stage because he needed to put a company of actors onstage. A tiny platform would have sufficed.

I think Walt held the meeting in the sound stage because the space had to be sufficient for telling a large and moving story that was worthy of a feature-length motion picture. The environment had to be one in which acting would seem natural. He wanted to do something extraordinary and, to convince his audience to experience it along with him, he needed to tell his story in a space that would make the telling appear ordinary. He had to put some theatrical distance between his listeners and himself.

That's why when I'm working with someone who is going to be telling stories to a group, I pay attention to the expected audience size and the throw, or distance, between the storyteller and the average listener in the venue.

If the setting is intimate—a table in a restaurant or a conference room—the story should probably be told the same way one would share a story with a group of friends. But, if the venue is larger, the method varies with the size.

> Tom's point here explains why the ice cream parlor encounter I had in college ended so poorly. (See chapter 1.) It also helps me understand why "performances" on video calls feel so awkward and it reminds me once again how important it is to find out beforehand the details of your speaking engagements—when, where, for whom, for what purpose, and who else will be appearing before you at the event.
>
> —STEVEN

THE MIDDLE GROUND

These are the sorts of venues that most people speak in, most of the time. They include locations such as most churches, your average school auditorium, or a community center.

These are also the ones that work well with your old drama teacher's maxim of exaggerating your gestures and moving around onstage.

And these medium-sized venues are the ones most people should practice for, as they are the type of venue in which most storytelling (and most speaking, in general) takes place. If you are asked to talk at a high school graduation, a civic meeting, the local chapter of a professional organization, and so on, this is probably the sort of venue you'll appear in.

When I'm storytelling in a venue this size, I plan to "play to the cheap seats." I'll mentally pick out one or two people near the back, and try to make eye contact with and address them at least half the time.

Stage and platform space may be at a premium in such venues: I've seen platforms with approximately the same amount of floor space as a residential bathroom. So, it's logical to assume you won't be walking more than a step or two. But you'll be near enough to your audience that gestures and most facial expressions will be understood.

Again, think of the folks in the back row as your audience. If they're following you, so will everyone else.

LARGE VENUES

The conference-center ballroom that's a good two hundred feet deep . . . The church that holds one thousand people . . . The auditorium of a major university . . . These are all cases in which the throw can easily exceed the audience's ability to pick up detail. Unless the event producers are using video to project a close-up of your face (more on that in a minute), your best option physically is to play to the farthest row you can easily see.

These are probably the most challenging venues in which to tell a story, and these are venues in which your audio delivery will be everything. When I'm speaking in a large venue, I like to imagine I'm both in front of a live audience and on the radio. The audience is my reminder that, if it's going to be hard to see my face, I should at least *sound* lively and animated, and the radio allusion keeps my voice alive and interesting (this is not the situation in which you want to drop into a monotone). Vocally, I keep up my pace, insert pauses where appropriate, and otherwise try to use a voice that compels the audience to listen.

SUPERVENUES

Okay, I made that word up. But you know what I'm talking about: extreme mega-churches, the plenary session at a conference where they've opened all the air walls to turn several already-large ball-rooms into the largest meeting space available at the convention center, or maybe an arena concert where you've been asked to share a humorous story in order to introduce the band.

These are all events where you can't even *see* the people in the cheap seats, let alone play to them. They, on the other hand, can almost always see you onstage, although it's like peering down at an ant on the sidewalk.

Fortunately, supervenues almost always use image magnification ("IMAG" in audiovisual jargon). These are giant video screens that give the audience a closer view of what's happening onstage. They're generally several feet high (sixteen feet by nine feet of usable display space is not out of the ordinary); if flanking the stage, there will usually be at least two of them, and a "video wall" may even make up the entire back wall of the stage. For deeper venues, additional screens may be "flown" (suspended from the ceiling) midway back, to make certain everyone in the audience can see the storyteller's smiling face.

When IMAG is available, it's usually possible to toggle between medium and close-up shots of you from one or more video cameras in the house, and a presentation, if your story is accompanied by images.

Even if it's just you onstage, storytelling, it's a good idea to do a "technical rehearsal" with the audiovisual crew ahead of time, and run through the story you are going to tell. That way, they'll know when they need to pull back to show the funny walk you're planning to make as you cross the stage, and when to zoom in to catch your facial expression.

If the venue is using IMAG, also ask whether there will be a confidence monitor. There probably will—it's simply a video screen aimed at the stage, so you can see what the audience is seeing on the big screens, and if your presentation includes images, there may be a second monitor to show you the next slide or graphic in the queue.

Personally, if I'm not using presentation software, the only reason I want the confidence monitor is so I can see that the IMAG is working and my image is being projected to the audience. If the confidence monitor goes black (or, typically, blue), that's my cue that the IMAG has cut out momentarily, and I need to use large gestures, walk as I talk onstage, and perhaps modulate my voice a bit more to give people something to concentrate on until the picture is restored.

> If you're part of a series of presenters, affirm the other speakers in the program. One time at a large international conference, I heard one of the best-known inspirational speakers in the world follow a comedian. He started by saying, "I'm not here to entertain you; I'm here to speak to you from my heart." As if the comedian hadn't been speaking from his heart! It was a terrible way to begin and immediately turned me off. Even if you don't agree with other presenters, don't be dismissive of them or insult them.
>
> —STEVEN

VIRTUAL VENUES

Media that have taken off in recent years are video teleconferences and webinars. It is now possible to be in your study in front of your computer, telling a story to listeners in twenty thousand or more locations around the world.

In the abstract, this can be daunting. The various teleconference apps keep adding audience capacity to their platforms and, when run through a sufficiently advanced control room and sent out over multiple feeds, the potential audience for a webinar theoretically has no limits in terms of audience size.

Now, if I ask you to share a story with a friend, you're probably ready to do so right now. But if I tell you that I've arranged for you to go online and share that same story with thousands of people . . . that's probably going to be a moment when you gulp a bit.

The thing is, thanks to technology, there is virtually (pun intended—thank you very much!) no difference between the two situations. Every one of those twenty thousand or more listeners will be viewing you as if you were sitting no more than six feet away. True, videoconferencing probably limits you to facial expressions and minimal hand gestures to convey emotion, but it is no more limiting than if you and each of your listeners were sitting across from one another at a conference table.

You probably have an educational channel available through your cable provider, and you've probably seen those shows where a historian is standing at a lectern and speaking about her latest biography. Chances are, unless the subject is of particular interest, you didn't stay tuned in for long. A person *pretending* to be onstage in a lecture hall is not the most captivating speaker.

Now, compare that to the historians featured in Ken Burns's documentary films. They are at ease, sitting in their living rooms or studies and telling stories as if they are chatting with an erudite friend.

You want to be the Ken Burns type of storyteller.

For some large, videocast events, I have worked with leaders who storytold on their feet, but I asked my speakers to turn and move a bit as the story unfolded (unless they are very experienced at standing and speaking to a camera, people standing in one place tend to sway, which looks terrible on-screen). If you are speaking to a fixed camera (such as the one on your computer or phone), you're often better off sitting.

It's worthwhile to pay attention to camera position and lighting. Just speaking to a laptop open on the desk in front of you is going to present you from an angle below your chin (rarely flattering to anyone) and illuminated in ghastly blue light from the screen.

To counter those things, move the camera up to approximately forehead level, position lights at approximately a forty-five-degree angle to either side of the screen (regular table lamps will suffice, or you can get color-adjustable LED video lights inexpensively online), and be sure that the image you're transmitting is in landscape mode—that is, if it is a smartphone or a tablet, turn it on its side rather than upright.

There are devices you can purchase that incorporate a holder for a tablet or a phone and a lamp that encircles the device (these produce weird halo reflections on eyeglasses, by the way), but it's possible to improvise using what you have. I'm a musician, and I have a six-foot tripod designed to hold my iPad (sort of a twenty-first-century music stand), and I generally rig this so that the screen-side "selfie" camera is sitting at approximately forehead height.

That works well, but in a pinch I've also simply piled books under a laptop to raise the height of my laptop to a more flattering level.

If I'm using my laptop, I plug it directly into my internet router. If I'm on my tablet, I make sure I'm close enough to my router to get a full-strength signal on its fastest band option.

This leaves one thing left to think about, and that is the camera lens.

Presumably, every maker of laptops, smartphones, and tablets is currently working on a way to place the device's camera lens in the center of the screen. But, as of this writing, it hasn't happened yet.

The lens is positioned in the margin surrounding the screen—in a phone or tablet, it's usually in the center of one of the shorter sides— and that's a problem.

You see, in most Western cultures, at least, we are conditioned, practically since birth, to convey trustworthiness to another human being by looking that person directly in the eye. But if we look a person "in the eye" on the screen, we are actually looking beneath, or to the side of, the camera. So, we think we look forthright and reliable, but we actually look as if we are trying to slip away with the listeners' wallets.

Even when addressing one of those Brady Bunch gallery images of listeners, it's human nature to seek a set of eyes to fix on.

The extremely low-tech solution I've devised to circumvent this issue is to take a red ink marker, draw an arrow on a large sticky note, and slap it on the screen, so the arrow points at the camera lens.

That's usually enough to remind most storytellers to look at the camera as they speak. And if you're looking your listener in the eye and speaking from the heart, half of your job as a storyteller is done.

Then just tell the story as if you are speaking to a single listener in the room with you.

That's the beauty of virtual storytelling. It allows you to keep the throw to just a couple of feet and speak to an audience in the thousands, using the same tools you would employ to tell a story to a friend.

SUMMARY

How you tell your story varies depending on your distance from the average audience member. If you're speaking in an auditorium, large gestures, a heightened voice, and exaggerated expressions may be necessary to convey your feelings to people sitting dozens or even hundreds of feet away. Yet if you take the same approach with listeners in a conference room, your delivery can appear over-the-top and contrived.

Oddly enough, extremely large venues are often best approached more subtly, because mega-venues often use large video displays showing the speaker's face. And, as far as virtual events, the conference may be beamed to thousands of people, but to the viewers it looks as if you are speaking to them from just a few feet away. Keep that in mind and speak in an informal, conversational tone rather than slipping into full-blown performance mode.

Key Points to Remember

- The primary purpose of a story is to entertain. It may educate or inform as well, but that part is secondary. A story can't accomplish anything unless it first engages and entertains.
- Acting and stagecraft are nothing more than doing what you do naturally, but planning those elements to work with the story that you're telling to the audience you're addressing.
- When you are being viewed from a distance, your actions—including your facial expressions and gestures—need to be more exaggerated to accurately convey your meaning.
- Gestures involve more than hands; use your entire body, if possible.
- Find out as much as you can about where you'll be storytelling, and plan your stagecraft accordingly.

CHAPTER 10

HUMOR

Adding a Light Touch
to the Stories You Tell
—STEVEN

"Deliberately trying to be funny or witty is a considerable drawback, and often leads to disaster. Honest responses are simpler and more effective. By the same token, making patterns and connections is much more important than making jokes."
—Kim Johnson, dramatist and author of *Truth in Comedy*

When one of my daughters was six months old (no, I'm not telling you which one), she would beat herself in the face with anything we stuck in the crib with her. When she turned eighteen months old, she would dig through the trash cans, pull out used Q-tips, and chew on them. And then when she turned three, she would take all her clothes off whenever we had company over and run throughout the house screaming, "I'm naked! I'm naked!"

I remember thinking, *Great. I've managed to raise a three-year-old, head-whamming, Q-tip-eating stripper.*

When she turned five, my brother got married. After the wedding, my daughter was sitting next to her new aunt and she started licking her arm.

"Stop that," I told her.

"I'm kissing her the grown-up way," my daughter said innocently.

"You mean with your tongue?"

"Mm-hm."

My new sister-in-law just sat on the couch staring at me as her niece licked her arm. I decided not to bring up the Q-tip chewing and stripping.

▪ ▪ ▪

Interjecting lighthearted moments into your stories can be a great way of entertaining your listeners while also keeping their attention and making your stories more memorable.

Rather than trying to be comprehensive here and attempting to pinpoint every factor that might invite someone to laugh or smile, let's take a look at a few specific, effective, and easy-to-use techniques to weave humor into the stories you tell—even if you don't think of yourself as naturally funny.

OFFER A UNIQUE PERSPECTIVE ON THE TRUTH

Both comedians and poets tend to notice the aspects of life that the rest of us miss. Comedians point out the absurdities and make us laugh. Poets show us the bloodstains and the beauty and make us cry. There is poignancy in both the laughter and the tears.

When we laugh at a comedian, we're not necessarily doing so because he's making fun of something. Often, it's because he's telling us something that we believe is true, but hadn't thought about in that way before. In essence, humor is often found by delving into observations about life or by pointing out truths that your listeners hadn't noticed yet. They recognize that this is the way things are in the world: *Yes! He's totally captured it. That's exactly what it's like to be in a middle school phys. ed. class!*

In a very real sense, humor is dependent on your listeners' perception of reality. Often, comedians who bomb haven't taken their audience's view of truth into account.

If your listeners don't think something is true or don't think you're offering them a fresh perspective on truth, they'll be less likely to laugh.

So, if you're speaking at the Save the Planet from Pollution's international convention and you poke fun at legislation that protects endangered species and how silly those laws are, your listeners are going to be thinking, *That's not true. That's not funny.* Rather than laugh, they'll bristle.

Think about this for a moment: Sometimes, conservatives complain that late night hosts don't give them a fair shake, that they poke fun at them more than at liberals. Well, where are most late night shows filmed? New York City and Los Angeles—two very liberal cities (at least compared to the heartland). The comedians are simply playing to their live audiences. They're not trying to be unfair; they're just trying to connect with the listeners who are sitting right there in front of them by presenting a perspective that those people believe to be true.

If your listeners hear you pointing out things that are overly obvious, they won't necessarily think that what you're saying is all that funny or original. So, look for ways to offer a fresh take on what your listeners will agree is true.

When you "go for a laugh," it becomes uncomfortable for everyone. Rather, showing people the irony, absurdity, or stupidity of life is what will make them smile.

So, stop telling jokes. Start making observations. There's nothing less funny than someone trying to be funny. Stop trying to be funny and start trying to be honest about life in what you say and the stories you tell.

> I mentioned earlier in the book that I landed my first speech-writing gigs because my old-school speaker liked to open with a joke, and I wrote some originals for him. That said, while I love opening with humor, I tend to avoid jokes because (a) they are difficult to deliver perfectly; (b) original jokes are hard to find and your audience will shut down if you open with one they've already heard; and (c) jokes have a huge potential to offend, even if that was not your intention. As Steven says, wry observation is a good way to open with humor, and it steers you away from the temptation to open with, "A rabbi, a priest, and a minister . . ."
>
> —TOM

EXAGGERATE FOR EFFECT

By using hyperbole (that is, exaggeration) to make your point, you can help listeners create a mental picture of what you're talking about. In one of my stories about my first-grade teacher, Mrs. Beale, I say, "She was nine hundred years old when I met her. She had blue hair—I knew because I knew my colors."

Of course my listeners realize that Mrs. Beale was not nine hundred years old, but to a little boy she might have seemed that way. And they can picture her.

In a story that deals with romantic relationships between teens, I say, "When a teenage guy sees someone he likes or thinks is cute, a change comes over his body. It's a scientifically, psychologically proven fact . . . he begins to act stupid. Girls, you can test this out any time you want. A bunch of guys are out there playing basketball—take a seat, flash 'em a smile, give 'em a wink, and those guys are gonna try to dunk when they can't even jump over a chemistry book."

LAUGH AT YOURSELF

Sometimes when you're the guest speaker, people will tell you strange things. I was at an event in North Carolina and this lady said to me, "Has anyone ever told you how handsome you are?" And I smiled and said, "No." And she said, "There's a reason for that."

Allow yourself to be the brunt of the joke. Fall on your sword. Look for ways to laugh at yourself rather than at others. Some people call this "self-deprecating," or "self-effacing" humor. Often, poking fun at yourself can be done simply through the turn of a phrase, where it ends in a way that your listeners didn't expect: "In high school basketball I couldn't jump very well, but I made up for it with a lack of quickness."

Sometimes I tell people, "I've written books on how to tell stories to preschool children and I write serial killer novels. My wife says it's kinda like inviting Stephen King over to do a puppet show for your kindergarten class. I admit, it's a little frightening, but it's all part of who I am."

Don't be impressed with yourself. Often, the funnier a person thinks he is, the less funny he really is.

When I first started in a career of public speaking, I had brochures printed up, but I forgot to proofread them. Everything was great except for the line that was supposed to say, "Steven James is available for public storytelling events," because I forgot the letter "l" in "public." Imagine the kind of events a mistake like that'll get you invited to.

As we looked at in chapter 7, tapping into times when you were naïve or overconfident can be a great mine of story material—it can also be a great source for humor.

Use dramatic irony to let listeners know about upcoming difficulties that the characters in the story aren't aware of. For instance, "At my wedding, I knew I was going to have a wonderful marriage, as soon as I got done changing my wife's opinion about leaving the toilet seat up!" Listeners will be shaking their heads or cringing, knowing that this guy is in trouble.

There are different moments in my life when I can remember thinking, *Sure, things didn't turn out so well for that person, but I'll be fine.* Or, *What's the worst thing that could happen?*

That's what I was thinking when I was in fifth grade and someone dared me to lick a metal fence post in Wisconsin. In January. In subzero weather.

If you tell your listeners, "It seemed like a good idea at the time," or "I was pretty sure I could handle this myself without a back-seat driver," you're allowing them to be "in on the joke" while you, as the character in the story, remain clueless. That's a solid setup for humor to come. You can lead listeners to think, *Oh, this is not going to turn out well!*

Now, remember, your audience isn't cheering for something terrible to happen—they don't want the character in the story to suffer *permanently*. That would drain the humor out of the moment. The audience is thinking, *He's an idiot, but I don't want him to really get hurt!* So, show that, in the end, everything turned out all right for the people involved.

My tongue is no longer attached to that fence post.

Take a minute right now. Brainstorm a time when you were about to start a big project and you thought, *How hard can this be?* That experience will likely translate well into a humorous story that your listeners will be able to relate to.

KNOW YOUR LISTENERS

There's a story about how some humanitarian aid workers brought battery-powered televisions to a remote village in Africa where the people would typically gather around the campfire each night and listen to the local storyteller for hours on end.

Somehow, the aid workers were able to set up the televisions to capture several different channels, and for two weeks the villagers sat glued to their television sets. But then, later that month, when the workers returned again, the people had left the televisions behind and were listening to the storyteller once again.

"Why aren't you watching the televisions?" the aid workers asked them. "They know so many stories!"

"Yes," the villagers said, "but the storyteller knows me."

The better you know your listeners and their culture, the more you'll be able to draw them into your stories and your presentations.

When I was a college sophomore, I volunteered to call people and ask if they'd be interested in receiving information from a certain community organization. (Yes, I was one of Those People.) It was free info—no strings attached! One day, a person answered the phone and it sounded to me like a six- or seven-year-old girl. In a singsongy voice I said, "May I speak to your mommy?"

"What?" she said. "Who is this? I'm twenty-eight years old. I don't even live with my mother!"

Needless to say, she wasn't too interested in the information I was offering to send her way. (Free though it may have been.)

PEOPLE WON'T LAUGH IF . . .

- they think you're making fun of them, but not yourself.

- they think you don't understand them or their culture.
- they don't agree that what you're saying is honest about life or human nature.

There's a saying that you understand someone's culture when you understand what makes them laugh. There's a lot of truth to that. Watch and listen to the reaction of your listeners. When considering using dialect or colloquialisms, ask, "Will this offend those who speak in this dialect, or will it affirm them?" Usually, imitating someone's dialect is not a good idea.

But what if you *don't* know your listeners that well? What if you've never met them before?

Look for (1) bridges between their culture and yours, (2) similar struggles you have, or (3) shared experiences you can tap into.

When I was storytelling in India, I found that some of my word-play humor didn't make sense to my listeners—especially when translated into Telugu or Hindi. However, the family unit is highly valued in India and I soon discovered that when I told stories about my children, the faces of my listeners brightened up. It was common ground.

By the way, the more confident you are when you tell your story, the more you'll put your listeners at ease. There's something very reassuring about someone who's comfortable being himself. As famed improv instructor Keith Johnstone told me once, "When a great performer steps onstage, audiences relax." A little confidence with a dash of humility goes a long way in bridging communication gaps between cultures, and between you and your listeners.

Also, let your audience know that they have permission to laugh at what you're saying. These days, some people are so sensitive about the prospect of offending others that they begin to feel uneasy if you mention any differences between various demographic groups. The listeners (rightly!) don't want to laugh if you're making fun of others or putting them down; however, they haven't necessarily been taught discernment that just because we're pointing out differences between individuals doesn't mean we're judging anyone. Help your listeners to relax and rest in the confidence that you're simply here to connect with them, not to mock or demean anyone.

TRUST YOUR AUDIENCE

After my daughter Ariel got her first pet, a hamster, I drove her home and we were setting up the hamster cage and the squeaky-spinny-wheel-deal when she turned to me. "I'm naming him Sniffer," she announced in her enthusiastic, eight-year-old way, "because that's the second thing he did when I put him in my hand!" When I tell the story, I say, "It's just a good thing she didn't name him after the *first* thing he did in her hand."

Do I need to tell the audience that he pooped in her hand? Probably not.

Avoid overexplaining.

Often, listeners will "get it," and the more you explain the point, the more impact you drain from it.

Sportscasters rarely ask questions that they don't already know the answer to. You have a newscaster at the Olympics and the second-place swimmer is climbing out of the pool: "You just lost a gold medal by a hundredth of a second. What's going through your mind?"

"I'd like to take that microphone and shove it up your—"

"And now back to you, Bob, at the studio."

RESPOND TO YOUR LISTENERS

The funniest comedians are often the ones who're the most responsive. Sure, they have their bits well prepared, but they also know when to play off an audience's response. They add material, insert callbacks (more on that in a moment), and adapt to the unfolding social encounter with their listeners.

You can do the same.

Timing in humor is important, but even if you don't think you have the best sense of comedic timing in the world, you can still milk pauses for effect. For instance, you might say, "If you fall asleep during my slide presentation, please don't snore . . . or you might wake up the person next to you." See how the humor comes not just from what is said, but was accentuated by the pause that preceded the payoff?

It's a delicate balance and depends on you reading the audience. For example, if you don't wait long enough for listeners to make the connection and laugh, but keep plowing forward with your story, when they do eventually start to laugh, they won't hear what you're saying. On the other hand, if you wait too long for them to laugh—and they don't—it'll create an uncomfortable pause. Crickets.

Developing a better sense of timing comes from experience, but simply watching and responding to your listeners will go a long way toward finding the sweet spot in establishing the length and frequency of your pauses.

By the way, affirm your audience; never diss them or cut them down. Don't tell your listeners that they aren't a very good audience or say something like, "Man, they really laughed at that story at the last conference. I don't know what's wrong with you guys."

Nope. Not a good idea.

I made that mistake once; I can tell you from personal experience that it's not one you'll want to repeat.

RESPECT YOUR AUDIENCE

My friend was speaking at a conference that was being hosted at a Baptist conference center. He was given his room key, but when he went to the room, he found that there was already someone in the room—a woman in bed! During his keynote, he told us the story and then ended by saying, "I know Baptists are hospitable people, but a fruit basket would have sufficed!" He was able to make light of the situation without mocking the people who were hosting the event.

Don't offend or insult your listeners, their subculture, where they're from, or their beliefs. Respect them in the way you relate to them, the attitude you portray to them, and the relationships you develop with them. Never make fun of where you are; just make fun of who you are.

Also, be careful not to stereotype a certain group or class of people or claim that they all act or look a certain way—especially if you're not part of that group. The more you generalize about others, whatever that stereotype might include, the more you risk offending someone or coming across as judgmental.

WHAT TURNS LISTENERS OFF:

- Trying to be funny
- Using sarcasm that cuts others down
- Coming across as judgy
- Appearing insensitive

Strive to speak with humility, integrity, and esteem. There'll always be those who don't like you or maybe don't agree with you. That's just the way it is. Don't let that stop you from delivering your message in a powerful, heartfelt, and humorous way.

Welcome listeners in rather than letting them feel left out of the joke or not part of the inside group that your humor is meant to appeal to. Remember when you were in high school and there were inside jokes in certain cliques that made others feel like outsiders? High-brow humor can do that. You want your humor to invite people in, not make them feel stupid because they can't understand the joke. Try to communicate to your listeners that you're one of them and that they're part of the "in group," not left out of it.

> You ever see those funniest home video shows on TV? People stand there watching the cruelest stuff happen! They're sadists, those people!
>> Man, I love those shows.

By adding that last line you make it clear that you're not belittling the people who love those shows because—guess what?—you're one of them. Rather than being judgy, you're confirming that we're all in this together.

By the way, don't tell people something is going to be funny. Don't say, "Oh! This is hilarious. You guys are gonna bust a gut! So, last night I was . . ." If it's funny, they'll laugh. If it's not, you don't need to draw attention to that fact.

Also, save the best for last. If you have a story that's really hilarious, build up to it throughout your program, or the end of your presentation might feel like a letdown.

PHYSICALIZE YOUR STORIES

Physical comedy can work—if you're comfortable with it. Children especially connect with physical comedy and slapstick humor.

I'm playing with a new story based on synchronized swimming. I started to brainstorm other sports that would be fun to watch if they were synchronized—and all the things that could go wrong. Like synchronized hammer throwing. Synchronized javelins. Synchronized shot putting.

There are lots of interesting directions this story could go—and with the natural appeal to movement, it lends itself well to physical comedy. As I develop that story, I'm going to work on the movement just as much as I am the words. (We also cover movement and gestures in chapters 9 and 18, so check them out for more ideas on physicalizing your stories.)

By the way, some people say that the "third time is the charm." However, more often than not, the third time is *the opposite of the other two*. So, if a guy slips and falls on the peanut butter sandwich his son dropped on the floor, it's funny. If it happens again, it's still funny. But if it happens a third time, it's not. It feels overdone. However, if, this time, he sees the sandwich, smiles to himself, steps around it, and clonks his head on the open cupboard door, knocking himself to the floor—that's funny (as long as he's able to shake it off and, with a grin, feed that hungry boy a fresh sandwich that hasn't been stepped on).

CAPITALIZE ON MISCOMMUNICATION

Over the years, I've taken note of odd and memorable signs from around the country. I was in California teaching storytelling at a conference held at a large Presbyterian church. I found this sign: "During the worship service, if you bring your infants, please sit near the rear." Someone had not given the wording on that sign quite enough thought.

On the door of a grocery store here in Tennessee, I once saw a sign that said, "Push. Do Not Enter." A friend of mine told me he saw a sign in West Virginia that read, "Free kittens for sale." I once saw a bookstore advertise that they carried "rare and nonexistent books."

Intriguing! At the Charlotte Douglas International Airport in North Carolina, on the people-mover conveyor-belt thing there was a sign: "Please. Walk on Left. Stand on Right." I tried my best. Didn't turn out so well.

In Virginia I saw a sign with lights around it near a construction site. The sign read, "Construction workers present when flashing." I drove by thinking, *That's the last thing I wanna see.*

Miscommunication is a staple for romantic comedies, and tapping into it can add a light touch to the stories you tell. Keep your eyes open for incongruity in life. Humor lies in those areas waiting to be tapped into.

CREATE MEMORABLE DESCRIPTIONS

If listeners don't see your story, it'll be difficult for them to get emotionally involved in it. As world-renowned storyteller Donald Davis once told me, "When someone laughs or nods, it doesn't mean, 'That's funny.' It means, 'I see that.'"

Before listeners will engage in a story, they have to picture it and care about the characters within it. Seeing precedes feeling.

So, spend a little time at the beginning of the story helping listeners build the setting in their minds. Help them to picture the scenery and the characters. Strive to do this not by flowery descriptions, but by succinct, evocative ones. Be aware that the more literary and formal your language, the more canned and the less authentic it'll sound. For example: "My somewhat overweight high school biology teacher strode languidly into the room, adjusted the collar of his dun-colored virgin wool sweater, and then pronounced, 'It is time for class to begin.'"

See how that doesn't come off as very natural-sounding?

Instead, you might say, "My high school biology teacher was shaped like a Weber grill. Tiny legs. Big belly. Wore ties from the

1970s. He had this vein on his head that would pulsate whenever he got angry. It looked like a big red worm slithering down his forehead. Worm Man terrified us."

Or, rather than saying, "There were a lot of cracks in the wall in the old farmhouse we used to live in," you might say, "There were so many cracks in the walls that you could have flown a flag in the living room."

Instead of, "He had a high, squeaky voice," try, "He sounded like Barbie on helium." Instead of, "She yawned really big," try, "She yawned so wide you could've driven a forklift into her mouth."

Be on the lookout for ways to evoke an emotion or create a certain mood rather than simply telling listeners what something is like.

WHAT WILL MAKE PEOPLE SMILE:

- Telling the truth
- Offering fresh insights
- Being responsive
- Using exaggeration for effect
- Sharing self-effacing anecdotes

USE CALLBACKS

What is a callback? Well, it's when you set up something early on and then refer back to it later in a different part of your presentation. These recurring images or references can tie a program together. Comedians often use them when one bit really worked early on and they want to build on that connection and laughter later in their performance.

One year, I was watching an Easter egg hunt at a local church and I jotted this down:

Easter egg hunts never end well. Whose idea were these things, anyway? They always end up with at least one kid in tears. Me! Me! Me! Me! Me! There's nothing like teaching kids anarchy and selfishness in the name of Jesus. No, Easter egg hunts are from the devil. I'm pretty sure they were invented by the same people who decided clowns would be fun for kids.

Now, to make this work in a set of stories, I began my keynote address by saying, "As an author, I don't get out of my basement much, so it's really nice to be here with you tonight. There really is a world out here and lots of really fascinating people! Sunsets and puppies and man buns and everything! The last time I got out was Easter. The church I went to had an Easter egg hunt . . ." Then, after including the observations about the evils of egg hunts, I transitioned into talking about clowns. Later in the program, I had the opportunity to call back to the eggs and clowns again.

Clowns. Ew. Terrifying. Even if they just show up in a callback. Stay far, far away. And never invite one to an egg hunt. Not ever.

LET THE AUDIENCE KNOW YOU'RE ON THEIR SIDE

I live in eastern Tennessee. Amazing views. Beautiful mountains. Warm and welcoming people. (Also, it's one of the epicenters of storytelling in the world—an added plus!) When I moved south from Wisconsin, I fell in love with the folks here right away. From the first time I stepped out of the moving van, I felt at home.

And here in the mountains, we have these amazing sayings: "Well, cover me with plastic wrap and stick me in the fridge." First time I heard that one, I knew I needed to start writing these down.

There's the practical: "He's tougher'n the lips on a woodpecker."

The experiential (and slightly stomach-turning): "That's slicker'n deer guts on a doorknob."

The impossible: "That's finer'n the hair on a frog's back."

And the philosophical: "That's bigger'n the color blue."

And maybe my favorite, which sounds like it could be quite intriguing (depending on what "awesome sauce" is): "Well, slather me with awesome sauce and lick me clean!"

Now, if I were to share all of this in a way that the listeners thought I was making fun of southerners, rather than affirming them, they wouldn't laugh. However, since these are my people and I'm admiring their colorful sayings, the observations bring a smile to listeners' faces.

SUMMARY

Truth will bring more laughter than jokes will. When people laugh, they're identifying with the truth of what was said, so spend enough time setting up the story to allow them to see it for themselves.

There's an old adage that "tragedy + time = comedy." Think about things that have seemed tragic to you, but that you later realized were humorous incidents. Tap into those for your talks. As storyteller and author Margot Leitman quoted in her book *Long Story Short*, "Most events in life can be categorized in one of two ways: a good time, or a good story."

As you tell your story, lock listeners in to a specific time and place. Use natural yet evocative language.

Often, humor is simply truth extended, or pointing out the truths that people haven't noticed yet. So ask yourself, "What does this audience think is true?" rather than, "What would this audience think is funny?" And know when to stop. Don't drag things out too long or overdo it. Whatever the humorous story is, kill it while it's still kicking.

Key Points to Remember

- Stop trying to be funny—there's nothing less funny than someone trying to be funny. Be honest instead.
- When appropriate, exaggerate for effect. Hyperbole is a tried and true pathway to humor—especially in descriptions of characters (as long as you're not precipitating stereotypes about a certain group of people).
- Learn to laugh at yourself. Self-effacing humor can be a great addition to your story.
- Strive to understand your listeners. Get to know them. Connect with them where they're at rather than where you wish they were at.
- Resist the urge to explain your humor. Trust your listeners to make connections themselves—and pause long enough for them to do so.

CHAPTER 11

WARTS AND ALL

The Truth, the Whole Truth, and Nothing but the Story

—TOM

"Life is composed of light and shadows,
and we would be untruthful, insincere and saccharine
if we tried to pretend there were no shadows."
—Walt Disney, filmmaker and visionary

'm stupid. At times, phenomenally stupid.

Let me give you a case in point: James Taylor.

James Taylor was inducted into the Rock and Roll Hall of Fame many years ago, and rightly so. His fingerpicking guitar style, influenced by childhood training in both cello and piano, is instantly recognizable, as is his voice, which has just enough nasal quality to appeal to the Everyperson in us all. Taylor's recording career has been a mixture of original music and covers, most critically acclaimed, and peers in the music industry, from Paul McCartney to Vince Gill, have recognized him as a musical genius.

Yet, years ago, I stopped listening to him.

It wasn't because of his early history of drug use (he's sober now) or his politics (which lean quite a bit left of mine).

It was neither of those. It was because of one song, and an album named after that song: *Sweet Baby James*.

Now, "Sweet Baby James" is not a bad song. It is in fact an indisputably great song, a combination lullaby and cowboy ballad in three-quarter time—waltz time—as opposed to the 4/4 time intrinsic to most rock and roll. Taylor himself is said to consider it his favorite song, and it is performed, virtually without exception, at every James Taylor concert—generally as the encore.

So, if James Taylor is easy to listen to, and "Sweet Baby James" is such a well-loved song, what was the turn-off for me?

It was the title.

I remember when I decided that. I was in an art class workshop in college, and a bunch of us were making gesso, preparing canvases for oil painting.

Prepping canvas is repetitive and tedious work, involving none of the creativity that one would normally associate with art. In that era, before streaming services (or even CDs), we passed the time in workshop by sharing vinyl LPs on a portable record player.

I was measuring ingredients into a double boiler when one of my classmates walked in late, having stopped by his apartment to pick up a James Taylor album he'd gotten over Christmas break.

He showed it to me; I remember that the picture of Taylor on the album cover bore a passing resemblance to my roommate, Fred. Then I read the name of the album.

"He called his album *Sweet Baby James*?" I asked.

"Yeah." My classmate nodded. "Ain't that cool?"

No. Although I didn't say anything at the time, I didn't think it was cool at all. What sort of flagrant narcissist would title his album *Sweet Baby (Insert My Precious First Name Here)*? I decided in that moment that there was plenty of other music that I could listen to. James Taylor could go drool over his own reflection in front of someone else.

Years—okay . . . *decades* passed. Then, one afternoon a few years ago, my wife and I were in the car, listening to satellite radio, and a short interview with James Taylor came on. He was telling the back-story to "Sweet Baby James," about how his brother and his wife had decided to name their firstborn son after him. James Taylor had written the song during a wintry drive up the Massachusetts Turn-pike to see the infant—his namesake—for the very first time.

Wait.

What?

A song I'd written off as shameless self-adoration turned out to be something very tender and endearing and highly appropriate: an uncle writing a cowboy's lullaby for his tiny, yet-to-be-met nephew.

Sheesh. Note to self: buy a James Taylor album . . . maybe two.

> First impressions are indeed lasting impressions—another reason to start off your story confidently and not with an apology ("I'm not really good at this, but they told me I had to speak to you today . . .") or an unnecessary mic check ("Testing—is this thing on?"). Let your first impression be one that sets your listeners at ease and lets them know that they are in good hands.
>
> **—STEVEN**

DIRTY LAUNDRY AND SKELETONS

I offer that anecdote as not only proof of my dull-wittedness, but also as evidence that, yes, I absolutely get it: some people will jump to conclusions and form biases—even decades-long biases—based on knee-jerk (and possibly incorrect) conclusions.

Add to this the brand damage caused to organizations when key individuals are revealed as something other than what they had long been perceived to be. A brand is only as strong as the stories shared about it.

The social media scion who was accused of stealing the code for his groundbreaking concept from a company that he did development work for; the NASA lunar-program genius who was revealed, after his death, to have been a Nazi that used concentration-camp labor to build rockets during World War II; the film producer who sexually assaulted numerous women and then used hush money and the threats of wrecked careers to keep them quiet . . . many times over, we have lauded the achievements of industry leaders and then had cause to regret it later on, when someone finally aired their filthy laundry.

Imagine, then, being the public relations person for one of the organizations involved. In every case, those revelations damaged reputations. In extreme cases, businesses have been destroyed when unsavory truths were revealed about people central to their legacies.

It's made us an extremely cautious society. At least, on the organizational side it has. Everyone's wary of saying the wrong thing and tipping over the apple cart.

A few years ago, I had a conversation with the chaplain at one of America's military service academies. He was wondering if I would like to come speak, and perhaps teach a master class on stories.

I told him I would be happy to.

He seemed overjoyed.

Then, for what seemed like an eternity, nothing happened.

I thought nothing of it. In the service, officers—including chaplains—get reassigned to new posts all the time. I assumed that's what had transpired, and the invitation had been forgotten in the transition.

Finally, a year and a half later, the same chaplain called and asked if I was still available to speak.

I told him I was, and then added, "To tell you the truth, I figured you'd forgotten all about me."

"Oh, no," he told me. "We just had a backlog, so it took us quite a while to complete your background check. Not for security clearance—that was quick—but we have to perform due diligence, just to make sure nothing might surface later on that could embarrass the academy."

Awkward silence. But it made sense, and I still have great memories of that trip and the conversations I had with students and faculty alike.

That raises a good question, though. What if you want to speak about your organization's legacy, but its founder, or someone else who was pivotal in the organization's past, has a skeleton in the closet? What if *you* have a skeleton in your closet? And what if you're the skeleton?

FACE THE ISSUE HEAD-ON

The tried-and-not-true method of dealing with that situation has been, to quote the 1944 musical-comedy classic *Here Come the Waves*, to "accentuate the positive, eliminate the negative . . ." and "don't mess with Mister In-Between."

That may have worked some of the time, back when doing research required a trip to the library or the local newspaper's back-issues "morgue." But today, when everyone has the virtual equivalent of the British Library or the Library of Congress accessible with just a few clicks on a smartphone, it is almost never the wisest tactic.

So, what do you do if there's something in your past of which you are less than proud?

Consider, for a moment, what Ford Motor Company did.

Ford was founded, of course, by Henry Ford, a technological genius who went on to be one of the giants of American industry. Contrary to popular belief, he did not invent the commercial automobile (the German automaker Benz beat him to that by a decade). Nor did he invent the assembly line; it had been common in the firearms industry for decades, and a form of moving-assembly-line shipbuilding had been used in Italy a full eight centuries before Ford adopted it.

But Henry Ford did change the automobile from a rich person's plaything to a dependable form of transportation that could be purchased by working-class families.

Along the way, touching and wonderful stories emerged about Ford.

More than once, upon reading in the newspaper that a local family had been put on the street for not being able to afford their rent, he would purchase a house, have his factory carpenters produce all of the furniture necessary to make it a comfortable home, and send teams of Ford workers over to move the displaced family into the home and present them with the deed.

Another time, while driving in the countryside near Ann Arbor (home of the University of Michigan), he saw a group of college students working at the roadside on their broken-down Model T. Ford leaned out the window and shouted, "Get a horse, boys!" But he also wrote down the license plate number, traced it, and had a brand-new Ford Model A delivered to their frat house the next morning.

He was kind to children who wrote him letters, and—for the most part—cordial with newspaper reporters.

But his privately held company allowed Ford to operate as he saw fit (Ford did not go public until 1956, nine years after Henry Ford's death), and sometimes his choices were alarming.

For instance, Henry Ford is often seen as a working-person's hero, largely because of his 1914 decision to pay assembly-plant workers five dollars a day—roughly twice the going rate for factory workers at the time.

Yet, at almost the same time, Ford created the Ford Motor Company Sociological Department, which dispatched a legion of investigators to check workers' homes for the presence of liquor bottles, tobacco, evidence of gambling, and generally any activity that did not align with the founder's vision of a temperate and conservative lifestyle.

Something as benign as behaving in a manner that investigators decided was "ethnic"—speaking a language other than English or favoring foreign foods and customs—could lead to a plant worker losing his job and its accompanying desirable wage.

Even if you're tackling difficult stories (or stories about difficult people), you can follow the same process for shaping your narrative as we've been emphasizing throughout the book. Here are six story-building questions to get you started:

- Character: "What are the characters like?"
- Setting: "Where and when does the story happen?"
- Struggle: "What goes wrong?"
- Pursuit: "How do the characters try to resolve things?"
- Pivot: "How does the story twist in an unexpected direction?"
- Payoff: "How will this benefit my listeners?"

Then, finish by asking yourself how the story ends and where it needs to start.

—STEVEN

Ford himself was not entirely xenophobic. His father had been born in Ireland, and Ford was proud of his Irish roots, so much so that he made Ireland the site of his first overseas Model T plant. But he viewed middle Europeans as simple and backward, and regarded the people of the Mediterranean basin as lazy.

Even that paled in comparison to his anti-Semitism. On camping trips, Ford would spend time around the campfire lecturing fellow industrialists about the dangers that Jews posed to American business. Labor strikes, materials shortages, and financial pitfalls were just some of the ills that he laid at their feet. The political issues that led to World War I were, according to Ford, a plot hatched by Jews.

Nor did he restrict his views to campfire conversations. He shared them with journalists and, when he decided that his views were not getting sufficient ink in the conventional press, he purchased his hometown newspaper (known, ironically enough, as the *Dearborn Independent*) and insisted on an anti-Semitic slant to its coverage.

"The International Jew: The World's Problem" was a front-page-headlined series of articles that ran in the *Independent*; its editor was so disgusted, he resigned his position—at which point Ford's personal secretary took over the role, hiring *Detroit News* chief editorial writer William Cameron to continue the tirade.

The most outspoken stories were assembled into *The International Jew*, a series of four booklets, the first of which had a reported print run of half a million copies. *The International Jew* was translated into sixteen languages and was especially popular in post–World War I Germany.

For most of the first half of the twentieth century, Henry Ford was seen as an enemy of the Jewish community. When celebrating events that included motorcades, synagogues on both sides of the Atlantic would stipulate "no Ford motorcars" to participants. And in 1939, when Nazi Germany presented Henry Ford with their highest civilian honor, the Order of the German Eagle, industrial achievement was the stated reason, but Adolf Hitler's sympathy for

Ford's views on the alleged "Jewish problem" was considered a contributing factor.

With their founder's biases such a matter of record (*The International Jew* was never protected by copyright, and copies are still for sale online today), it would be futile for modern Ford spokespeople to deny them, so the company frankly admits that Henry Ford had his flaws. At The Henry Ford, a nonprofit historical preservation organization founded by Ford himself, the Benson Ford Research Center will even give visiting scholars a printed bibliography of its collection of materials related to the Ford Motor Company Sociological Department, in order to help expedite their research.

So, when talking about their founder, Ford executives will admit his faults and even share stories about the mean streak that was a characteristic of his personality.

Allegedly, Ford would sometimes borrow his bodyguard's handgun and discharge it into the ceiling of his office, just to frighten the junior executive working on the next floor. Once, when Ford's son suggested updating their product offerings during a board meeting, Ford expressed his displeasure by moving his son's desk into the men's room and making him work there until the founder's anger had subsided.

THE FIVE OKAYS

If you work for or represent a great company that has some not-so-great history, you can sometimes get past that, as long as the firm has grown past it in one or more of these ways:

1. It's okay to have a dark period in your organization's history, as long as you have acknowledged it, changed, and become reputable. Automakers who fudged on their emissions figures, bankers who forced loans onto

individuals—we've seen both in recent years, and the companies in both cases have cleaned house and moved on.

2. It's okay to have a founder or leader who was considered less than admirable, as long as you admit the alleged actions were wrong and you have striven to right those wrongs. Steve Jobs is reported to have overworked and browbeat his employees, yet Apple is now an admired company.

3. It's okay to make bad decisions, as long as you grow past them. Coca-Cola once changed their time-honored recipe to create "New Coke," and nearly bankrupted the company. They returned to doing what worked, and now they're doing just fine.

4. It's okay to have stupid mistakes in your past if you fixed them. Early in the twenty-first century, the Lego Group came to the staggering realization that it was selling some of its products for less than it cost to make them. The company reorganized, introduced new and profitable lines, and regained its former international prestige.

5. It's okay to change an organization entirely if it's best for everyone concerned. One company, in the highly competitive nineteenth-century agricultural-implement market, noticed that its porcelain-coated hog scalder was selling more quickly than expected—because farm families were using them as bathtubs. That company—Kohler—went into the plumbing-fixture business and became the new standard in that market.

You can use these "okays" to rectify issues. Ford Motor Company is currently viewed as altruistic, despite several shaky elements in its past. Indeed, Bill Ford, a great-grandson of Henry Ford and past president of Ford Motor Company, has frequently said that, "Good companies build quality products and provide a reasonable return to their shareholders; great companies do the same thing, but also make the world a better place."

In such a situation, a founder who could swing between good deeds and unfettered bigotry can be a baseline—useful to show how a company has matured over the years.

More importantly, when companies admit that the people in their histories had flaws, those people emerge as fallible: like you, like me, and like every other human being on earth. Doing the opposite—presenting key figures as perfect—paints them as people with whom you and I have nothing in common.

The word for such a portrayal of a seemingly infallible person is "hagiography"—literally, "to describe the saints." I grew up in a church that had images and statues of saints all over the interior. They were carrying the baby Jesus across a river, being pierced by arrows while gazing longingly to heaven, or performing one or another miracle while appearing, Mary Poppins–like, "practically perfect in every way."

I couldn't relate.

Hagiographic depictions just aren't that interesting. They don't seem real. Indeed, if you examine the lives of actual, canonized saints, even they have the occasional rough spot or two. Even Mother Teresa has been accused of mismanagement, slipshod medical practices, and questionable politics—and she seems much more approachable to me as a result.

DON'T TIME TRAVEL

In your storytelling, it is almost always a mistake to impose emerging values and priorities onto earlier times, yet well-intentioned organizations do this with alarming frequency.

During the growing environmental consciousness near the end of the twentieth century, one automaker's publicists discovered that, long before the Roaring Twenties, their founder had instructed his plant workers to disassemble the oaken boxes in which machine parts arrived and reuse the wood in the floorboards of his cars.

The publicists were elated: this was evidence that their founder recycled to preserve the environment long before any other industry did so!

And this news was very well received . . . until historians familiar with the founder's values pointed out that he was also notoriously frugal, to the point of stinginess. He wasn't reusing the wood to keep from cutting down trees. He wanted to avoid purchasing new wood; he was simply being cheap.

▪ ▪ ▪

I often tell speakers not to worry if the public will discover that someone in their company has a questionable history; and then I tell them the reason I say not to worry is because it's a certainty that it *will* be discovered. The public affairs term for that is "bad news known," and it is always best to control how it becomes known by sharing it oneself—and then balancing that unpleasantness with the story of how the organization has moved past and made amends for that behavior.

Was an early leader of your company a misogynist? Explain how those actions so appall your organization's leadership today that you are a leading supporter of women's charities, and that your company has made it a priority to work toward a board and a C-suite in which women occupy as many positions as men.

Or you can do as one leading chemical company did, and reveal how—decades ago—the gross mismanagement of one of their local operations contributed to a pesticide chemical release that killed thousands of innocent residents of a village in India. After considerable reorganization, which included acquisition by another firm in the same industry, the company is now a leader in corporate safety. They coach other businesses on how to become safer, and sometimes open their presentations with an account of their own failures, to demonstrate how recovery is possible.

Of course, if hagiography is bad practice when talking about the predecessors in your organization, it is equally ill-advised when you're talking about yourself. (See Steven's discussion of this in chapter 7.)

Fortunately, most of the speakers I work with understand this intuitively. We all learned as children that it's considered rude to brag about oneself, so we tend to take a more humble approach and oftentimes even lead with our faults.

When most of us compose our stories about ourselves, we'll share them with others to try them out. This is good—I'm a big fan of practice—but you need to be aware that friends, colleagues, and family members naturally tend to want to see you in the best possible light, so they'll often urge you to edit out anything that appears self-deprecating or self-critical.

They mean well. Thank them for their advice . . . but don't take it. The more perfect you appear to your listeners, the less they'll be able to relate to you. We all see ourselves as flawed people, and we gravitate toward and identify with others who acknowledge that they have flaws as well.

Besides, especially when shortcomings are presented as a baseline from which someone grew, they can contribute powerfully to the development of their story.

Want proof? Look at what Guinness recognizes as the bestselling book of all time: the Bible. One of the Bible's most prolific authors is Paul, who wrote about a quarter of the New Testament. Like many biblical writers—Moses, who lost his temper and killed a man;

David, who had an adulterous relationship with another man's wife; Peter, who denied association with Jesus in order to avoid arrest— Paul had a checkered past and he was vocal about it.

Paul describes how he, a Roman citizen of considerable stature, systematically persecuted Christians, whom the Roman Empire considered a threat to the security of the state. When Paul himself converted to Christianity, and suffered for that decision (a sizable portion of his writing was done while he was under house arrest, prior to his execution), he became reformed, and someone to whom we all can relate.

SUMMARY

Nobody's perfect. We, our families, and our organizations frequently have events in our past that paint us less than favorably, and, in an age of internet searches and muckraking media, the chances of covering up such instances of imperfection are slim to none. The best course is to acknowledge our shortcomings and show how we—our organizations and ourselves—have grown beyond our mistakes.

Story is an excellent tool for this because, to listen to a story, a person has to accept you as an individual with whom they have *something* in common. You can use story to start building community upon that tiny bit of common ground.

Key Points to Remember

■ Realize that you cannot cover up flaws, shortcomings, or failings surrounding the visible individuals in your organization's history (including yourself). In this online age, in which everyone has the ability to become an investigative reporter, flaws will eventually be discovered and shared.

- Remember: "bad news known" is much more readily handled if your organization is the one making it known.
- Perfect characters appear distant to us and are far less interesting, because no one can relate to them.
- We all see ourselves as flawed individuals, so we naturally identify and empathize with others who describe themselves as flawed.
- Stories are narratives of overcoming, and vulnerable, imperfect characters work best in them.

CHAPTER 12

THE KUNG FU LESSON, THE LLAMA SWEATER, AND THE ICE CREAM COOKIE STACK

—STEVEN

"An eloquent man must speak so as to teach,
to delight, and to persuade. To teach is a necessity,
to delight is a beauty, to persuade is a triumph."
—Marcus Tullius Cicero, Roman statesman
and orator (106 BC–46 BC)

If you haven't noticed yet, we believe that the most effective speeches contain stories and the least effective stories contain speeches.

So, how can we map out our speeches or presentations in a way that really engages listeners and makes the most of the storytelling principles we've been exploring?

Well, for each story you intend to tell, you'll want to identify the main struggle within it and how your listeners will connect with that, find a unique point of view you can bring to the story, and then think through how this story might fit in with the rest of your presentation.

In this chapter we'll explore three effective approaches for tapping into the power of storytelling to engage listeners, inspire them, and motivate them to apply the life lesson you're trying to convey.

THE KUNG FU LESSON

Maybe I should explain why I call it this. Growing up, I loved watching—and imitating—kung fu movies. Eventually, I outgrew the urge to strike a dragon or mantis pose and launch a flurry of kicks, but those cinematic fight scenes stuck in my head, and I still use them as metaphors when I teach storytelling.

This technique overcomes many of the pitfalls inherent in traditional approaches to speeches, is flexible, and can be used for almost any talk. It's a good way to teach without seeming too overbearing or didactic, and it's easy to remember.

It involves applying (up to) six very specific kung fu movie–inspired moves.

Kung Fu Move #1—Grab 'em by the throat.

Sometimes you'll hear the advice to start a speech with humor, or to break the ice with a joke. This can be very effective *if you know your audience*. Otherwise, if no one laughs at your opening joke, you may find yourself in trouble. Starting with a joke that no one thinks is funny is the last thing you want to do. It's tough to recover from an opening routine that bombs. Believe me. I've been there.

So, rather than a joke, often it's more effective to start by hooking listeners' attention by telling them something surprising before moving into the more lighthearted or humorous part of your talk.

Once, when I was talking to a group of ministers, I started my message by saying, "The first time I tried cognac was in a Ukrainian prison." Believe me, that got their attention! Then, once I'd snagged their curiosity, I moved into telling the story of how that experience had played out, what I learned, and how it applied to their lives.

Remember, when you walk onstage, everyone wants you to succeed. They really do—both for your benefit and for theirs. You have their attention right off the bat. It's up to you to keep it.

Often, they don't know who you are or what you're going to say. So, try something that makes them think, *Huh. I wonder where this is going.* It might be an opening anecdote, an object lesson, or a presentation slide that sparks their curiosity.

When starting your talk, appeal to curiosity by using *surprise.*

Kung Fu Move #2—Tickle 'em in the funny bone.

Humor can draw in listeners, and, if you're naturally funny, humor can form the core of your talk and become what people remember the most.

People love to laugh, so if you don't start with humor, now, after you've captured their attention, is a good place to inject it. But how do you do that?

1. Point out truths that your listeners haven't noticed yet.
2. Tell a story about a time when you were naïve, overconfident, or underprepared.
3. Use exaggeration to accentuate eccentricities.

We covered humor in depth in chapter 10, so check that out for more practical ideas. For the moment, though, remember that truth—not trying to be funny—is one of the principal keys to humor.

Avoid anything that will make your listeners think you're making fun of them or their culture, or that you're being insensitive. For instance, don't joke about mental illness, race or ethnicity, other people's body size or shape, disabilities, or suicide and homicide.

Puns can cause people to groan or mutter, "Ha ha," but they rarely ignite genuine laughter, so be careful with them as well.

Most talks can be enhanced with the judicious use of *humor*.

> The Gilbert and Sullivan comic opera *The Mikado* debuted in 1885. "I've Got a Little List" is a piece sung in that opera by the character Ko-Ko—the Lord High Executioner, who has yet to execute anyone—and the lyrics of that piece have changed countless times over the last century. That is because, by tradition, the lyrics are updated to reflect current events at the time of each production. Current events are always potential fodder for humor . . . provided you and your audience share similar views on them.
>
> —TOM

Kung Fu Move #3—Hit 'em in the head.

There's quite a bit of bad writing advice out there. Lots of misconceptions.

For instance, authors are often told that there are "plot-driven" stories and "character-driven" stories. However, this leaves out a third type of stories (relationship-centered stories). Also, it's simply not true that either plot or character drives a story forward. Instead—as we covered in chapter 1—all stories are driven forward by *tension*, created by unmet desire, whether that's internal (a question that needs to be answered), external (a problem that needs to be solved), or interpersonal (a relationship that needs to be initiated or restored).

So, when I teach at writers conferences and I start talking about how stories are driven by tension and not by plot or character, I need to anticipate the objections my listeners might have to what I'm saying because of what they've previously been taught. If I don't do so, those misinformed ideas become a distraction and the attendees won't be as likely to listen thoughtfully to what I have to say. People's objections and natural resistance to change can cause them to tune out rather than engage in what you have to say.

So, go ahead and acknowledge that not everyone agrees with your position. Perhaps say, "Some people might counter . . ." Or, "Some people believe . . ." Or, "Maybe you've been taught that . . . and I understand where those folks are coming from, but here's another view . . ."

Anticipate objections. Avoid simplistic answers and trite advice in your talk as you challenge your listeners' *intellect*.

Kung Fu Move #4—Sock 'em in the gut.

Years ago, I heard a fable, attributed to Aesop:

> Once upon a time, Dog became friends with Wolf. Every day, Wolf would visit Dog and they'd talk and play and romp in the yard. One day, Wolf said, "Hey, why don't you come over to my place in the woods? We can play there!"
>
> But Dog replied, "Well, actually, I can't leave the yard. I'm chained to that tree over there. But why don't you stay here with me?"
>
> Only then did Wolf notice the sturdy chain that was attached to Dog's collar. "You can't ever leave the yard?"
>
> "Oh, it's worth it," Dog told him. "My owner brings me food and water and takes care of me. It's safe here. If you stick around maybe he'll give you a chain too."
>
> "No thanks," Wolf replied, trotting toward his forest home. "I'd rather be hungry and free than well fed and in chains."

This short fable packs a lot of punch. Without overexplaining itself, it speaks to the issues of freedom, trust, friendship, and the different types of things that might enchain or enslave us. It's the kind of story that sneaks up on us, and the last line really impacts people.

Rather than bending over backward trying to be "relevant," simply tell the truth—which is always relevant. Truth impacts us and shocks us and angers us and inspires us and changes us. Though we might not always want to hear it, we need to.

Don't hold back when it comes to sharing gut-level *truth*.

Kung Fu Move #5—Touch 'em in the heart.

It's been said that a story told from the head reaches the head; a story told from the heart reaches a heart; but a story told from a life reaches a life. Or, as author John Burroughs put it in his 1879 essay *Speckled Trout*, "When you bait your hook with your heart the fish always bite."

Bait the hooks of your talks with your heart.

Tell the stories that matter to you and, more often than not, you'll find that they also matter to your listeners. Be passionate about them. When great storytellers speak, people are moved, not just informed. "I don't get it," isn't nearly as bad a thing to hear when you're done as, "I don't care."

Emotion is a powerful pathway to change, so rather than simply exhorting people to change, let them feel the importance of the change by inviting them to empathize with the story character's struggle, pursuit, and transformation.

Stop telling people what to feel and move them to feel it instead.

For instance, when I was in first grade, I thought that my two pet turtles were the perfect subjects for show-and-tell, but then I found out there was a rule that we couldn't bring live animals to class. I was devastated. When my teacher, Mrs. Beale, found out how upset I was, she smiled and reassured me softly, "Everything will be all right."

Then, since I couldn't take my turtles to school to meet her, Mrs. Beale arranged to come over to my house to meet them for herself.

I still remember how much it meant to me when she showed up and let me introduce her to Tommy and Jerry. When I share the story, I often close by saying, "When I was a kid, I thought Mrs. Beale came over because she loved turtles. Only when I got older did I realize that it was something else that mattered to my first-grade teacher."

Without being overly sentimental, it's a story that warms listeners' hearts.

> Going for the heart is especially important if you have also used humor in your talk. If you share nothing but humor with your audience, you risk sounding silly, and if you share nothing but heartstring-plucking sentiments, you risk sounding maudlin. But if you can use a bit of each end of the emotional spectrum, the elements will balance each other, and the result will be more satisfying to your listeners.
>
> —TOM

For most people, emotions cannot be called up on command but are the result of identification. Telling people "Be happy!" or "Be sad!" doesn't usually work. Instead of trying to manufacture emotion, build a relational connection and appeal to the struggles and desires your listeners have. Then they'll feel. Then they'll care.

Entertain your listeners even as you move them with emotionally resonant stories. Engage *emotion* without manipulating your audience.

Kung Fu Move #6—Let 'em show some backbone.
Another fable. (Yes, I love Aesop.)

Long ago, there was a war between the birds and the beasts. Bat was fighting on the side of the birds, but it looked like they were going to be vanquished by the beasts, so in the middle of the night, he sneaks over to the other camp. Shocked to see him, all the beasts exclaim, "What are you doing over here? You're a bird!"

"No," he tells them, "I'm a beast just like you. Look, I have fur. No birds have fur. I'm a beast."

Well, the beasts talk it over and can't think of a way to refute that. They say to him, "Okay, that is true. No birds have fur. You must be a beast. You can fight with us."

The war continues, and soon it looks like the birds are going to win, so Bat slips over into their camp at night, and they say, "Hey, you were fighting with the beasts! What are you doing here?"

"No, you're mistaken," he explains. "I'm a bird like you. Look, I have wings. No beasts have wings."

They can't argue with that, so they let him join them. But once more it looks like they might lose, so Bat goes over to the beasts' side once again.

"We know you were fighting with the birds!" they tell him, but he just shakes his head. "No, my friends. Look. I have teeth. No birds have teeth. I'm a beast just like you."

"Well, it is truth that you have fur and teeth. No birds have either. Okay, you must be a beast."

Eventually, there was peace between the birds and the beasts, but all of them said to Bat, "From now on you must live by yourself in a cave in the dark, and you will be considered neither a bird nor a beast, for you could not decide which side you were fighting for."

This story can be used in a wide variety of circumstances to call listeners to act, to choose their side, or to stick with the fight.

Close your talk with a call to action, a specific application of the principles you've covered, or a final reminder of what you, yourself, have learned that—by implication—your listeners can learn as well.

Invite them to put the principles of your talk into practice by appealing to their *will* and their desire for change.

REMEMBER THE SIX KUNG FU MOVES:

#1—Grab 'em by the throat.   (use surprise)

#2—Tickle 'em in the funny bone.   (inject humor)

#3—Hit 'em in the head.   (challenge intellect)

#4—Sock 'em in the gut.   (tell the truth)

#5—Touch 'em in the heart.   (evoke emotion)

#6—Let 'em show some backbone.   (appeal to will)

■ ■ ■

You certainly don't need to include every element of the Kung Fu Lesson in every presentation you give, and you don't need to include the kung fu moves in this specific order, but the approach is an easy way to remember a presentation's central elements.

By the way, can you overdo it by trying to pile too many stories or anecdotes into one talk?

Certainly.

The length of a message, the setting, the goals of the speech, and your own personality will all come into play when determining which stories you tell and which kung fu moves you use.

THE LLAMA SWEATER

When my daughter was a college junior, her professor assigned her to give a speech and, since she was attending a Christian college, she decided to speak about how God can work in the background of people's lives and weave things together so that, even though we might not see the pattern now, something beautiful can be formed in the end. She wanted her listeners to know that there's a bigger plan at work that will one day become visible.

While we were brainstorming ideas for her talk, I recalled hearing about an illustration of a rug that has a pattern on one side but tied-off threads on the other. She considered that, and then went to her room and returned carrying a llama sweater that she'd bought while volunteering for five months at an orphanage in Ecuador.

"There's a llama on one side," she explained, "but on the other you can't see the llama at all. It's just a tangled mess of threads."

"That'll work!" I said.

During her speech, she held up the llama sweater inside-out. No one in her class could see the pattern, just those tangled threads. Then, when she finished her speech, she turned the sweater right-side out and everyone saw the llama, reinforcing the point of her talk that order can be brought out of the apparent chaos and disorder of our lives.

When I think of the approach she used—showing an object that caused listeners to think, *I don't get how all this fits together . . . Where is she going with this?*—I think of that llama sweater. And, although she used it to teach a spiritual lesson, the approach can be used just as effectively to teach any life lesson.

Lock your story in the minds of your listeners by using imagery that ties together the truths you're sharing.

Stories have characters (subjects), struggles, emotion, and a meaningful pursuit. Outlines have main points (objects), descriptions, logical progression, and a list of concepts. Rather than an outline, present a mosaic of images that the listeners can inductively connect for themselves:

- Begin with a controlling metaphor or image rather than a theme statement.
- Weave the message and teaching time together organically rather than mechanically.
- Allow your audience members to make their own discoveries and connections between ideas.
- If you have multimedia capabilities, consider ways to include music, imagery, and video in the presentation.

To use this approach, first choose your llama—this will be the controlling image of the speech. Often, if you can represent your image or metaphor by using an object, you can make the concept memorable to your listeners, as my daughter did. This will be the takeaway, the lesson that your listeners will remember. It's the idea that you'll be hanging every anecdote or illustration on.

So, let's say that you're hoping to share a message that includes one of the following insights. Choose something that ignites curiosity. For instance, you could use the suggested objects to create a visual aid to your presentation:

1. The greatest struggle is not between people but within them. (An X-ray)
2. Truth is the sharpest scalpel of all. (A scalpel)
3. Humility is the strength you're not even aware you have. (Exercise equipment)
4. Life is not about getting ahead of others, but about lifting them higher than they could ever climb on their own. (A ladder)
5. Play is an attitude we have, not an activity we do. (Toys)

6. It's better to say, "I tried and failed," than, "I failed to try." (A participation trophy)
7. Wealth is so slippery that, no matter how much you have, you always try to grab more. (A pile of pennies—too many to hold with both hands)
8. You soon resemble the masks you wear. (A mask)

Rather than introducing a new idea at the end of your talk, circle back to your story's central idea and let people make the connection for themselves. Finally, "turn the sweater around" to show how all the threads of your message weave into a coherent whole that your listeners won't soon forget.

THE ICE CREAM COOKIE STACK

Think of a warm and gooey chocolate chip cookie. You scoop some ice cream on top of it, layer on another cookie, dollop on more ice cream, and top it off with a final cookie. There's nothing like a multi-layered ice cream cookie stack. Yum!

In this approach, you'll tell one story (the cookie), then include a refrain that ties the whole message together (the ice cream) before stacking another story on top of it.

Story stacking can be a powerful tool in your teaching and story-telling, as you convey a poignant message to your listeners and reinforce its different facets through numerous stories.

First, choose your ice cream: the refrain you'll use to tie the stories together. Then, pick your cookies—the stories, anecdotes, illustrations, or examples that you'll stack on top of each other. Each additional story or comparison will echo the main idea of the others, and serve to interpret and enhance the point you're making.

STORY STACKING . . .

- solidifies ideas.
- ignites wonder.
- raises important questions.
- builds impact.
- invites listeners to make connections.

Tell a story, then either show a slide with your summary statement or mention the refrain. You won't have a three-point outline. Instead, you'll have a one-point outline, and every cookie (that is, every story) clarifies or reinforces it, often by providing a fresh perspective on it.

Where do you get the cookies from? If you tap into L.I.F.E., you'll always have a source of stories to tell. Choose stories from literature, imagination, folklore, and your own personal experiences.

L—Literature: Stories you've read (or seen)

Try thinking of stories you've read, or films or TV shows you've seen. Consider using examples from books you liked as a kid, or the ones your teachers read to you. The whole world of literature is open to you.

I—Imagination: Stories you've made up

You have within you the potential to create stories that teach powerful truths. If you give yourself the freedom to explore your imagination, you might be surprised at what you'll be able to come up with.

F—Folklore: Stories you've heard

Use both ancient and contemporary folklore, fables, and myths in your presentations. Fairy tales, urban legends, hero tales, and even local history and lore can all add powerful illustrations to your talks.

E—Experience: Stories you've lived

Telling personal and family stories is a way to share your values, explain your heritage and history, help listeners understand and apply discoveries you've made, and deepen your relationship with them. (Chapter 15 will take a deep dive into ways you can explore your memories to develop material.)

Look for similar action, emotion, or symbolism as you examine stories from literature, your own original stories, tales you've heard, and experiences from your own life that exemplify or illustrate your message. Then, stack your stories together for added impact.

▪ ▪ ▪

Can you combine aspects of the Kung Fu Lesson, the Llama Sweater, and the Ice Cream Cookie Stack in one speech? Sure. Capitalizing on the strengths of each approach can be a powerful way of teaching or sharing insights. The shape and structure of the resultant hybrid speech will depend on the audience, how much time you have, and the message you're trying to convey.

A number of years ago, the principal at a local high school asked if I could speak to their student body. "Sure!" I said immediately, as any good storyteller would. "No problem!"

"There's a lot of gossiping," he explained. "I want you to get the students to stop gossiping."

"Oh. How much time do I have?"

"Maybe twenty minutes?"

That sounded like a challenge to me. Since shorter stories can sometimes pack more of a punch than longer ones, I figured I'd shoot for eight to ten minutes, tops. But as I began working on the speech, I started thinking, *What have I gotten myself into?*

It was an intimidating task, especially when I realized that if I just told the students, "You shouldn't gossip!" my message would have only a negligible effect—if it had any effect at all. And, as we covered in chapter 3, we want to avoid telling people what they already know in a way they already expect.

How could I encourage these students not to gossip, and do so in a way that would sneak beneath their radar, touch their lives, and impact their attitudes as well as their actions? I decided to go about it backward and not give them any advice at all.

Let me explain.

Often the best way to teach a virtue isn't by giving an example of the positive effects of putting it into practice, but by sharing the *negative consequences of doing the opposite.*

So, rather than talking about how well you acted and all the good things that happened as a result, you do the exact opposite. For instance, if you're exploring the different aspects of forgiveness, don't tell people they should forgive others, but show the consequences of unforgiveness. If you're teaching about the importance of respecting coworkers, tell stories that show the consequences of failing to do so. If you wish to encourage your listeners to communicate better, show the consequences of miscommunication.

Also, taking my audience into consideration, since I was twenty years older than they were, I knew I'd need to find a way to enter their world and connect with life in high school—something they could identify with.

I wanted to grab their attention right from the start, get them curious about where I was going, and give them a memorable image that would summarize the message.

In the end, I decided to use a combination of the three approaches: grabbing the students by the throat and then socking them in the gut (from the Kung Fu Lesson), using a controlling metaphor (a Llama Sweater), and stacking a folktale and a personal experience story together (from the Ice Cream Cookie Stack).

I started the speech by saying,

You know how sometimes you hear a story and you can't seem to forget it, even when you want to? It sticks with you over the years—kinda climbs inside you and changes the way you view things forever. I heard a story like that. And now, whenever I think of it, I think of her.

After that teaser, I told a short folktale I'd heard:

There was this guy who felt bad about spreading rumors and gossip, so he went to his priest to confess. The priest told him that God forgave him and so did he, but there was still one thing he needed to do.

"What's that, Father?"

"Take a pillow up to the bell tower and rip it open," the priest said. "Let the wind catch the feathers and blow them over the town. Then return here to speak with me."

The guy thought this was kind of weird advice, but he wanted to have a clear conscience, so he took a pillow to the top of the church's tower and ripped it open. The wind scattered the feathers all over town. Then, he returned to the priest.

"Good. Now, go and gather the feathers," the priest said. "Collect every one of them from every street and meadow and tree. Bring them back and re-stuff your pillow."

The man gasped. "How could I ever do that? The feathers are scattered too widely!"

"Remember that the next time you're tempted to gossip," the priest replied.

Admittedly, this story could come across as a bit didactic or "preachy," but since I'd started with the teaser about remembering "her," and there was no "her" in this anecdote, I still had those students' attention and their curiosity as they naturally wondered, *Who's "her"?* Then, I entered their world the best I could as I told the story of a girl I knew when I was their age . . .

Everyone had heard about a girl at my high school; we'll call her Kami. She was like this living legend at our school—two years all-state in basketball, all-conference in volleyball; she'd broken a ton of school records. She was looking forward to a full-ride scholarship in either sport she chose. I'd have to say she was one of the best athletes to ever attend my high school. Everyone talked about how great she was.

It was early in the fall of her senior year when she disappeared.

Here, I'm introducing tension. Now, I had curiosity on my side as well as concern.

It was autumn and I can still remember when the phone call came. My sister played on the same volleyball team and her coach was calling up all the team members to give them the news. He wanted to stop any rumors that might be going around.

Apparently, the day before, Kami had been out on a speed-boat with her older sister Lindsey and their boyfriends. It was Saturday morning, they were hanging out, and everyone was having a great time. They were just cruising around the lake when, little by little, the wind whipped up. The water got choppy.

Now, I'm dramatizing the incident based on what I later learned about what had happened. I could have just summarized this part, but I wanted the students to be drawn into the story. And hey, I had eight minutes. Notice how those Story Cube elements are present here: first, I introduced a character, then a setting, then foreshadowed a struggle. The pursuit is twofold: locating Kami and discovering the truth. (Later on, the payoff and pivot will appear together in the story's final paragraph.)

The waves turned into little frothy mountains. John, whose dad owned the boat, was showing the girls what it could do. He began slamming straight into the waves, whooping and hollering.

"Watch this! I can make this turn without even slowing down!" he called, steering the boat into a sharp right turn.

At first, zipping around the lake was cool, and both Lindsey and Kami were laughing and screaming and holding onto the railing of the boat.

As they cornered the turn, Lindsey shouted, "Wow, Kami! Isn't this awesome?" But when she looked behind her, the boat's deck was empty.

For a moment, she froze. Kami had been there just a minute ago.

"Kami? Kami! Where are you?" By now, Lindsey was screaming at the water and the wind. "John, stop the boat!"

He throttled back on the speed. "What's wrong?"

"Kami!" Lindsey's voice was swallowed by the wind. "She was just here. She must have fallen in somewhere. Go back. Quick! Go back! We've gotta find her. She doesn't know how to swim!"

John spun the speedboat around and they scanned the water. For a half hour they sped around the lake shouting and calling and crying out in disbelief. It didn't seem real. How could she be there one moment and gone the next?

The search went on into the night, but the police and the local search and rescue teams found nothing.

My sister hung up the phone and told me all about it. "She'll probably be there at school tomorrow. I'm sure it's some big mistake or something."

Kami was still missing the next morning when we went back to school. Everyone was talking about it—you know, in the halls, at lunch, even passing notes in class. For a few days we all thought Kami would be found, or at least that her body would be found.

A week later the rumors started. No one could understand why the search teams still hadn't found her body.

The tension of the story now escalates—not that things get worse for Kami, but they do get worse for her family.

"Someone like Kami couldn't drown. She's like this awesome athlete, right? She must have been pushed in and left to die. There's something suspicious about this whole thing."

"I heard she was taking swimming lessons but wasn't telling anyone. Maybe it was all faked. It's like this movie I saw a few years ago where this lady fakes her death by . . ."

"Did you know Kami was pregnant when she disappeared? Only a couple weeks along, I guess. The family is super religious and they're trying to keep it quiet. I know it's true because my cousin heard it from Kami's boyfriend's sister."

Word leaked to her parents. I think even the local newspaper ran a story about it all. Her parents insisted she'd never learned to swim and wasn't pregnant. But soon, word around the school was that they were covering for her. They'd helped plan the whole thing, which explained why they didn't seem so upset about her death.

"I heard they didn't even cry when they got the news."

"Yeah, and not only that, but my mom saw Kami's mom at the grocery store and she was laughing with the checkout lady. Laughing right after your daughter dies? Yeah, right. I don't think so."

"They orchestrated the whole thing. Her dad is a writer and I guess he got the idea from some book or something."

None of us knew what to think. Everyone had a different version of the story that they'd heard from someone they trusted. I wanted to believe she was alive, but faking your death? I mean, why put everyone else through all this? I only spread the parts of the story I knew for sure were true. We all did.

Those last two sentences aren't meant to excuse me, but to reveal what I was telling myself at the time—and what so many people tell themselves when they gossip. I'm hoping that students will personalize the story at this point.

Two weeks after her disappearance, her parents had a closed casket funeral at my church. I remember sitting there wondering if it was all being faked. Was Kami dead or alive after all? They still hadn't found a body. I guess her parents wanted closure and they thought maybe the funeral would put a stop to the rumors. That afternoon, they buried an empty casket.

In the next few months, the stories about Kami became more and more bizarre. She had faked her death, people said, to move to another town three hours away, take on a new identity, and have her illegitimate baby. Every week or two, some juicy bit of news would surface and spread like wildfire around the school.

Then winter came. Ice covered the lake.

Four months later, in the spring, after the ice had melted, some fishermen found a body washed up onshore. After it was positively identified as Kami, the rumors stopped abruptly.

What had those rumors done to her parents? Her sister? Those of us who spread them?

"I don't know if this is true, but I heard . . ."

"You won't believe what Rita told me . . . !"

"Remember when Kami disappeared? Well, did you know that . . ."

Some people excused themselves. Others denied having heard or passed on the rumors at all. A few people admitted what they had done and apologized to her family. But most of the people at my high school just stopped gossiping about Kami, and started talking instead about Jessie . . . and Charles . . . and Monica . . . and Julie . . . and Donald and Tracy . . . and me.

And the feathers still flutter through the halls of that school to this day.

That was it. My anti-gossiping speech.

If I would have thought of it, I could have ripped open a pillow and scattered the feathers across the floor of the gym at the end of the story, but as it was, I let the stories and the imagery speak for themselves.

Did the talk work? Did the students stop gossiping? Well, I wouldn't be telling you the truth if I said that they gave up gossiping entirely. But I heard later from the administration that the story did have an impact on the students and reinforced what their teachers were trying to impress upon them about not spreading gossip or hurtful rumors. So, at least we took an eight-minute journey in the right direction.

SUMMARY

By utilizing these three patterns for presentations, you can appeal to curiosity, teach to both the head and the heart, and create messages that your listeners will remember—and be impacted by.

Employ the techniques that are most appropriate for you as a storyteller, for the message you're sharing, and for the listeners who are present. Be wary of including too many stories, tell them each in your own way, and stay nimble to shape them toward your audience's needs and reaction.

Key Points to Remember

- Use surprise, inject humor, challenge intellect, tell the truth, evoke emotion, and appeal to the willpower of your listeners.
- Rather than starting with a joke, begin by inspiring curiosity, establishing common ground, or building a bridge to your listeners' lives.
- Instead of explaining the truth, unfold it one crease at a time, one image at a time, so that, at last, your listeners see its landscape stretching out before them.
- Let your listeners discern meaning on their own—they'll often understand more than you give them credit for.
- Explore ways to create your own hybrid speeches by intertwining the three presentation patterns found in this chapter.

CHAPTER 13

GOING FROM DRY TO DRAMATIC

When the Facts of the Matter
Really Do Matter

— TOM

"Sometimes, reality is too complex. Stories give it form."
—Jean-Luc Godard, screenwriter and film director

I've met many people who, although they agreed that story could perceptibly raise the level of a presentation, did not feel that it had a place in *their* presentation.

I think of them as the rhetorical equivalent of those voters who will happily support the tax levy to construct a new freeway and then, when the time comes to get it built, protest, "Not in *my* backyard!"

It is not that these folks dislike a good story. Most enjoy stories. But often they feel that their subject matter, or their audience, does not lend itself to narrative. What works for others doesn't seem right to them.

"My subject is too technical," they say. "It's science, not art; it's grounded in fact, not fiction. Story is for the softer subjects, not for those that deal with measurable facts and proven principles."

That's a common assumption, but it's incorrect.

A CENTURY REMOVED FROM A WAR

Consider Michigan historian Bruce Catton. A century after the American Civil War, he sat down to write a definitive account of that conflict.

The timing was both a blessing and a curse. A blessing, in that the centennial was raising new interest around the war and its events, and a curse because historians had already raked its ashes cold.

There was nothing new to be said. The war had been less than four years long, and academics had been examining it for a hundred. Everything to be learned about the war—everything of significance—had long since been learned, and much of it was known even by people who usually took little interest in history. Lincoln, Davis, Grant, Lee, Fort Sumter, Gettysburg, and Appomattox were all familiar to every schoolchild, so Catton had no revelations to make—no fresh information to present.

He did have, however, a fresh means with which to present it.

With nothing more than a few years of college in the way of academic training (his only degree was honorary), Catton had honed his writing skills in the newspapers, initially as a stringer and eventually as an editor. That experience gave him a taste of the sort of storytelling that people liked to read, a taste that he carried to *American Heritage* magazine when he became its founding editor.

The success of the magazine proved what Catton knew in his heart. Historians may look at the past in terms of facts and figures, but everyday people wanted to know what it all *meant*. A historian could tell you that William Tecumseh Sherman said, "War is hell," but it would take a storyteller to explain why. A storyteller could add the detail that facts and figures hid: that burning black powder smells like brimstone; that the ground fog of battle smoke could so confuse men fighting in close quarters that infantry would fire on their own lines; that the creeks which meandered through so many Civil War battlefields would run red for days following a battle; and that the low-velocity weapons of the day could wound so grievously that, often, it was better to have been felled by the shot than to be doomed to live with its aftermath.

Catton knew this. He also knew that the Civil War could only make sense to people if viewed from the perspective of the healing that followed it. In an editorial for the first issue of *American Heritage*, he had written, "Our American heritage is greater than any one of us. It can express itself in very homely truths: in the end it can lift up our eyes beyond the glow in the sunset skies."

What Catton was after, then, was a perspective that tied it all together: a resolution. Yet histories don't resolve.

But stories do. And, because they do, Bruce Catton became the most notable of a new breed of scholars: a narrative historian. For an entire generation, he changed the ways we viewed and thought of the past. And his Civil War trilogy—*The Coming Fury, Terrible Swift Sword*, and *Never Call Retreat*—remains popular today.

Ask yourself, "What aspect of this information is new or hasn't been shared before?" If there's nothing new about it, you'll want to find a way to impart it in an unexpected way. If it is new, that novelty alone can grab and hold the attention of your listeners—if it's presented with authentic passion. Ask, "Does this data surprise or shock people? How could I present it in a way that it will?" Then, rather than simply listing facts, choose one person who was impacted by the work you're doing and tell their story. It'll make the data more contextual, relevant, and memorable. And rather than considering simply how to make the information *understandable*, look for a way

> to make it *unforgettable*—by embedding it in a story. As researcher and storyteller Kendall Haven puts it, "No one ever marched on Washington because of the facts on a flowchart."
>
> **—STEVEN**

REACTION . . . AND ACTION

Bruce Catton presented facts—facts reviewed and verified by respected peers. But he did not simply release those facts into a vacuum. He shaped them through narrative, and he told those narratives with a purpose in mind.

With his trilogy, Bruce Catton wanted the citizens of his nation to feel proud of their heritage, and to know that the passions that raged during four years of conflict ultimately did not leave the nation divided, but eventually bound it together more closely than ever before. He wanted Americans to feel proud about being American.

I'm a novelist, but I also have a "day job," and in that day job, I work with and advise people before they speak to groups. When considering such an event, one of the first things I ask is: "What do you want people to *do*, once they have heard what you have to say? Do you want them to write to a legislator, change a habit, adopt a philosophy . . . what?"

If speakers do not have an answer to that question, I suggest that they decline the engagement. If their only reasons for speaking are to present facts and communicate basic information, a bulletin board or an email might fit their needs better than a lectern. Both communicate facts more effectively than a speech, because both can be reviewed by their recipients at their leisure, while the exact words of a speech begin to blur, blend, and fade just moments after they are heard.

But if the speaker's intention is to elicit an emotional response, to move an audience to act . . . in that case, we have something to work with.

Sharing a vignette from the birth of a company or an organization can remind an audience that they, too, have the power to become the pioneers that others will celebrate for generations to come.

Facts have the power to leave listeners energized, inspired, and moved to action.

Tangible evidence can be presented in a manner that moves an audience to tears or releases their joy in laughter. It can turn a fact in a file or a number in a ledger into a moment that will resonate for months. It all depends on how the information is presented.

Have you ever seen the movie *Schindler's List*? It can be summarized by a statistic: during World War II, German industrialist Oskar Schindler spared the lives of 1,200 Jews by employing them in his factories.

Yet the story of *Schindler's List* shows how Schindler faced increasing jeopardy and literally lost a fortune in his quest to save lives. The film ends with an epilogue containing actual footage of some of the 8,500 modern-day descendants of the *Schindlerjuden* arriving in a long, long line, to place pebbles on Schindler's grave.

The statistic is impressive. The story will haunt you for years.

When the purpose of your talk is to summon a power that can touch people's hearts, there is no better way to do that than through story.

A confession: I was never much of a fan of history class while I was growing up. Maybe it was because I mostly had teachers and professors who emphasized names, dates, deaths, and dusty facts rather than tales of bravery, discovery, or intrepid adventurers.

Then, one day, long after college, while I was on vacation on the East Coast, I happened upon a book called *That Others Might Live*. It covered the history of the U.S. Life-Saving Service from 1878 to 1915.

At first I thought, *Bleh. History.*

But then I flipped it open and found myself transported back in time as I read about the heroic exploits of those ill-equipped lifesavers rescuing survivors of shipwrecks. History came alive. The stories leapt from the page as I read that book on the same wind-whipped Atlantic shoreline where those brave men had battled the surf and the vicious storms that lashed the coast, trying to save others. Since then, I've loved hearing stories of shipwrecks, sailor lore, haunted lighthouses, and voyages on the high seas. That one book of history opened up whole new worlds to me through the stories it shared. That's the power of storytelling.

—STEVEN

THE MAGIC OF *MAINTENANT*

Let me explain the final word in that heading. It's French. It means "now."

I have spoken French, after a fashion, since Miss Rambeau very patiently introduced me to the language in her classes at Dwight Township High School, a place where you could see Illinois cornfields from the windows—as far removed from the Champs-Élysées as one could possibly imagine.

In bits and pieces, what I learned there stuck with me. Today, I possess a sufficient knowledge of French to get through most travel situations—ticket counters, the front desks at hotels, and conversations with waitstaff at restaurants—without needing to reverse gears into English.

On conference calls to Paris, as soon as they hear *"Bonjour,"* colleagues will, often as not, shove the speakerphone toward me, so I can open the call in halting French, before our counterparts across the Atlantic pick up on my horrible accent and fractured syntax and shift the conversation into their practiced and impeccable English.

That's about all I ever expected from those high school French classes: a sort of disjointed, conversational ability to avoid looking like a complete imbecile, should anyone ever address me in the language.

Then I got accepted into graduate school, and guess what? If you want to be a Master of Arts, you have to pass an exam, showing that you are fluent in a second language.

This was not welcome news. Yes, I spoke French—sort of—but whenever I spoke with someone who actually grew up with the language, I could practically feel them wincing, even if it was on the phone. "Fluency" and I were not even in the same area code.

Then I looked into the requirement further and learned, to my relief, that the university didn't expect me to actually *speak* French to demonstrate fluency in that language. Nor would I have to write in it. All they wanted me to do was *translate*; the exam consisted of someone from the French department opening a book from my area of study, marking a spot in it, and asking me to translate a chunk (five hundred words, as I recall) within the forty-five minutes allowed for the exam. I even got to use a French-English dictionary.

This seemed both reasonable and doable (and let's relieve the suspense here right now—I passed the test). But I needed to practice, so I started reading books in French—literary criticism, novels, and other subjects that interested me.

Some of these books were histories, and I noticed something intriguing: they were written in *present tense*. And not only were they told in present tense; often as not, the reader was invited into the situation being described. So, as I practiced my translation, I found myself penciling down sentences that began like this: "You are standing with Napoleon on the field at Waterloo . . ."

That was . . . so . . . *cool*!

It turned history—an area of study practically synonymous with dust, mildew, foxed page-edges, and dimly illuminated rooms—into this bright, vibrant, and immersive experience.

Here's something to try: tell a story in "third person," even if it's about yourself.

For instance: "He toddles into the kitchen and looks around. He's less than a year old, but is getting around well for someone his age, already walking. He's alone there—left momentarily unsupervised by his parents. He sees a cord hanging over the edge of the counter, drooping down toward the floor. Curious, he goes closer. He doesn't know what the cord is attached to. He knows nothing about the boiling grease in the deep fat fryer above him. Just that cord. That intriguing cord. He's close enough now. He reaches out for it . . ."

And so, I start the story of how I was badly burned as a toddler. Try it with a scar story of your own. How does it feel to tell the story that way? Does it give you more emotional distance, or less? It can add a unique angle to a talk!

—STEVEN

I'm really not sure why French historians stumbled across this technique, but I suspect it's because history is something the French have in such abundance. I mean, the Louvre, parts of which date back to the twelfth century, is not thought of as a particularly ancient building. In comparison, American history spans a relatively brief period of time—its events can practically be thought of as "current events." The French wanted a way to spice up history, give it some vitality, and make it relevant to modern readers, and they found a way—by simply changing "was" to "is."

You know where this is going, so let me express the obvious: present tense works really, really, really well when you're telling a story.

Stand-up comedians have known that for decades. The time-honored way to open a joke is, "A guy walks into a bar . . ." No past tense there.

But present tense, and particularly the historic present tense, is also a great, vibrant, and non-boring way to integrate historical material into a talk or presentation.

Consider this anecdote, which I used a few years back in a talk to auto-industry observers:

It is 1896, and you are in Detroit, Michigan—specifically, in a small, brick garden shed behind a modest, rented home on Bagley Avenue.

It is late on a June evening, and there is a light breeze blowing through the open shed windows, a spring breeze, barely touched by the usual nineteenth-century evening city scents of coal smoke and manure. Down the alley behind the shed, a horse nickers, answered by the confused cluck of a chicken startled awake in the night.

With you is Henry Ford, still dressed in the clothing he'd worn for his ten-hour shift as an engineer at the Edison Illuminating Company. Only two things are different: he has removed his hat and celluloid collar to rest them on the workbench and, to protect his white linen shirt, he has donned a well-worn leather mechanic's apron.

Ford looks tired, his shoulders sag with fatigue, and it makes him appear older than his thirty-two years. But when he raises his face, his steel-blue eyes twinkle with excitement.

He has just made one tiny, final adjustment on his labor of love: the Ford Quadricycle—the very first automobile to bear his name. It looks like the front half of a buckboard wagon, resting on four bicycle wheels, the front two movable by a tiller. Never before has it tasted the open road. But tonight is the night.

Standing straighter, Ford extends his hand to you, asking for a tool.

He is not asking you for a micrometer, a drill, a tap, a wrench, or a screwdriver.

No. What Henry Ford needs to finally bring his achievement to life is . . . a sledgehammer.

This last part always worked even better if I brought out the sledgehammer (which I'd concealed behind the lectern) to illustrate what I was talking about (no kidding—I had a prop made of rigid foam, so I wouldn't look like a weakling when I picked it up). Then, to answer the question this last statement raises, the vignette would conclude:

You see, after months of machining to tolerances bordering on a thousandth of an inch, Henry Ford realizes that there is one thing he had not measured accurately; his creation is too wide to fit through his garden-shed door.

Wincing at the thought of the repairs he'll have to make over the coming weekend, he swings the sledge at the doorframe, knocking bricks loose with a clatter. Ten minutes and several swings later, the opening is just wide enough for the Quadricycle to inch through.

It's a moment of humor that, combined with the you-are-there proximity of the present-tense narrative, turns Henry Ford from a historical figure into a living, breathing—and fallible—human being. Setting aside the liberties we have taken by putting the audience into the shed with Ford, it has the additional merit of being absolutely true.

I usually segue with the observation: "Henry Ford was a genius, but Henry Ford was fallible. Not everyone in this auditorium is a genius, because I know for a fact that the guy on the stage is not. Yet I can guarantee you that everyone here is fallible. Ford got his car on the road. It's how we deal with that fallibility that counts."

That anecdote does more than convey the fact that Ford built his first car by hand, on his own. It allows the listener to share in the thrill of that moment.

> Notice how, in Tom's anecdote about Henry Ford, he captures the six aspects of the Story Cube—he describes a vivid *setting* (both in time and place) to help listeners see the scene, brings an iconic *character* onstage, shows his *struggle* ("his shoulders sag with fatigue"), elaborates on his *pursuit* of creating the Quadricycle, and weaves in a *pivot* with the introduction of that unexpected sledgehammer. Since this is an anecdote, Tom clarifies the *payoff* himself, after the story has closed. As you develop your stories, keep each of those six elements in mind.
>
> —STEVEN

SUMMARY

We've all told real-life stories: how we caught a fish, how we landed a job, how we got up the gumption to first speak with that amazing person we eventually married. When we tell those stories, we often unconsciously shift into the pattern of narrative: a desire, an obstacle, how that obstacle was overcome, and the afterglow that resulted. It's the oldest form of entertainment. People love to hear stories.

They vastly prefer a story to a mere recitation of facts, and stories bring the storyteller to life as well; your listeners will feel that they know you better after you have shared a story with them. That is why stories work so well in presentations, and present-tense stories usually work best of all.

Business typically deals with the concrete and the technical: matters that, at first blush, may appear entirely unsuited for the seemingly soft delivery of storytelling. But a story is especially well suited for explaining esoterica. Frankly, sometimes it is the only way to bring the heart of a technical matter across to a general audience.

Key Points to Remember

- Virtually any subject can be presented through narrative.
- Before consenting to speak, consider what you want your audience to do with what they have heard, and whether a story can motivate them toward that action.
- A memo or an email can present the facts; a story can convey why the facts matter.
- Narrative offers the opportunity to depict historical figures as three-dimensional (and fallible) human beings.
- Using present tense is often the best way to bring an audience into a historical narrative.

PART IV
THE STORYTELLER
What You Bring to the Story

Every storyteller is unique, and as you share a story it'll be an extension of your individual, distinctive, incomparable personality. In this section, we'll explore how to develop your own innate storytelling skills and how to look at your experiences through a storyteller's eyes to tap into your memories to find powerful stories to tell.

CHAPTER 14

TRANSFORMATIVE TECHNIQUES TO IMPROVE YOUR DELIVERY

—STEVEN

"Humans are truly homo narratus, *story animals."*
—Kendall Haven, storyteller and author of *Story Proof*

When I was in middle school, I entered the Conservation and Environmental Awareness Speaking Contest for Jefferson County, Wisconsin, on a quest to win the whopping $10 first-place prize. For dozens of hours I labored over my three-minute master-piece, carefully perfecting every gesture, pause, and facial contortion in front of our bathroom mirror.

And it worked too. Sort of. Though I never took home the first-place ribbon, I did place in the top ten each of the three years I entered (even on the year it snowed and only one other contestant showed up). My monologue about the importance of soil conservation told from a worm's point of view left the judges in stunned silence. And my storytelling career was up and running.

Or at least squirming.

I think I might even have won that $10 prize if the judges could have visited our bathroom and watched me rehearse in front of the mirror. I was brilliant.

Unfortunately, they couldn't come over and at the time I didn't know these five secrets to practicing and telling stories.

SECRET #1—
RECITE LESS, RESPOND MORE

My high school basketball coach had a saying: "Practice doesn't make perfect, it makes permanent."

The same is true for storytelling. Practicing stories is important—no doubt about that. But practicing a story doesn't necessarily improve the way you'll tell it.

It may improve how well you remember that story. It'll probably impress upon your mind and body one way of moving or acting or speaking. But if you practice your story over and over the same way in front of a mirror, it doesn't mean it'll become "perfect." It's just much more likely that you'll learn to tell it that way.

Every time.

Forever.

So, use practice time to develop proficiency at storytelling skills. Tell the story in a variety of settings to a variety of audiences in a variety of ways. Become so familiar with the story that when it's time to deliver it you'll be able to tell the most natural, appropriate, genuine version of your story on that day. You'll know the *story*, not *one version of it*.

Effective storytellers strive to respond to the audience rather than recite their story. To shape their stories, they react to the ongoing feedback of the listeners. They tell a story differently in front of a bathroom mirror than in front of a live audience. If a storyteller practices in front of a mirror, it shouldn't be to perfect the story, but simply to become aware of what the listeners see during the story.

The best communicators combine diligent preparation with a warm sense of spontaneity. Think of the most effective speakers you've ever heard. Maybe they were comedians. Maybe authors or actors or pastors or professors. What made them so good? I'll bet one of the reasons was the connection they established. You didn't feel like the whole speech was canned, but was being told personally to you.

The delivery of your story is based on four factors: the story, the listeners, the context, and the storyteller. This is no surprise. It's Communication 101. These four elements (message, receiver, context, and sender) are present in all communication events. As with any message that needs to be shared, each factor affects the communication process: story (content, truth, emotion) + listeners (readiness, familiarity, response) + context (setting, venue, expectations) + storyteller (goals, gifts, personality) = delivery. That's why this book is divided into four parts, each probing into one aspect of story delivery:

Story + Listeners + Context

+ Storyteller = Delivery

Many speakers fail to take all four aspects into consideration in their preparation and delivery. This is what happened with me when I replaced telling to actual people with telling to a mirror—and ignored the listeners and the social context entirely.

If you leave out the story, you're doing improv.

If you don't consider the listeners, you'll have a tougher time reaching them.

If you fail to give thought to the context, you'll end up undermining your message.

And finally, if you don't add your own take on the story, you'll sound like you're imitating someone else.

Bring it all together in your delivery: think about the story itself, the readiness of your listeners to accept what you have to say, the venue, and your own style and communication skills. And remember, as a storyteller, you're not only responding to the listeners, but also to the story itself as you tell it.

If you hone a knife too long, you'll eventually make it more brittle. It's the same with story preparation. Practice until the story is sharp, then stop. Don't over-polish your stories or they'll lose their edge. The best stories are polished (well honed), but also contain an air of spontaneity.

As you deliver your story, pay attention to what's happening right now; don't worry about how the story is "supposed to go" or how it went when you were practicing it. Be present. Notice how it's unfolding as you speak, and respond to how your listeners are responding to you.

If you pay attention, your listeners will help you write your story as you deliver it.

Shoot for a connection, not a reaction—the reaction will come naturally when the connection is made.

The power in the story comes when the listeners can identify with or empathize with the character or emotions at the center of the story, when they can see the events, and when they can find themselves in the narrative. Try to find emotionally resonant moments, and then don't overplay them. Melodrama results when there isn't enough emotion in the story to justify the response you're asking the audience to experience. Avoid that. Instead, strive for authenticity.

A technically "perfect" story may fall flat. Why? Because listeners would rather hear a storyteller who relates to them, who touches them with the story, who communicates with them—even if he fumbles for the right word once in a while—than watch someone go through the meticulously rehearsed actions of telling a story that they don't feel a part of.

STRIVE FOR . . .

- preparation in how you develop your story.
- authenticity in the way you tell your story.
- clarity about the direction of the story.
- emotion because of the tension within the story.
- responsiveness to your listeners as you deliver your story.

As we've stressed in different places throughout this book, don't try to memorize your story. Yes, you need to be prepared. Yes, learn the story and practice your pauses and gestures. Yes, move naturally through it. But don't worry about retelling the story "word for word." Instead, be flexible. Strive to tell it naturally to this audience today rather than reciting it the same way you did earlier in front of your mirror.

Your listeners will be turned off if they think every gesture, pause, and vocal utterance is identical this time to the last time you told the story. They want you to tell the story to *them*, not to an imaginary bathroom mirror. They want you to experience the story with them, sharing its poignancy, warmth, spontaneity, or humor. This can only be done if you're attentive to the story as you tell it, and are continually filled with wonder and curiosity about the story. So, focus on responding rather than reciting.

SECRET #2—
CONCENTRATE LESS, RELAX MORE

My basketball coach also had us practice numerous drills in ball handling, shooting, passing, and playing defense. He used the drills to teach us how to respond when we faced similar situations in the game. He wanted us to become so proficient at shooting that we wouldn't even have to think about it when someone threw us the ball.

I remember one game when I became frustrated and started to concentrate on everything I was doing: *Okay, Steve, keep that forty-five-degree trajectory and good rotation on the ball, flick your wrist, follow through with your hand, keep your eye on the basket . . .* That game I couldn't hit the broad side of a barn. And that's pretty bad. Especially for a kid from Wisconsin.

Instead of overthinking things, I just needed to play the game. I'd become proficient at the skills during practice. The moment I began to think about how I was *supposed* to shoot the basketball, I became too distracted to actually shoot the ball well. Rather than *concentrate*, I needed to *relax*.

When you practice a sport, you do the drills and exercises to improve. But when it's time for the game, you play. You don't think about the drills during the game. Practice is practice; play is play. There comes a time to *play*. When you get up to tell your story, put away the watch and the notebook and your expectations and inhibitions. Let loose. Have fun. And play.

When practicing a story, it's important to explore and refine body movement, voice inflection, facial expressions, gestures, and so on. But, during a story performance, don't focus on the mechanics of the story. *Experience* the story with the listeners.

Tap into the energy of the moment. Embrace the audience's attention. Telling stories can be intimate and thrilling and exhilarating. When you're well prepared and connecting with your listeners, the human connection can almost feel like magic.

Practice will give you the confidence to tell the story well—but don't get distracted by how properly or how poorly you're telling it. Relax and enjoy. If you must concentrate, concentrate on what's happening in the story, not on what could be going on, or what should be going on, or how well it went in rehearsal. Pay attention to what's happening in your story *right now*.

Attend to the moment. Abandon all your expectations, worries, and distracting thoughts, and let the story flow naturally.

SECRET #3—
PRETEND LESS, BELIEVE MORE

Unnatural gestures will look unnatural, but if you believe the story as you tell it, your body will respond naturally and realistically. An effective storyteller is observant, both toward the story she's telling and toward the audience she's telling it to.

When you're in the middle of a story, stop acting *like* the person you're portraying, and start acting *as if you were* that person. Perhaps you've seen a movie or a play in which one of the characters seemed real. For example, the actor stopped looking like someone imitating Mark Twain, and suddenly you *saw* Mark Twain. But how can you get to that point? How can you attain that? Stop acting and start responding.

Enter the story and act *as if.*

Let your belief inform your response.

During an acting class that I attended years ago in a barn that had been transformed into a theater, the instructor placed a sneaker halfway across the barn, then handed out blindfolds to us. He pointed across the room. "I want you to pick up the shoe," he said, "while wearing that blindfold."

The shoe had to be fifty feet away.

We just wanted to do improv games, but we sighed and, one by one, my classmates shuffled forward blindfolded, bent over, and reached down. No one was even close to picking up the shoe.

Then it was my turn. I told myself, *I'm going to get that shoe!* I started calculating how many steps it would take me to get there, taking into account the length of my stride, the speed of the earth's rotation, the Coriolis effect, the force of gravity—heck, anything and everything I could think of. At last, figuring that I had this for sure, I put on the blindfold and strode confidently across the room toward the center of the barn.

Counting off my steps, I walked forward until I came to the spot where I was certain the shoe would be right beside my right foot. I bent over and smiled as I closed my hand . . . on thin air. I was shocked. I felt again. No shoe.

I took off the blindfold and saw the shoe waiting eight feet in front of me. Embarrassed at how confident I'd been, I returned, somewhat humbled, to join the rest of the group.

After the activity, the instructor lined everyone up, and then walked directly up to me. "Steven, you were the only one who closed your hand. Why did you close your hand when you reached for the shoe?"

"Um . . . I'm a little embarrassed to say this, but I really thought it was there. I mean *really*. I could hardly believe it when it wasn't."

"That's right!" He jabbed his finger against the air just inches from my face. "And that's how much you need to believe your stories when you tell them."

He went on to explain what he meant. "You were certain that something was there, even though you couldn't see it. Your mind knew what the shoe would feel like and how much it would weigh. You couldn't fake your hand's reaction. I could tell you thought the shoe was there. That's how real your story has to be when you tell it. Then you won't be pretending when you tell the story; you'll be responding to it as it happens around you."

I hadn't practiced closing my hand, hadn't even planned on doing so, but I believed so much in what I couldn't see that my body simply responded as if the shoe were there.

That experience at the barn opened my eyes to the importance of belief and stepping into the stories I tell.

Tony Montanaro, a well-known mime who trained numerous professional storytellers, emphasized this point in his book *Mime Spoken Here*: "When I lean on a wall, I honestly *believe* that the wall is there. When I fly through the air as the legendary Icarus, I *see* the Aegean waves surging beneath me. My ability to believe these things, these images, determines the clarity of my gestures and the integrity of my sketch. My belief ignites my audience's belief, and they join me in my adventures."

In my worm monologue, I felt ridiculous acting like a worm, and because of that I looked ridiculous. A lot of *pretending* was going on, but very little *believing*.

The best storytellers don't pretend. They actually imagine the story happening, and then respond to it as it unfolds. Strive to see the story around you and disappear into it.

And then reach for the shoe.

FOUR STEPS TO TAKE

- Tell your story in your own words.
- Believe in the story.
- Imagine what's happening as you tell it.
- Respond to your audience.

SECRET #4—
EXPLAIN LESS, EVOKE MORE

I heard about a dancer who was approached by an audience member after a stirring performance. "Wow!" the lady gasped. "Your dance was incredible. But I have to say . . . I didn't really understand it. What does it mean?"

And the dancer replied, "If I could tell you what it meant, I wouldn't have had to dance it."

Some things cannot be explained, summarized, analyzed, or tied up with a neat little bow. Sometimes, explanations aren't sufficient. The dancer embodied her message through movement since that was the only way she could express what was truly in her heart.

Stories should stand on their own and communicate what cannot be easily explained.

Think about it: You don't read a novel and then flip to the last page to read the author's explanation of the story to you. You don't watch a movie and then have someone come on during the last scene and explain to you what the film was supposed to mean.

In *Mystery and Manners*, novelist Flannery O'Connor wrote, "When you can state the theme of a story, when you can separate it from the story itself, then you can be sure the story is not a very good one. The meaning of a story has to be embodied in it, has to be made concrete in it. A story is a way to say something that can't be said any other way, and it takes every word in the story to say what the meaning is."

If you can summarize a story, you probably don't need to tell it.

Stop looking for ways to clarify the point, and start looking for ways to dance what cannot be stated outright. If readers can ferret out the theme, they're not on the way to being moved, but on the way to being bored.

If the poet or the storyteller could explain her point to you, she'd do it. Actually, it would save a lot of time and stress and ink and crumpled-up sheets of papers. Marriages, too, probably. But the thing is, she *can't* explain it. That's why she *tells* it. The novelist, the artist, the poet, the dancer can't summarize her tale, painting, poem, dance. The story can't be reduced to theme statements and plot out-lines or, if it can be, it wasn't a very good one to begin with.

The greatest storytellers don't set out to simply teach us lessons. Instead, they try to strum a certain note of pain or joy or wonder in our souls, and to play that tune in such a way that it resonates with us and awakens something deep within us that could never be awak-ened by mere explanation.

A good story carries more of an impact than its explanation would. It defies explaining. It has more depth, detail, passion, and truth than any description about it or summary of it would contain. Explanations tend to shrink rather than expand a story's meaning. So, rather than explain your story, look for ways to use the story to evoke, expose, examine, or explore topics that matter to your listen-ers. As storyteller and playwright Kevin Kling told me once, "If you have to tell us the moral, you haven't told us the story."

A story found throughout the world tells of a poor family where the grandmother lived with a little girl and her father. Food was scarce and they never seemed to have enough to eat. Finally one day, the girl overheard her dad muttering to himself in the other room, "I'm going to have to ask Grandma to leave. There just isn't enough food for all three of us."

The little girl came into the room and said, "We should give Grandma half a blanket when we make her leave."

"*Half* a blanket!" her father gasped. "Why would you say such a thing?"

"So I can give you the other half when I make you leave one day."

It's not necessary for you to elaborate on what the story means. Listeners get it.

As speakers, performers, and educators, we're sometimes tempted to trust our explanations of stories rather than the stories themselves. We seem to think that the more we explain a story, the better it will be—but exactly the opposite is true. The more you explain a story, the less impact it has. Let the story impact your audience before you explain too much. *And even then, don't explain too much.*

As we covered in chapter 4, if you need to interpret a story or tell your listeners what it means, you have an anecdote on your hands. *Anecdotes* depend on context and an explanation to bridge to the application. In that case, listeners will appreciate the time you take unpacking the meaning. A *story*, however, contains the context and requires no explanation—in fact, people may be annoyed by an explanation. They'll feel insulted by it.

> When Steven says people will be insulted by an explanation, I'm reminded of a person I used to work with who, every time someone said something of substance, would immediately jump in and say, "What Bill is trying to say is . . ." and then he would paraphrase what had just been said. Finally, one time, when he was beginning his usual jump-in, the person who'd just spoken said, "No, Frank. I am not *trying* to say anything. I just *said* it."
>
> No one in the room peeped a word. But—inside—I'm pretty sure we were all applauding.
>
> —TOM

At the end of your stories, include a choice that shows the change within the character. That transformation might be from an internal revelation; it might resolve an external problem; or it might impact an interpersonal relationship.

That choice is what allows the story to embody its meaning, rather than require some outward moralizing. Was there a change of heart? A lesson learned? An insight gained? Rather than stating it outright by saying something along the lines of "So, I learned . . ." or "That's when I realized that . . ." it's usually better to show the choice that reveals the change. Strive to show the change by noting what you *did* differently, not just stating that you *thought* differently.

So, share with your listeners how you acted after that incident rather than delineating the lesson to them. For instance, "I crumpled up my to-do list and tossed it into the garbage. Then I took my daughter's hand and we headed to the park," rather than, "I'd learned that I needed to spend less time working and more time playing with my daughter."

You are the story's spokesperson, not the interpreter.

Include all six elements of story: an intriguing and vulnerable character, an evocative setting, an intimate struggle, a goal-directed pursuit, a surprising pivot, and a resonant payoff. Then, let your listeners infer the story's ultimate meaning on their own.

I'm not saying that you want to annoy or confuse your listeners or leave them scratching their heads, just that you can often trust them to draw conclusions on their own rather than feeling like you need to unpack everything for them. Focus more on telling the story well than on "getting the point across." Trust the story to do its work.

Incidentally, with anecdotes, the best transitions are invisible. Getting from the account of the time you nearly burned down half of Oklahoma when you were setting off fireworks with your best friend behind the barn back in ninth grade to the problem of little destructive habits getting out of hand in our lives is like the handoff during a relay race at a track meet. If the runners drop the baton, everyone notices, but if there's a smooth transition, hardly anyone notices. When you move from anecdote to application, you don't want anyone to notice that you've switched runners.

This is how most people make the transition: "Just as the fire started small and got out of control . . . so also . . ."

It's a little more subtle to say, "Every time I think of that fire, I'm reminded of the time I . . ." then launch into a personal story about how a negative habit got out of control in your life.

Or, "Recently, I thought of that fire when I read these words . . ."
Or, "Lately, I've been learning that . . ." Or, "I'm beginning to realize
that . . ." Or, "That's similar to something I experienced myself . . ."

Sometimes the best transition is no transition at all. Rather than
feeling that you have to spoon-feed your train of thought to your
listeners, let them discern the application themselves.

SECRET #5—
IMITATE LESS, EMBODY MORE

Every one of us has different DNA.

Our storytelling DNA is different as well.

The spirited eighteenth-century preacher Charles Spurgeon
(who preached more than six hundred sermons before he even
turned twenty years old) emphasized how important authenticity is
when he said, "Your mannerism must always be your own, it must
never be a polished lie."

Some people are soft-spoken and shy. Others are dramatic and
outgoing. Let your storytelling style grow from your unique personality, from your own comfort zone. The most effective storytellers
are always those who bring the story out of who they are, instead of
pretending to be someone they're not.

So, when you tell stories, don't try to imitate how someone else
would do it. Instead, use your own specific gifts, talents, personality,
and abilities to tell it in a way that only you can.

There's a Hasidic story that one morning a Rabbi named Zusia
awoke, pale and trembling. He was so visibly shaken that when
he went to speak to his followers, they immediately asked him
what was wrong.

"I had a dream," he said, his voice trembling. "And in my
dream, the Angel of the Lord asked me a question. And after I

heard the question, it upset me so much that I couldn't sleep another moment."

None of his followers could understand what question could have caused him such concern. After all, he was very devout and religious. "But you're a holy man!" they stammered. "You know the Torah. You follow God's Law! What was the angel's question?"

The rabbi replied, "The Angel of the Lord did not ask me, 'Zusia, why were you not Moses, leading God's people out of slavery?' That was not the question the angel asked . . . The angel did not ask me, 'Zusia, why were you not David, conquering kingdoms in my name?' The angel did not ask me that . . ."

"But what was the question?" his followers asked him once again.

And he responded, "The Angel of the Lord asked me, 'Zusia, why were you not . . . Zusia?'"

The Angel of the Lord isn't going to ask me, "Steven, why were you not Tom Morrisey, writing thousands of speeches for business execs?" He's not going to ask me, "Steven, why were you not James Patterson, selling hundreds of millions of books all over the world?" But I should hope that one day I wouldn't hear these words: "Steven, why? Why, when from an eternity you were shaped and planned and formed and given just the right amount of enthusiasm and creativity and . . . stupidity . . . and placed on just the right planet at just the right moment in history . . . to cause the least amount of damage . . . Why? Why were you not Steven?"

Embody your story and leave your DNA on it. Let it flow naturally. *"Zusia, why were you not Zusia?"*

When you hear that question in the still of the night, it can be enough to keep you awake until morning.

Or, at least, it should be.

SUMMARY

Develop a storytelling style that's comfortably and uniquely "you." Your most natural storytelling voice will sound like you when you're talking to someone you trust rather than someone you're trying to impress.

Respond, relax, believe, evoke, and then embody your stories. Spend more effort imagining them occurring and less effort worrying about how they're going as you tell them.

Okay, so these aren't the only secrets to storytelling, but maybe, just maybe, if I'd known them when I was in middle school, I would be $10 richer today.

Key Points to Remember

- Believe the story is happening. Actually step into it and become a part of it. Attend to the moment.
- Remember that a vibrant delivery will take into account all four factors: the story, the listeners, the context, and the storyteller.
- Let your gestures flow out of responding to the story rather than planning them beforehand and then rehearsing them.
- Tell the story in your own distinctive way rather than trying to be funny or literary or impressive or sound like someone else.
- Avoid the temptation to summarize and explain everything. There's always more to a good story than its explanation could contain.

CHAPTER 15

DUSTING OFF YOUR MEMORIES

Crafting Personal Experience Stories

—STEVEN

*"There is no greater agony than
bearing an untold story inside you."*
—Maya Angelou, poet

Whenever I move to a new house or apartment, I scrutinize everything I own and ask myself, "Does this still belong in my life? Is it worth packing up, carrying along, and hanging onto, or should I just get rid of it? What does it mean to me? What is it *worth*?"

The last time I moved, I filled a dozen boxes with trash. By uncluttering my possessions, I found out what I truly valued. And here's something I discovered: often, an object's value and significance was intimately tied not to its commercial value but to its *narrative* value. Though some items might've sold for only a handful of spare change at a yard sale, they'd become invaluable to me because of the stories I associate with them.

Sharing stories from personal experiences involves a similar sorting process. You sift through memories, examining them for significance, filtering through the trivialities of everyday life until you find moments that grab you and simply won't let you go.

Tapping into your own experiences can give you powerful stories to tell and stirring anecdotes to share. Here are some specific ways to explore and examine the stories you've experienced so that you can more effectively share them with others.

If you're like me, you're glad Steven brought up that decluttering image.

I, for one, find it almost impossible to declutter. I'll start to empty a shelf or a drawer, and an hour later my wife will find me looking at a pocketknife, a fishing lure, a shiny pebble, an old camera, or the trumpet I haven't played in two years, and she'll ask, "Why aren't you cleaning?"

Now I know why I'm not.

Next time my wife asks that question, I'll tell her, "I got lost in a collection of stories."

—TOM

FOSTER POIGNANT MEMORIES

Jog your memory however works best for you—by paging through photo albums (physical or virtual); pulling out souvenirs or childhood toys; revisiting old haunts; or flipping through school records, scrapbooks, or adolescent love letters. Review favorite books you've read over the years, peruse old diaries, or take a look at heirlooms and memorabilia.

As you file through your past, reliving your dreams and fears, your triumphs and traumas, you'll find some memories that stick with you and that you can't seem to shake—missed opportunities, lost loves, vacations that ended not-so-grandly. And also stolen kisses, secret crushes, and unlikely or unforeseen celebrations as well.

Devastation. Delight. Despair. Discoveries.

"I was a sophomore in high school when I found out I was adopted . . ."

"When I heard the door slam, I knew my dad had been drinking again . . ."

"On my twelfth birthday, my friend Brad and I decided to investigate the old deserted house on the far edge of town, out by the pond . . ."

When I'm developing stories, I sometimes think about people who inspired me or moments I wish I could experience over again—or do over again. Usually, there's a story crouching there waiting to be discovered. As author John Shea wrote, "We turn our pain into narrative so we can bear it; we turn our ecstasy into narrative so we can prolong it. We tell our stories to live."

Think of . . .

- a struggle you had when you were younger. What resolved it? Or, is it still a part of your life?
- a dream you had when you were growing up. How did it actually come true in a way that you didn't anticipate?
- a favorite teacher you had. What illustrative event comes to mind?

Think about a pivotal moment in your life. What was altered? What became clearer? What did you discover? Start there—with what you felt, learned, or feared. Think of something that hurt, taught you something profound, changed your perspective, or helped make you who you are. As John Yorke, author of the screenwriting book *Into the Woods: A Five-Act Journey into Story* told me, "Write about a wound that needs healing or a joy you want to share."

The best personal experience stories have a character that listeners can relate to, an intriguing problem or struggle, vivid details that help them envision the story, and emotion that impacts their lives.

Begin with whatever you have, and nurture that fragment of a memory: the smell of your grandmother's cookies, the charming way your father used to whistle, the chill in your soul as you rushed to the hospital in the middle of the night, the taste of salt spray that summer at the ocean, the tender warmth of your daughter's tiny hand when you held it for the first time.

Whatever sparks your imagination, fuels your passions, or ignites your emotions can fill your stories. Turn those memories over in your mind; carry them with you. You may not know why this particular memory is so powerful to you, but explore it. Start there and see where it leads.

SEARCH FOR CONNECTIONS

When I think of lessons learned the hard way, I think of diaper water.

One day my wife and I took our three young daughters to the beach and I stayed out in the sun about, well, nine hours too long. My back was burnt to a crisp—very close to the color of a boiled lobster's claws. When I went to bed, I couldn't sleep and tossed and turned all night, until finally, I got up cranky and angry at 5:14 a.m. to take a shower and get on with the day—only to find that the water heater was broken. Water that was ten degrees colder than ice poured over me. The expression on my face looked like those guys melting at the end of the first Indiana Jones movie.

So, after a four-second shower, I decided to catch up on some writing. I spent an hour editing three articles that were due that day, saved them, and, as I did so, they mysteriously vanished from the computer into the black hole of cyberspace. Like magic. *Presto! You will never see those articles again! Watch and be amazed!*

I stomped back upstairs and my wife handed me our youngest daughter, who was six months old at the time. "Would you change her this time?" Then she turned and headed back to bed before I realized it wasn't a question.

That's when I began to mumble incoherently to myself.

And I wasn't quoting inspirational quotes from my favorite authors.

In an effort to be environmentally conscious and to save money, we were using cloth diapers. Because of that, we had a huge diaper pail in the bathroom that we stuck the nasty diapers in until we could wash them. On this morning, it was filled to the gills with disgustingly polluted poo water. The older two girls (ages six and four) had now gotten up and were crowded, curious, in the bathroom doorway. Twice I told them to go to the kitchen to eat breakfast, yet they lingered. I was clenching my teeth. "Pleeeeease go into the other rooooooom."

They stayed. I think they were enjoying the show.

I leaned over to get the diaper wipes and hit my head on the shelf, and that did it.

"Aaaaaaah!!!" I kicked my leg backward and it hit the diaper pail, sending reeking, yellowish brown water splashing all over my two oldest daughters. All three girls started crying and screaming. My six-year-old was yelling, "Daddy got diaper water on my face!" over and over again. "Daddy got diaper water on my face!"

That's when my wife came into the room.

It was not one of the high points of our marriage.

She inhaled through her teeth so intensely that I was afraid she might create a vacuum that would disrupt the space-time continuum. She took over diaper-changing without a word while I started to clean things up, penitently, on my knees.

Just another day in paradise.

Finally, when things calmed down, I apologized to everyone, and life trudged on. A little later that morning, I found my oldest daughter coloring at the kitchen table. "You know what rough mornings remind me of?" she said.

"What?"

"Bricks."

"Bricks?"

"You know, rough mornings like we've been having and rough days and rough nights like we sometimes have, they make me think of bricks because they're rough."

"Oh. And what kind of a day would you like to have?"

"Smooth."

"What's smooth and soft that you'd like to have a day like?"

"A blanket."

"A blanket instead of a brick?"

"Uh-huh." She didn't look up from her drawing. "That would be nice."

What do you say in a moment like that? There's nothing to say. No matter how hard I try, I end up with just as many brick days as blanket days. As many diaper water days as beach days. That's life. Not always easy. Awfully messy at times, yet always holding out the promise of a repaired water heater somewhere down the line—maybe out of sight, but not out of reach. Not completely. Not forever.

Then, she looked up, leaned over, and gave me a hug.

"Ouch."

"What, Daddy?"

"Sunburn."

"Oh."

But, hey, I could deal with that. The moment wasn't a perfect blanket, but it was close enough.

EXPLORE THESE IDEAS:

1. Warnings: "I wish I could warn my younger self that . . ."
2. Lessons: "The greatest lesson I ever learned from my dad was . . ."
3. Insights: "One of the most self-destructive things a person can do is . . ."
4. Secrets: "I am secretly . . ."
5. Questions: "I used to wonder . . . but now I know . . ."
6. Growth: "I used to believe that . . . but then I learned . . ."
7. Transformations: "I used to be . . . but now I'm . . ."

Now, you won't necessarily say those phrases to your listeners—it could come across as too heavy-handed—but examining these seven areas can be helpful to you personally as you develop and brainstorm new stories.

■ ■ ■

Often, the most powerful insights come not from the exotic but the familiar observed in a new light. In a guidebook on preaching published in 1954, author Webb B. Garrison wrote, concerning sermon illustrations, "In order to be usable, the strange must not be too strange. It must be linked with the known by at least a narrow causeway." It's a good observation. Philosopher and theologian Helmut Thielicke made a similar comment: "Often we miss the inner mysteries of the very things with which we are most familiar."

Little moments often hold more easily accessible truths than the big ones. Life tilts or changes in some small, subtle way, and something inside of us shifts, irrevocably, in a new direction. As award-winning storyteller Matthew Dicks puts it, "Seek out the moments when you felt your heart move. When something changed forever, even if that moment seems minuscule compared to the rest of the story."

So, for story material, look at the familiar and search for something unique within it. What makes this moment, experience, or observation extraordinary or noteworthy? How does it deviate from your normal day-to-day existence? It's exceptional, it's memorable—why?

Think about it: What draws our attention to one rose over the others in a bouquet? It's not how similar it is to the others, but how different—whether that's because it has unfolded more than the others, or perhaps has wilted prematurely. Our attention is drawn to incongruity. So, when you're preparing your stories and evaluating which events from your life to include, look for those moments when things didn't quite fit, when something was altered, or when your attitude pivoted into a new direction. Look for discrepancies between what you expected and what resulted. That's often where the stories that resonate the most deeply with listeners will be found.

NURTURE MEMORIES THAT WON'T LEAVE YOU ALONE

There's a Portuguese proverb: "What is difficult to bear becomes sweet to remember."

Let's say that you have a vivid memory or something humorous happened to you and you want to share it in your next speech. How do you frame it? How do you find out what it means or how it will apply to your listeners' lives?

Once you find memories that you can't leave behind, it's time to search for how they might develop into stories. This integration involves searching for connections between seemingly unrelated events, sometimes across the years. Look for parallels to other stories you've heard or read. Then, identify specific ways to apply the story to your life or the lives of your listeners. Ask yourself, "What does that incident mean? What did I learn? How did I change? How does that connect with a lesson I'm trying to teach or a virtue I'm trying to convey?"

We make sense of our experience by combining our memories (both the facts and the feelings) with meaning (the lessons or truths we attribute to that experience). As you shape your story, ask yourself:

1. What is it about this memory that grabs my attention or seems significant?
2. What happened, and what was my role?
3. What question or crisis did I face? How was I hurt or what did I struggle with?
4. What eventually caused the tilt or pivot in my circumstances or attitude?
5. What did I learn, discover, or understand—or how did I mature as a result of this experience?
6. How has this lesson changed the way I live? What insight did the experience give me?
7. How can I help others identify with this struggle or lesson as well?
8. What do I need to add, change, or cut from my story to better impact my listeners?

Without struggle, you have no story, so concentrate on your challenges, trials, wounds, and obstacles; or maybe the problems you've faced, or the approval you've sought. Remember the cost of sacrificing for something you believed in? Dealing with loss or tragedy? Recovering something important? Life is full of things that go wrong, and every one of them is a story waiting to be told.

Once, while teaching a class on writing memoirs, I told the class, "A good story has conflict. If nothing goes wrong, it's not a story."

One woman, who was close to seventy years old, raised her hand. "My life has been a good one. I don't have any conflict in my life. I guess I don't have any stories to tell."

Just then, it was time for a break, so after I excused the class, I asked her to tell me a little more about her life. Within five minutes she'd told me about her forty years of marriage and how she and her husband had moved thirty-six times. She shared with me the tragic news that her sister had a terminal illness and that the two of them were trying to mend their relationship. She explained that she was late for class each day because she stopped to visit a woman with Down syndrome who lived alone at the end of her street.

This woman's life was rich in stories—we just needed the right way to help her understand that.

Since then, I've stopped talking about "conflict" and encouraged people to look for struggles, transitions, and challenges instead.

FOCUS ON PURSUIT INSTEAD OF PLOT

Don't worry about finding the plot of your story. (Remember from chapter 1: plot is simply the journey that the *character* takes through the *setting* to overcome her *struggle* during her *pursuit*.) Instead of trying to figure out the plot, simply look for instances when you faced a problem and struggled your way toward a new understanding or situation, most likely learning an unexpected lesson along the way.

When telling stories from personal experience, you've already lived the plot, but since life doesn't always seem purposely directed, you'll need to sort out the everyday irrelevancies and incongruities to find the thread of meaning winding through those moments. Your listeners will want to be able to see the causes and effects, the motives that shaped your choices, and the results those choices had.

Something caused that revelation to come to you. What was it? For instance, "When I saw that, I knew ..." Or, "After that, I couldn't help but think ..." Or, "That's what changed things for me ..."

It might take you a while to discover for yourself what the story means to you before you can shape it into a meaningful story to tell others. Often, an isolated memory isn't enough for a complete story. Even if it was hilarious or heart-wrenching, painful or profound, in order to be meaningful to your listeners, it needs a context. Strive to include all six elements of the Story Cube: character, setting, struggle, pursuit, pivot, and payoff:

1. Character: Help listeners identify with the main character's questions or desire by highlighting one they share (that is, she wants to find love or adventure or freedom or acceptance or belonging, and so on ...). This encourages empathy.
2. Setting: Describe the scene with enough details for your listeners to see it and feel something toward it.
3. Struggle: Weave in tension as you tell the story—now that the audience can see it and cares about the character, show how things go from bad to worse.
4. Pursuit: The story will progress as she tries different ways to avoid, overcome, obtain, or withstand something—and fails, escalating the tension or sharpening the emotion.
5. Pivot: Build up to a climax that listeners wouldn't expect, but that makes sense, given the context of the story.
6. Payoff: Wrap things up with a final twist or revelation— usually by showing the choice the character makes that she wouldn't have been ready to or capable of making at the start of the story.

Here's one framework for understanding your stories and what you've taken away from them: "I used to . . . until . . . Since then, I've . . ."

You don't necessarily need to say this sentence to your listeners. This is simply for you to better process the experience's impact on your life. However—that being said—as a teaser, you *could* start your presentation by saying it to your audience. For instance, "I used to think that I wanted things to be fair until I met that little girl in Fayetteville, Tennessee, and since then I've realized I don't want life to be fair at all."

Intriguing. Why would you say that? Isn't "fairness" a good thing? Immediately, your listeners' curiosity will be piqued and they'll be drawn into your story.

Audiences want to know what causes the transformation in a story. Even though it might be tough to identify the specific event that caused you to make a decisive change in your life, it's worth the effort of looking for it. Try to identify the impetus to change. It won't do to say, "I thought about it for a long time, weighed the pros and cons, evaluated everything, and finally decided to become a police officer, like my dad," or "I prayed about the situation day and night, and finally, last week, all of our marital problems were resolved." What unforeseen event caused the decision in the first example or the reconciliation in the second? That's what your listeners want to know—the cause and effect that led to an unexpected pivot and unforgettable payoff.

What did you desire? What did you do? What got in the way of you getting what you wanted? How were you surprised? How did things resolve in a surprising way? What was the residue of emotion that you felt and that you want your listeners to feel?

Remember, they are interested in how you were affected by the event or encounter. If bad stuff just happens to you and you don't react, it won't be nearly as interesting as it would be if you actually make meaningful choices when the struggles come.

Relevant stories contain shared personal experiences, realistic situations, and memorable characters. They address issues listeners can identify with and believe are important. Effective personal stories contain easily pictured locations, meaningful choices, and a natural application of the main character's journey to real life as the listeners are experiencing it.

A personal story is more than simply a recollection of what happened. It needs that pursuit, pivot, and payoff we explored in chapter 1. Often, storytellers fall into one of three traps when telling stories from their lives:

- Trap #1: Portraiture—The "sweet old lady who died" story. The teller basically starts by saying, "So and so is a saint, and I'm going to tell you why . . ."
- Trap #2: Nostalgia—The wistful memoir story: "Ah . . . the good ol' days . . ." The only problem is, no one wants to hear you relive the illusion of an idyllic childhood. Life was never a Norman Rockwell painting, for anyone.
- Trap #3: Bravado—The thinly veiled bragging session where you just sing your own praises or subtly put others down: The teller grunts and says, "Huh. When I was your age, we didn't have kale. We ate bark. No one was allergic to gluten—it hadn't even been invented yet."

WRITE YOURSELF OUT OF
THE SPOTLIGHT

Your story, even though it might be about your life, is not about you; it's about what you (or someone else) learned or observed. Rather than being in the spotlight, you're standing behind it, directing its focus on the story instead.

You don't want to end up as the actor taking bows after the curtain closes—and don't become the victim either (as we covered in chapter 7). Be the one who fumbled the ball, not the courageous overcomer; you're the recipient of grace rather than the savior, the problem-haver and not the problem-solver. Emphasize not how you triumphed but how you floundered and took something meaningful away from the experience. You were the knucklehead, not the champion holding his hands up high in the center ring.

Listeners don't want to hear how great you are; they can't identify with that. Reveal your vulnerabilities instead. They want to hear how you faced a problem and made a surprising discovery. Be authentic by being honest, sincere, and vulnerable. Then they'll identify with your story.

When telling personal stories, remember that there's a difference between openness and honesty. You can tell a story that is completely honest—that speaks the truth—but you don't need to be 100 percent open about your struggles. Use discernment in your use of self-disclosure. Don't overshare.

Tell your audience about your difficult decisions, identifying what you learned as a result of them, and pinpointing how those lessons shaped or changed your life. Remember, listeners want to hear more than what happened; they want to know how you felt, how you reacted, and how you gained a new insight or matured as a result. So, as you share your struggles, pinpoint what you discovered as a result of the difficulties you faced.

Sometimes that's an inspiring story.
And sometimes it's a heart-wrenching one:

Cathy had blonde hair and eyes that could leap over tall buildings in a single bound. She told me she'd recently graduated from college and was only working as a receptionist at the local children's museum temporarily. "I'm gonna move to Los Angeles and become an actress." Her eyes flashed as she said the words. "I'm gonna be famous someday."

"I hope you make it," I said.

Since my daughters were the right age to enjoy the museum, we visited it often. One day, Cathy mentioned that she was still living with her parents, but not for long, just until she saved up enough money to move. "The day is coming," she told me. "It won't be long until you see my name in lights."

"I can't wait," I said.

A week later, she smiled at me and whispered, "I visited L.A. this weekend. It's great. In two weeks, I'm quitting and moving there."

"We'll miss you," I said.

Three weeks later, I found Cathy still sitting at the front desk. When she saw me, she shook her head. "I don't have enough money, but I think I'll probably work for one more month before quitting."

"Okay," I said.

Six months later, I walked past the museum on my way to a nearby coffee shop and glanced in the window. Cathy was sitting behind the counter, rearranging the papers beside the phone.

Oh, I thought.

She happened to look up as I passed.

For a long, uncomfortable moment we stared at each other, then she lowered her head and went back to work.

And as I headed on my way, all I could think of was the look in her eyes the first time we met and how it compared with the look in her eyes now.

So tragic—yet it's a powerful memory that won't leave me alone. If I were presenting Cathy's story in a program, I would probably look for an inspiring story, one about someone who was able to pursue their dreams as a counterpoint to Cathy's experience, to overlay against hers so that I could end on a more inspirational note.

For instance, perhaps this one:

In Wautoma, Wisconsin, Z's Drive-In sat on the corner of Highway 21 and Highway 22—although it wasn't technically a drive-in because you had to walk up to the window to order.

A screened-in dining area with picnic tables and a pinball machine rested by the kitchen. Behind the restaurant, a grassy lot with a swing set, picnic tables, and a child-sized merry-go-round sprawled back to a white picket fence. A crooked gate led to a small garden nestled in along the edge of the lot.

A wooden sign half the size of a billboard on the corner of the parking lot announced "Z's Drive-In" in hand-painted letters—at least, that's what the sign read when I first visited there one summer, many long years ago.

The place used to have another name. You could tell by the way the sign was painted. Faded, barely visible letters peeked out from behind and between and underneath the new ones, like a scene from a movie that hadn't quite faded away when the next scene began. I guess the previous owners went out of business. I'll bet if you asked the folks who live around there, not too many would remember what the place used to be called. To them, it was Z's.

I had Tuesdays off that summer. So, one hot Tuesday in early June, I took my wife to town for lunch. We'd never been to Z's; it looked fun and within our budget, so I pulled into the lot and we walked up to the ordering window.

We were the only ones in the parking lot.

Everything on the menu started with the letter "z." I ordered the "Z-burrito," my wife got a "Z-burger," and we had two ice cream "Z-bars" for dessert. It cost $5.95. The ice water was free.

We were in our mid-twenties at the time and a friendly, curly-haired woman maybe a decade older than we were hummed through the window as she prepared our food. She delivered the tray to us outside at the picnic table where she had encouraged us to "sit and enjoy the breeze." A few feet away, the garden gate hung awkwardly on one hinge, creaking occasionally. Just beyond that lay a freshly planted garden.

"Nice place you've got here," my wife said.

She smiled and nodded. "Thank you, we like it."

"We?"

"My friend and I. We spent all our savings to buy it."

Then she looked away from me and stared toward the garden. Tourists and water-skiers, sunsets and long walks, Z-bars and summer romance flashed in her eyes. She was about to add something else, but stopped.

I thought it was a remarkable thing to move with a friend to a vacation town, spend all of your savings to buy a restaurant with a view of the horizon across a cornfield, and grow a garden.

I tried to think of something profound to say. All I came up with was, "I'll bet it's been an adventure."

She turned from the garden, glanced at me, smiled again, and walked back to the kitchen. She was humming when she left.

Throughout July and August, my wife and I enjoyed visiting Z's Drive-In almost every week on our day off. We introduced our friends to the Z-bar. And as the summer passed us by, we watched that charming little garden grow tall.

One day, after the summer had floated by and autumn was nipping the air, I drove to that corner of Highway 21 and Highway 22 on my way to town. The tourists were gone. Trees had turned from green to orange and red and gold. The stiff wind and wild skies reminded me that winter was coming quickly to Wisconsin. And when I glanced toward the restaurant, I noticed a flashy new sign on the corner of the parking lot. The words "Z's Drive-In" had been painted over. In bold, bright letters the sign read "Dragon Drive-In."

Someone I didn't recognize was locking the place up for the winter and as I turned the corner, I noticed that the garden where fruit had grown all summer was withered and brown, and the gate was locked.

But that fruit had grown. That garden had flourished for a whole summer.

And sometimes, that's enough.

It's been more than twenty-five years now, and I suppose most folks around there don't remember Z's Drive-In and the dream behind it anymore.

Most folks, maybe. But there are a few of us who do.

DELVING DEEPER INTO YOUR PAST

Stories about the events that shape our lives can be moving, inspiring, and even profound. Use your personal story as a way of introducing your lesson, as a bridge into the lives of your listeners, or as an example or illustration of the life principle or moral you're trying to share. To find ideas, consider milestones, turning points, and times of transition:

adoptions	holidays
anniversaries	homecomings
arrivals	honeymoons
baptisms	hospitalizations
births or birthdays	houses
body image	injustices
building projects	jail sentences
camping trips	meals
confirmations	money
decisions	moving
divorce	new family members
dreams	new homes
empty nests	new ventures
environments	priority shifts
funerals	remodeling
going back to school	retirements
going back to work	reunions
graduations	rivalries
grandchildren	separations
health issues	vacations
heroes	weddings

You can also spark memories by scrolling through old social media posts, visiting meaningful places where you've lived or worked, cooking favorite childhood foods, or reminiscing about the more unusual people and events that have shaped your life.

Many of our deepest memories are rooted in the first time we did something, owned something, felt something, or realized something.

As you glance at the list below, consider not only the memory but also the story that swirls around it. Remember the first time you . . .

got made fun of?	fell in love?
went on a sleepover?	broke up with someone?
walked into your high school?	bought a house?
had a death in your family?	broke the law?
got a car of your own?	got hired for a job?
went on a date?	got fired from a job?
got cut from a sports team?	left to "seek your fortune"?
moved away from home?	returned home once again?

SUMMARY

Your memories provide a virtually limitless well of stories for you to tap into when you're looking for material to tell. To find your stories, foster poignant memories, search for connections between the memories you have and the lessons you've learned, and write yourself out of the spotlight as you direct the attention of your listeners not on your accomplishments but on your discoveries.

In Appendix C, you'll find 365 Story Starters that will help you discover stories from the experiences of your life. When you read them, note how they each relate to memories of the two things that lie at the heart of all personal narratives—struggles and discoveries. Don't be intimidated or overwhelmed! Start with something manageable. Choose three numbers at random between 1 and 365 and see if you can come up with stories for those three memories. Give it a shot and let the stories you've lived inform the stories you tell.

Key Points to Remember

- Your life has ample material for you to share. If you mine your memories deeply enough, you'll never be without stories for your speeches.
- Spark stories by dusting off your memories and exploring in depth the ones you just can't seem to shake.
- Examine times of transition in your life, struggles you've faced, challenges you've had to overcome, and people who've inspired you—those memories offer rich material for stories.
- Consider what caused you to change your views, then explore those moments, unpack the memories surrounding them, and search for a way to show the change in your life without "beating listeners over the head" with the insight.
- Tell stories that matter to you, that touch on the universal desires or wounds we all have, and you'll find that the stories will matter to your listeners as well.

CHAPTER 16

SHAPING STORIES
LIKE A SPEECHWRITER

—TOM

"Any life isn't just one story. It's thousands of them."
—Dean Koontz, author, in his novel *False Memory*

We'll begin with some assumptions here.

You've accepted an invitation to speak. The audience is one worth making a connection with, the event is worth the effort it will take to put together a talk, and—seeing as you're reading this book—you understand the value of story in your presentation.

How do you decide on the story (or stories) you'll use?

Here are some of the things I consider as I help a leader put together a talk.

WHAT'S THE CALL TO ACTION?

If you're making a trip, before you even head to the airport you'll have to know where you're planning to land. That is, after all, the purpose of a trip. If you're going to Miami, fly to Miami.

If you're preparing a talk, before you even start sketching it out, it's wise to know how you want your listeners to feel, and what you want them to feel motivated to do when you stop talking. That is the purpose of speaking—the resonance or the directed energy that you are imparting to your audience.

That may seem obvious, but it's easy to get so wrapped up in minutiae that you forget why you're putting together the speech. So, as you create elements, test them against the state of mind that you want everyone in the room to have at the end of your talk. Ask the metaphorical question: "Is this getting us any closer to Miami?"

HOW MUCH TIME DO WE HAVE?

As far as practical construction—assembling the bits and pieces of a talk—the initial factor to consider is the budget, and by budget I'm not referring to dollars, euros, or pounds sterling. What I'm thinking about is *time*.

Consider how well the time allotted matches the subject proposed.

It is not simply a matter of whether you're getting enough time to cover the topic; it's also whether you're getting too much.

Different cultures have different expectations when it comes to speech length.

In September 1960, Cuban leader Fidel Castro addressed the General Assembly of the United Nations for 269 minutes (just under four and a half hours). Twenty-six years later, he spoke in his home nation for a reported seven hours. If that sounds like a lot, consider that Venezuelan leader Hugo Chávez once spoke nonstop for *eight* hours.

True, neither Chávez nor Castro were likely to get pulled off the podium by a stage manager. Still, there are some contexts in which audience members all know to arrive at a speech armed with empty bladders and a sandwich.

In North America, Britain, Australia, and New Zealand, though, unless the speaker is engaged in a filibuster, oration tends to be considerably more concise, and the expected length of a speech becomes even *more* concise with each passing year.

For instance, in the years following World War II, a forty-five-minute commencement address was not considered excessive. By the 1990s, seventeen and a half minutes, precisely, was considered the edge of the envelope by most speechwriters. By the time the twenty-first century rolled around, nine minutes was the typical target length for a university commencement.

Today, when I get a commencement request, it frequently comes with a suggestion to limit remarks to five minutes.

> Most conversational stories are brief—sometimes only a few paragraphs (or even less). Keep your story lean, evocative, and moving. Sometimes all you're going to share is the recollection of a moment in your life when your eyes were opened and you saw things in a new light. Don't pressure yourself to shape every story into a finely honed, performance-worthy, twenty-minute-long narrative. It's better to share a story that errs on the side of brevity rather than one that's bloated and top-heavy. Often, less really is more.
>
> —STEVEN

Thing is, five minutes doesn't mean you'll have those full three hundred seconds for talking. Some of that time will be consumed by other things.

Applause, for instance. Most people never think about applause (other than the fact that it feels good to be applauded), but it eats up seconds. In a five-minute speech, if you allow enough opportunities for the audience to clap, an audience making noise to show their support can easily burn forty-five to sixty seconds of your very limited speaking time.

That's one reason that, if the audiovisual team is capable of playing a sound clip, I ask them to play walk-on music as the speaker approaches the lectern.

You've experienced walk-on music before—it's music played while someone is making the journey from the stage wing to a microphone, to cover extraneous noise. Well-known people will even have their own "theme songs" that are used for the walk on (think of Bob Hope and "Thanks for the Memories"). As such, walk-on music establishes the mood for the start of a talk, *and* it has one other merit—when it stops, the audience accepts that as their cue to cease clapping. You can begin with no time lost to opening applause.

But let's say you don't have your own theme song . . . No matter. Keep preliminaries to a minimum. If someone just introduced you, shake their hand, and mouth, "Thank you." If the audience has seen that, they don't have to hear it.

Try also to reduce "junk" applause. Place the thanks to the sponsoring organization and compliments to the audience after the beginning of your talk. Keep that part brief and, if you are in, say, Chicago, resist the urge to say, "The Windy City! I love it here!" . . . because that is going to evoke junk applause—people clapping just because they heard a reference to their town.

Speakers think they're supposed to do that whole "It sure is great to be back here in Cleveland" opening because they've seen touring comedians and musicians do it. But those folks do it because they *want* junk applause. In stand-up comedy, junk applause loosens up the audience and makes them more likely to respond later in the set.

That's not you. If you only have five minutes at the microphone, you'll want to move as much applause as possible to the end of your talk, where it won't use up your speaking time.

Of course, most good talks will evoke some reactive (non-junk) applause and possibly laughter as you speak and storytell. Estimate where that occurs and budget for it. A five-minute talk may consist of four and a half minutes of you speaking and thirty seconds of audience response.

If your host has asked you to speak for five minutes and you step away from the microphone at three hundred seconds exactly, you come across as professional and you'll probably be invited back.

At the other end of the spectrum is the host who asks you to speak for forty-five minutes. That's nearly three times longer than most audiences want from a single speaker (there's a reason TED Talks cannot last more than eighteen minutes).

A good reply to such a request is, "That's longer than I usually speak. Would you mind if we kept my part down to twenty minutes?"

That will usually work, but some hosts have forty-five minutes ingrained as the amount of time a speaker should be onstage. Plus, cutting your talk shorter might disrupt the agenda.

If the event is one you really want to be part of, and your host really wants you onstage for three-quarters of an hour, interstitial elements can break the talk up into smaller, more easily digestible sub-talks.

Some of the more unusual interstitial elements my speakers and I have used include a gift flood when helpers entered the ballroom through every doorway to hand out gifts (often corporate swag) to the audience, and live music as a performer stepped onstage to set the mood for your next element. For an outdoor event I've even employed brief pyrotechnics.

If you don't have that sort of budget, never fear. Promotional videos—such as company "sizzle reels" or a video introducing a new product—can serve the same purpose.

And (you knew I would get to this eventually) so can stories.

The wonderful thing about a story is that it has the power to reset your listeners. You may be seven minutes into your time onstage, but if you begin a story, it's like a fresh start.

One executive I work with is frequently invited to events for students and young professionals. The program window is typically forty-five minutes. So, rather than negotiate a smaller window, we use a special "stump speech" (one that can be repeated at multiple venues).

It consists of five minutes of preliminary comments, followed by eight five-minute stories. Each story is about how the executive navigated or overcame an obstacle in his career—for instance, deciding between a job that would pay more money and a job that would give him new and essential skills, or how he reacted when he did not get a promotion he was promised, or how he dealt with a boss who seemed determined to tank his career.

Each of these instances lends itself perfectly to the classic story structure: goal desired, goal denied, obstacle overcome, and afterglow. Because they are full-fledged stories, rather than anecdotes, they require little or no explanation. And because we are conditioned to think of stories as self-contained elements, that executive's talk was not one long, forty-five-minute presentation; it was nine presentations strung together, and audiences were regularly astounded to see that three-quarters of an hour had gone by as they were listening.

Regardless of how long you're asked to speak, always strive for excellence. Don't just phone it in. It's not just your reputation that's at stake, so is your brand (whether that's a professional one or a personal one). Under-promise and over-deliver. Rage against mediocrity in your storytelling. It'll raise the bar and show a deep level of respect for your listeners.

—STEVEN

HOW CAN WE TOUCH THE HEARTSTRINGS?

A good story can reset an audience and make them feel as if a talk is starting fresh, but that's not the only—or even the primary—reason to use storytelling in your talk.

Telling a story helps you to sound more genuine. If you're delivering platitudes such as, "We are proud to be a member of this community," or "Our people are our strength," it sounds as if the script was written by HR, PR, or some other acronym with an "R." You sound like a company talking. But encapsulate those thoughts in narrative, and you're much more likely to sound like a person talking.

That's better. Organizations don't talk—people do.

Also (we've touched on this already, but it bears repeating), stories and anecdotes are dead-simple to learn and rephrase in your own words. When you were in school, it probably took you days to memorize, say, the Gettysburg Address or the Pledge of Allegiance. Yet if someone told you a funny story in the schoolyard at recess, you'd have no problem telling that same story to someone else that same day, after school.

I use story in just about every talk because of how it (1) makes speakers sound human, (2) can be learned quickly and easily, and (3) can be delivered naturally. While each event is different, I frequently advise a leader to open and close with a narrative—usually an anecdote to introduce a topic and then, to wrap things up, a longer story that contains its own point.

Back in chapter 4, we mentioned the "serial recall effect"— basically, people remember best what they heard first and last. If, in your talk, the initial and final elements are ones that you deliver naturally and that your listeners can take easily to heart, chances are they'll remember your entire talk fondly.

WHAT STORY SHOULD WE USE?

Ask someone, without preamble, to "Please, share your story..." and you're likely to get a deer-in-the-headlights reaction.

There's good reason for that. Simply recounting your life wouldn't make a good story. Start with your earliest memory and narrate what happened—even generally—up to this moment, and what you'll have is an extraordinarily lengthy and circuitous mess.

Happily enough, though, lives are collections of *many* stories. The way you met and wooed the love of your life; the way you overcame being canned from the job that was supposed to be the pinnacle of your career (this actually happened to one leader I knew); the process that showed you that, while you'd gotten a degree in psychology and pre-law, you were really much happier cleaning hotel rooms (this one's true too)—every life is heavily sprinkled with fascinating nuggets of narrative.

> In her book *Stories That Stick*, Kindra Hall examines the four essential stories that every business leader needs to tell: the Value Story, the Founder Story, the Purpose Story, and the Customer Story. Whatever organization you work for, consider telling the stories of its history, its priorities, and its constituency. These are great places to start when searching for appropriate stories to tell.
>
> —STEVEN

The same is true with company histories. If you don't believe your organization has a virtually endless supply of stories, go to the next celebration for employees celebrating milestone service anniversaries, and listen in on the conversations. You'll hear enough stories to fill a book.

Stories are easy to find, but difficult to choose. Pick the ones that will lead people to feel and act the way you want them to at the end of your time together.

It's uncanny how, if you think of the talk this way, the right stories will usually come to mind almost immediately.

Try it out: think of a time when you've felt like an imposter in your chosen profession.

For me, that moment came the first day on my job as a speechwriter with a new company.

I was not a new speechwriter. I'd been doing it for years. It had helped me establish a pattern: interview the leader who'd be giving the speech, write the speech, send it in, do a quick phone call to make sure the script ticked every box, work with the leader's administrative assistant to make any tweaks, and wait to hear how it all went. Sometimes I attended the event to hear the talk for myself, but if I did, I sat in the audience.

Then I got the new job, and as the leader and I finalized the script, she said, "And you're getting there to set everything up, right?"

"Of course," I told her.

Inside, though, I was thinking, *She wants me to be the production manager, as well as the speechwriter? That's a completely different job!*

Different job or not, I had moved across half a continent for this speechwriter role, so I showed up at the venue three hours before showtime—the epitome of the mantra "Fake it 'til you make it."

I looked at the venue and tried to imagine myself as the one giving the talk.

The event was being recorded on video and I saw that the camera lighting was aimed right at the lectern, making it impossible to see a script on the lectern. I asked the lighting crew to position two camera lights offset on either side. The stage manager was planning to have ice water available for the speaker, and I asked it to be replaced with water just slightly cooler than room temperature (cold tightens throat muscles). I rehearsed the speaker entrance with the emcee, and made sure he knew when and where to make his exit and what path he would travel.

After that event, the leader smiled as she said, "That was the smoothest event of my career; I knew we made the right choice when we hired you."

I hope my sigh of relief was inaudible.

Needless to say, I spent much of the next year getting smart about stagecraft. I got to know producers and picked their brains for details. Planners began inviting me to their meetings so we could build my speakers' desires into their events. And today, I often teach other speechwriters the basics of stagecraft.

That's the story of my imposter moment. Yours was probably very different, and that's good—because it's *your* story. In both cases, though, the role—the job—gets laid bare and a fallible and approachable human being emerges. Tell that sort of story, and you cannot help but become closer to your listeners.

To decide what story *you* should tell, ask yourself some strategic questions:

- What lesson or sentiment do you want your listeners to have as their takeaway from your talk? For instance, I've found that my "fake-it-'til-you-make-it" story ended up being great for helping recently hired or recently promoted people overcome their feelings of being inadequate for their roles.
- What story is most approachable for your intended audience? Newly hired salespeople may welcome a story about feelings of inadequacy for their roles, while airline pilots or cardiologists may not.

- How applicable is the story to your topic? This doesn't mean the story has to be about your topic, specifically, but it should at the very least clearly make your point.
- How easy is the story to remember? This doesn't just mean that the story should be brief (although brief, in general, is not a bad idea). It should use concepts with which your listeners are familiar, so they aren't presented with a steep learning curve. For example, if you're sharing a story about musicians with teenagers, refer to artists they'll know, not the icons of classic rock.
- Is it a story your listeners will love? I once had a gray-haired executive win the hearts of his audience— young college students studying engineering—by sharing a story on how he learned to do a skateboard trick . . . which he then performed onstage. Fortunately, we budgeted time for the standing ovation that he received.

As you ask strategic questions, a story will very likely pop into your head. Keep brainstorming if you want, but write that initial thought down. In my experience, that first story to come to mind is the one that will work well with your talk.

Some people have attributed the following outline to St. Augustine (I don't know if he came up with it or not, but it's worth having in your back pocket—so here you go!): (1) What is it? (2) What's it worth? (3) How do I get it?

This technique tracks the significance of the message, moving from clarification (head) to value (heart) to action (hands). If you follow this pattern, focus first on clarity in what you're hoping to convey, then touch on why it's precious, and finally highlight the application and either how to obtain it or how to put the principle into practice.

This template gives you a simple way to choose three stories that will lock together and naturally lead to application on the part of your listeners. *Voila!*

—STEVEN

Story also does a wonderful job of bringing facts to life.

Let's say you are celebrating the twentieth anniversary of your company's arrival in its current city. The standard public affairs spiel might be to talk about the number of jobs created, what the company contributes to the domestic product of the region, and how much the company donates annually.

All of that is good and worth sharing, and your listeners might remember a figure or two.

Imagine, though, if you then continued like this:

What I remember best are the stories we've created together. I was here on the day we were interviewing applicants to work the second shift on the line at the plant. I got to talk with one of the applicants, a young man named Joe.

Joe was visibly excited about the prospect of working with us. When I asked about that, he said he already had a job with a different company. It was paying his bills, but just barely, and he had a twelve-year-old daughter who played violin with the middle school orchestra, but she was using a secondhand instrument. She wanted to get something better and take private lessons to become a country-and-western fiddle player.

Joe and his wife had been scrimping and saving to provide both of those things for their daughter, but it had been slow going, and it kept him up at night, knowing that his little girl had this unfulfilled dream. A job on our line would provide enough to pay for that dream.

Joe got the job, and his little girl, Phyllis, got her fiddle and the lessons she so earnestly desired.

Today, Joe is the first-shift manager at our plant. And Phyllis? If you turn on the TV tomorrow night, you'll see her. She's touring with the most popular country band in the world.

Our company didn't get her there. Her talents and Joe's belief got her there. But we are very proud to have played some small part in that success.

That is only 250 words total. It takes less than two minutes to deliver. But it's a story. People will remember it long after they've forgotten the exact amount that your company donated to local nonprofits.

SUMMARY

Regardless of how long you are speaking, story almost always has a place. Extremely brief appearances may best be handled with a single story and virtually nothing else. Lengthy speeches can be broken up with interstitial stories that "reset the clock" for the audience and make the time in their seats feel shorter. Add to this the way stories breathe emotion into facts, and story becomes a natural tool for any appearance.

Key Points to Remember

- Begin with the end—imagine how you want people to feel at the end of your talk, and work toward that moment.
- Think of the time allotted for your speech as a budget that you cannot exceed, and remember to account for

time-consuming elements (such as applause) and factor them into your budget.

▪ Bear in mind that anecdotes and stories are much, much easier to remember than scripts, and they allow you to look up from the page and speak directly to your listeners.

▪ When sharing personal reminiscences, ask yourself strategic questions to discover which story to share; the first one that pops into your mind is very likely the one you should use.

▪ Facts fade, but stories are remembered. Find ways to express the essence of your facts in a story.

CHAPTER 17

STEPS TO GROWING YOUR OWN TALE

—STEVEN

"Love is not a subject unless the writer of the song is in love."
—Wallace Stevens, Pulitzer Prize–winning poet

Okay, so once you have your idea and your audience in mind, how do you even get started with preparing your story? Are there any specific techniques to help you remember stories better?

Yes. Absolutely.

Let's walk through the steps you can take to develop, learn, and recall your story.

GET TO KNOW THE STORY

Before sharing your story, you'll want to get acquainted with it. You need to get to know your story.

Notice that I didn't write simply that you need to *know* your story, I wrote instead that you need to *get to know* your story.

What's the difference?

The process of getting to know someone takes time. It only takes a moment to meet someone, and you might say that you know them—but really *getting to know them* takes longer. It's only through the process of becoming better acquainted that a deep relationship can be built.

The better you know someone, the easier it'll be for you to introduce them to others. Only then are you really familiar with the characteristics and traits that make them unique.

It's the same with your story. The more familiar you are with it, the easier it'll be to tell it to someone else. The deeper the relationship you have with your story, the deeper you can plant it in the hearts of your listeners.

So, go through it aloud several times. Ask yourself, "What would I be experiencing if I were in this story? What would I see? What would I be hoping for? What's this story really about?"

Before introducing others to your story, take the time to get better acquainted with it yourself. Look at what's happening in it by (1) identifying the main character, (2) visualizing the setting, (3) noticing what the character struggles with, (4) tracking with how they try to solve or resolve things, (5) identifying any surprises or twists, and (6) clarifying, in your own mind, the story's ultimate payoff.

Then, tell yourself *about* the story. Explain it in your own words. Walk through it. Watch the story happen. Don't worry about performing it. Just imagine it happening around you as it unfolds.

In the real or imagined world of your story, what happened just before it began, and what transpired right after it ended? I'm not saying you should share these things. To the contrary, one way to make a story memorable is to get into it as late as possible and to leave it as soon as practical. But I find that, if I have in mind the context of the story—how it fits into the world in which it exists—it makes it easier for me to get to

> know it. Then, the better I get to know it, the easier it becomes
> to share.
>
> **—TOM**

As you tell the story, step into it and become part of it. Great storytellers disappear into the story, take your hand and lead you through it, and then reappear for the applause at the end. When you're watching and listening to them, you feel transported into the story yourself.

Here's something I perhaps should have mentioned earlier: I can't tell you the right way to tell a story. No one can. Why not? Because it doesn't exist.

Or, to put it another way, any story can be told effectively, and there's not just one way to do that. There are countless ways.

This is one reason why you'll want to avoid writing down your talks. If you do write them out, you'll be tempted to think of that version as the "right" one or "the way the story should go." But there is no "should."

Each time you tell a story is a unique experience with different people, expectations, and goals. I can give you examples of how I might tell a story, ideas on learning new stories, and suggestions on how to improve the stories you already tell—but that doesn't guarantee that my words or techniques will work for you individually or connect with your specific audience.

It might sound intimidating, and you might be thinking, *If there's no "right" way to tell it, what am I supposed to do?* However, the insight is actually quite freeing. It takes the pressure off. You're free to share the story in your own way and in your own words on this particular day with this particular audience.

Yes, be prepared. Yes, do the best you can. But don't pressure yourself to get the story *right*. Focus instead on simply telling it well.

Remember the reason you're telling the story in the first place; you're there to connect with your audience.

Strive for connection rather than perfection.

TEST-DRIVE YOUR STORY

I'm over six feet tall, so it's tough to find a car that has enough legroom (and headroom) for me. When my wife and I go car shopping, I need to actually sit inside the vehicles and make sure my head isn't jammed up against the ceiling and my legs aren't too cramped.

Other people worry about cup holders and Bluetooth capabilities and color-coordinated seat covers. For me, it's whether I actually fit in the car.

If you were shopping for a new car, you'd probably test-drive it before handing over your money. You'd want to consider whether the options are right for you. You'd evaluate the whole package to see if it really fits your needs and lifestyle.

You need to test-drive stories too.

After you've become acquainted with your story, hop into it and start the ignition. Tell it to yourself. Test how fast it should go, how smooth it feels, how it handles curves and the traffic of real life.

Ask yourself, "Where does this story really take off? Where is it too slow? Where does it meander too much? Is it even the right story for me to tell?"

Make sure that the way it's told fits you as a storyteller and fits your listeners as an audience. Some stories won't be a good fit. They may need to be modified so they feel natural for you to tell or so they really connect with your listeners.

As we've covered elsewhere, authenticity is one of the most vital wild cards you hold. Allow your own personality to come through. Delivery is as much an extension of your personality as it is mastery of the material.

If you're working on a literary story, read it aloud to yourself, and then put the book down and tell the story to yourself. As you do, look for surprises in the narrative. Try to notice something new every time you go through it.

At this point, don't try to polish or perform your story. There's no need to worry about that yet. Just talk through the story and try to notice what's going on inside it.

Stories grow as you tell them. So, explore the story as you practice it, adding details and descriptions where appropriate or necessary.

As you prepare your story, think of the Story Cube and ask:

- Character: "Is the main character believable, empathetic, and realistically vulnerable?"
- Setting: "Is the setting (both in time and place) clear enough for listeners to picture this story?"
- Struggle: "Is the struggle something my listeners can identify with or that they face in their daily lives?"
- Pursuit: "Does the character make meaningful, goal-directed choices?"
- Pivot: "Is the ending unpredictable, logical, and impactful?"
- Payoff: "Is the lesson (or takeaway) natural, or too contrived?"

LEARN TO FORGET

Your attention is like a river wandering through the countryside. There may be many dry creek beds that it can channel into, but the more divided it gets, the less force the river has, until finally it slows to a trickle or dries out completely.

Don't let too many distractions drain the impact and presence out of your delivery.

Even when you're rehearsing, it's easy to get distracted by things that have nothing to do with your story—how cold the room is, or how you forgot to eat lunch, or how your ankle hurts from twisting it trail running yesterday afternoon. You may be nervous or worried about how well your listeners will like your story, or how well they'll like you.

All of these factors (and many others) vie for your attention. And, as they do, they distract you from the task at hand—connecting with your story and your listeners.

So, as you work on developing your story, focus on being present in the moment. Take the time to iron out difficult sections, rehearse intricate phrases, and practice transitions from your introduction—if you have one—to the story itself. But when you're actually telling your story, don't let those preparation details distract you. As strange as it may seem, your goal when practicing a story is to learn *to forget*. Forget your practice time. Forget the script. Forget everything that might divide or distract your attention.

I find that the clearer my mental images of the story are, the less likely I am to get distracted. The more I can enter the story and imagine it happening around me, the more my listeners will be able to see it in their imaginations as well.

Remember, when you tell a story, none of your listeners are seeing exactly what you are. They hear the same words, but each person sees a different set of images in their mind. If you showed a video to your listeners, they would all see the same thing. But when you *tell* them a story, they all conjure up different mental images.

Several factors contribute to how well you'll be able to imagine the story yourself:

- your familiarity with this story
- your confidence level in telling the story
- your ability to clearly see and experience the details within it
- your comfort level with this particular audience

As you become more familiar with the story and practice telling it a few times, try to observe what's happening in it and tell it as you see it—don't just try to remember the words you used the last time you went through it.

NAVIGATE THROUGH YOUR STORY

Storyteller Jim May says, "Let's say you go on a journey, and it's the difference between memorizing only the path or learning the whole landscape . . . if you know the whole story, if you learn it well, know its emotional content, its general direction, its landscape, then if you get off the path, you can always find your way back."

Think of it this way: Imagine that you're driving home without any GPS or cell phone to assist you, and you come to a "Road Closed" sign. If you're familiar with the streets of your city, you could choose an alternate route and still make it home. But if this was the only route you know, you'd be stuck.

Memorizing the words of a story puts you in the same position. What would happen if you forgot the next word? The road ahead would be closed off.

That happened to me once, and I hope it never happens again.

I was doing a presentation with another speaker. We'd both memorized our talks and were alternating speaking our parts, line by line, through the story. The idea was to allow people to hear the messages one line at a time and then thread the meaning together for themselves on their own, coming to the same conclusion we were working toward.

It was a fine idea, and it might have worked well if I hadn't forgotten one of my lines.

Halfway through the story, my friend said his line and I opened my mouth to say mine, and nothing came out. My mind went blank. I was standing there in front of six hundred people who all knew it was my turn to talk and that if he went on with his next line, the story wouldn't make sense.

I found myself totally out on a limb. There was no escape—because of the intricacy of the story and the presentation style, my partner couldn't continue without my response and I couldn't improvise my way out of it or make something up. I had to remember!

Terrified of looking stupid and ruining the talk, I frantically tried to remember the page I'd memorized. I stood there for a long, frozen, uncomfortable moment (that seemed to last an hour!), trying to visualize the page I'd committed to memory. Mentally, I scrolled down it until I came to the line I was supposed to say. Finally, I rattled it off and the story continued.

Afterward, the man who'd invited us to speak came up to me and said, "Was that just a dramatic pause there, or did you forget your line?"

"Dramatic pause." I winked at him. "Definitely a dramatic pause."

"Ah," he said. "Gotcha."

When you memorize a story, you only know one way through it. If you forget your line or suddenly lose your train of thought as I did, you're in a tough spot. When an audience thinks that you've forgotten your line, they become uncomfortable. And remember, you're here to serve your listeners, not the other way around.

That day, I knew only one way through the story. When I found the road before me obscured, I didn't know what to do. I had to mentally review the map.

Dramatic pause?

Yeah, right.

On the other hand, if you've explored alternative routes through the story, you can maneuver past forgetting a word or two and still make it safely home, to the end of the story. If it's appropriate, you might meander along the scenic route, or, if you need to, hop on the interstate to zip to the ending. And, if you find that your listeners really like the view, you can drive around the block a few times before heading home.

> What if you do lose your place while telling your story, or you suddenly remember something that you should have mentioned earlier? Simply say, "Something that hasn't come up yet is that Julie was an elite powerlifter..." Or, "Oh, by the way, my uncle owned two ponies, named Nellie and Fred, in his fenced-in suburban backyard . . ." Or, "Now, it's important for you to know that . . ." Or, "What I haven't told you yet is . . ." Then, simply fill your listeners in and go on from there. Most of the time they won't even be aware that you intended to tell them that information earlier.

Storytellers are concerned with helping their audiences picture the story. Because of that, images and sounds are more central to storytelling than printed letters and words. I know that might sound a little strange—of course stories are made up of words, right? To a certain extent, yes. However, when we communicate orally, it's through sound, not text.

So, as you begin to learn your stories for telling, don't think of it as a process of memorizing and reciting the right *words*, but of creating the right progression of images.

How?

First, write it with your mouth. Rather than typing it up and then trying to commit it to memory, speak it into existence. Talk about the story. Work your way through it, and pay attention to what you're saying, what actions seem appropriate, and what inflection and tone of voice seem to serve the story best.

There's a saying among storytellers, attributed to Donald Davis: "My work is not the result of a script—a script is the result of my work." I can identify with that. Eventually I might write a story down to keep a copy of it, but that only comes after I've presented it to numerous audiences.

During my preparation time, I often go on a walk carrying a notebook. As I talk my way through the story, I take notes on what wording sounds good, on phrases that I want to make sure I remember, and on details or descriptions that I like.

The next time I go through my story, I might pretend that I'm telling it to a huge audience and use exaggerated facial expressions and gestures. Then I might sit down and tell the story as if I'm talking to a friend on the back porch. Each time through it, I'm working on getting to know the story's layout, not trying to take exactly the same route to the end.

I sometimes teach people in my seminars to "never tell the same story twice." Really? What is that about? After you spend all that time learning it, you can't tell it to another group someday? Well, yes . . . and no. As we pointed out earlier, every storytelling event is a unique social encounter. Each time you tell, you're at a different place in your life and your listeners are at different places in their lives as well, with different states of mind, different outlooks, assumptions, and desires.

All of these factors will change (sometimes in very subtle ways) the way in which you tell the story. Because of that, every time you tell a story is the first time you tell *that* story. Allow it to be shaped by the context of the event and the mood of the audience. Focus on telling it well to those listeners on that day rather than trying to perform it like you did the last time you went through it.

Every life is a work in progress, so every story is a work in progress as well.

By the way, keep only the mistakes you like. One time I was telling a story and rather than saying "lawn mower blade," I accidentally said, "lawn blower maid." Now, whenever I tell that story, I digresss for a minute and do a bit on lawn blower maids. It adds some humor and shows that I'm not perfect (as if the audience needed to be reminded of that!). If you make a mistake and it adds something memorable, humorous, or unique to the story, consider including it the next time you tell that story.

ELEVEN TIPS FOR REMEMBERING YOUR STORIES

To remember a story well, strive to have more than one mental association with it. Each of these techniques will help you remember the story, but when you combine several together, it'll make recalling your stories even easier:

1. Episodes—Remember a story by events, or "episodes." Limit yourself to seven major events or it may be too tough to keep them all straight.

2. Movement—Movement triggers memory. The more gestures and movements you have tied to specific story events, the easier that section of the story will be to remember.

3. Storyboarding—Some people find that they can remember the story better if they draw a series of pictures that represent the scenes of the story. Each scene shows the progression of the action in the story. (Don't worry about drawing masterpieces; just use simple pictures to help ignite your memory.)

4. Objects—Objects, costumes, and props will help spark your memory. As you pick up each object, it'll help you remember the next section of the story. (Presentation slides and visuals can serve the same purpose and be effective as well.)

5. Images—Some people imagine the story and watch it as though it were a film. Watch the story in fast forward to get the big picture, and then in slow motion to notice the details.

6. Escalation—Stories naturally progress to a climax. Just think about what has to happen next to move the story forward. If you get lost, ask yourself, "What would naturally come next?"

7. Repetition—If you can find events or phrases that are repeated throughout the story, it'll make it easier to remember.

8. Practice—You guessed it: Tell your story! Practice it different ways—while seated, walking around, with no gestures, or with exaggerated ones. Tell your story whenever you can, over and over. By hearing your voice, you'll learn what needs to change in the story.

9. Encouragement—Practice with a partner. Find someone who'll encourage you as you begin learning your story, and then give you constructive feedback as you develop and improve the way you tell it.

10. Listening—Record your story (either an audio or video version) and then listen to (or observe) the way you tell it. If you do this, listen to the story several times and listen for (or look for) different things. First, listen for the overall impact. Second, listen for timing, pauses, and flow. Finally, listen for words or phrases that aren't as clear or concise as you'd like. Change them and improve.

11. Outlining—Outlining a story, summarizing it, or even writing down a version of it for later reference is helpful for some story-learners.

KEEP THE MOOD IN MIND

As you work on the story you're preparing, take into consideration the "feel" of the story and try to reflect that in the way you tell it.

For instance, a tense, suspenseful story will mirror that mood, while a humorous story will be told in an entirely different manner.

Let the way you tell the story grow from the content and message of the story. Don't tackle a serious topic (untimely death or sexual abuse, for instance) in a lighthearted or joking manner. Speak with passion as well as sensitivity. Years ago, I attended a seminar by author and preacher Fred Craddock, and he said, "There are some things you can shout. Some things you can say. Some you can hardly say."

If you started a story with, "The nurse came into the room, tears in her eyes. She sighed and softly closed the door behind her," your audience is not going to be expecting a comedy routine.

Practice your story with your listeners in mind. Think about what you want them to experience during the story or to conclude by the end of your story. This is the destination your story is attempting to reach (that flight to Miami that Tom mentioned in chapter 16). If you can't delineate it in specific words, don't get frustrated. The meaning of a story may be hard to succinctly articulate. Can you feel the emotion you want your listeners to experience? That's a good place to start. Go from there. Aim for the heart, not just the head.

FOUR FACTORS THAT WILL INFLUENCE YOUR DELIVERY

- Substance—Locate the resonant moments in the story.

- Style—Find your authentic voice.
- Presence—Step into the story.
- Responsiveness—Adapt your delivery, as necessary, to your listeners' reactions.

The first minute of your story will set the mood for the rest of the story. Make sure you know the beginning well and that you're comfortable telling it. Also, hone the ending so you don't have to concentrate on the words so much, but can focus on seeing the story conclude, and observing your listeners' reaction as it does.

Let your understanding of your listeners help shape the way you prepare your story. You can derail an audience from listening to your story by choosing material that isn't age- or culture-appropriate. Think about what techniques will best communicate your story and reach these listeners, today. Avoid techniques that might distract them or make them uncomfortable.

SUMMARY

Get to know your story—really become acquainted with it. Test-drive it to make sure it's the right one for you to tell. Focus your attention on the story as you practice it and as you tell it. Think about and talk about the story, but don't worry about "perfecting" it. Try it out. Explore the possibilities (gestures, inflection, visuals, movement, etc.) for retelling it.

Forget about reciting or performing your story; just share it genuinely, moment by moment, from your heart. See it play out. Each time you practice it, try to notice different aspects of the story. Pay particular attention to the beginning and ending—you really want to make sure the story starts and ends strong. Find a personal connection with the images or emotions of the story. What moments draw you in or speak to you personally? Connect with those first, and then build the rest of the story around those sections.

Become familiar with the city streets and back alleys of the story rather than memorizing one route through it. Finally, practice your story with the audience in mind. By doing that, you can nurture the right environment both in your imagination and in the presence of your listeners for your story to grow and mature.

Key Points to Remember

- During rehearsal, hone your story, but stay open to possible changes in the way you might tell it when the time comes.
- Focus your attention on the story. Picture its images. Be aware of what's happening in your story as you tell it.
- Practice the story, not the words. Tell it with your whole body, not just your mouth.
- Never tell the same story, exactly the same way, twice. Avoid the temptation to memorize your story.
- Practice your story with the audience in mind, and relax and enjoy yourself when you deliver it. It'll help your listeners relax and enjoy it as well.

CHAPTER 18

ORCHESTRATION

Bringing It All Together

—STEVEN

"Learn the exercises and then forget them. The key to becoming proficient is to learn the language of the activity so well that you speak it naturally. Then, you don't concentrate on the specific actions, gestures, words, but rather the moment."
—Tony Montanaro, world-famous mime and author of
Mime Spoken Here

I have a friend who works as a music producer in Nashville. He told me one time that many of the top musicians he works with don't read music.

"How is that possible?" I gasped. "How do they know what to play?"

He went on to describe a system they'd developed for moving from key to key through a combination of number values based on the song's key, and playing by ear and by instinct. He talked me through it twice. Not being a musician, I had a tough time following and couldn't tell you how to do it yourself, but the approach amazed me.

And, as a communicator, it inspired me.

Here's the thing. Your storytelling delivery isn't about a series of rules that you have to follow to the letter; it's more about the result: the story that you produce.

When a musician plays, he doesn't want people to exclaim afterward, "What appropriate finger positions he used!" Or, "Clearly, this man has practiced his scales!" No. Instead, the musician just wants people to be immersed in and moved by the music.

When you finish your storytelling presentation, you don't want people to walk away saying, "My, what a clever use of dialect!" Or, "What poignant facial expressions that storyteller used! Masterful! To die for!" Instead, you want to bring all of the communication skills at your disposal together in a way that listeners don't even notice—all they notice is how great the story works with all of those instruments playing in sync with each other.

CHOOSING YOUR INSTRUMENTS

Some instructional books on public speaking and storytelling spend lots of time explaining all about voice, posture, gestures, stage presence, and so on, but forget to emphasize the importance of the final goal—creating a resonant story that connects with listeners. With those books, it can be easy to lose sight of the whole point of storytelling and work instead on developing various oral presentation skills in isolation rather than merging them into one integrated whole.

It's like a musician who studies the history of each instrument, polishes the brass, collects guitar picks, and delves into music theory but never actually plays anything. It's much more important for a storyteller to tell a story in a way that listeners engage with than to worry about his proficiency at each specific storytelling skill. (Which is why this chapter is the final one in the book—we wanted to emphasize such vital aspects such as passion, belief, connection, and responsiveness first.)

With that in mind, it *is* helpful to develop your presentation skills—as long as you remember to focus foremost on *telling your story well* so that the end result touches and moves listeners.

Once you're familiar with the instruments of storytelling and how they interact with each other, you can begin mixing them together in new ways to create fascinating arrangements of your own.

Instrument #1—Voice

The most basic instrument of all is your voice. While it's certainly possible to communicate a story effectively without using your voice (mimes, dancers, and those in the deaf community come to mind), most of us rely on our voices to tell our stories.

You can use your voice to differentiate characters, develop sound effects, express emotions, and create suspense.

In the few instances when I've taken on interns or protégés who don't sing or play an instrument, I've bought them ukuleles and taught them basic chords and rhythm. That's because language is a type of music, and it's best approached accordingly. Certain sounds are sad; others are joyful, intriguing, or profound. If a person can understand that, they have a grasp on one of the most effective tools in spoken communication. So, when interviewing people who want to work for me, I always ask what instrument they play, whether they enjoy singing, and what music they enjoy listening to. It sounds like chitchat, but it's not.

—TOM

It's smart to take care of your voice. Many actors and singers spend long hours training their voices to be resilient and strong and to sound clear and pleasant rather than strained and weak. There are lots of breathing exercises and vocal warm-up exercises for the serious voice student, but let's be realistic—if you're telling stories a couple of times a week, you probably don't have time to train your voice like a professional singer.

However, there are a few simple things you can do to care for your voice:

- Before telling your story, take the time to warm up your voice by singing a little, exploring different levels of pitch and volume, and trying out some of the different voices or the inflection you'll be using.
- Relax your jaw muscles and loosen your neck, throat, and shoulder muscles before speaking. Tension in the throat, neck, and jaw causes vocal strain. (Yawning is a great way to relax your throat muscles!)
- During rehearsal, experiment with different types of sound effects or voices for your stories, but only use those that are comfortable for you. Don't strain your voice. Avoid yelling, screaming, shouting, or other activities that can damage your voice. (Speaking in cold, wet weather can also cause you to lose your voice.)
- Drink lots of lukewarm water before and during your speaking engagements (rather than tea and coffee, which actually constrict the muscles in your throat).
- If you find that you frequently strain or lose your voice, contact a voice coach or singing instructor for more activities and guidelines for caring for your voice.

If there's a large group, one of the best ways to take care of your voice—and be easily heard by the audience—is using a microphone.

There are different types of microphones that you might be asked to use. Sometimes there'll be a variety of them available. Don't be intimidated.

Basically, there are three main types of microphones: a headset mic, a lapel (or lavalier) mic, and a handheld mic.

A headset mic will usually have a way of wrapping around the back of your head or have a hook to go over your ears. Let the sound technician adjust the mic so that it fits snugly and comfortably. Move your head around to make sure there's enough play with the cord to allow you to move without causing the microphone to tilt away from your mouth. This type of mic is a good choice if you use both hands to gesture during your talk.

A lavalier mic, also known as a "lapel mic" or a "lav," clips to the front of your shirt. It should typically be worn at chest-level. If you know that you're going to be using a lapel mic, wear a button-down shirt rather than a turtleneck or blouse. Lapel mics aren't typically as ideal as headset mics because they don't pick up the sound of your voice as well when your head is turned to the side.

A handheld mic might be wireless or have a cord attached to the bottom of it. In either case, hold it about eight inches from your mouth. The most common mistake people make when using a handheld microphone is holding it too close, not too far away. If you can lick the mic, it's too close! Handheld mics are good for doing sound effects because you can move the mic closer to or farther from your mouth for effect. They also work well for telling humorous stories. (Think about it—how often do you see stand-up comedians use a lapel or headset microphone?)

Be careful to speak clearly so people can understand the words you use. Many of us have certain words that we mumble, especially at the ends of sentences. Try to identify these words and then practice saying them more clearly, and finish your sentences without fading out.

If you speak too slowly, you'll bore your listeners. If you always speak quickly, you'll tire them out. Use variety to increase interest—slowing when appropriate for dramatic impact, speeding up during the parts that can be easily summarized.

One more thing: speak naturally. Some people start talking in an angry, scolding manner as soon as they step in front of a group. Other people speak with an annoying, condescending, or "preachy" tone. Avoid both extremes and talk in a natural, pleasant speaking voice.

Instrument #2—Face

Your face is a magnificent storytelling tool. With your face you can show nearly every emotion and reaction imaginable: from joy to sadness, from anger to contentment, from fear to surprise, from confusion to delight.

To communicate clearly, it's important to express the same emotions with your face that you feel in your heart.

Try this at home. Turn away from a mirror and try to make a face that clearly expresses one of the emotions or reactions listed below. Then, turn and look at the mirror to see if you're accurately portraying it. You may be surprised to discover that some of the emotions you think you're clearly expressing actually look like something else. Choose five of them at random. Give it a shot!

afraid	disgusted
alluring	ditzy
amazed	enthusiastic
angry	furious
bewildered	grumpy
bossy	guilty
concerned	happy
confident	hateful
content	hesitant
depressed	hopeful
determined	infatuated
disappointed	innocent

insane	relieved
intelligent	romantic
intrigued	sad
joyful	sarcastic
lonely	shocked
mean	shy
mischievous	sick
naggy	silly
nervous	sleepy
pleading	stressed
pouting	surprised
powerful	thankful
regretful	tired

One other note: you can overdo it. Don't get caught up trying to do too much with your face. Instead, simply use this exercise to expand and refine the facial expressions you have in your repertoire so you can naturally start using them in your presentations.

Instrument #3—Eyes

While I was studying storytelling in graduate school, I took a seminar with professional storyteller Ed Stivender. He pointed out that one of the differences between actors and storytellers has to do with the dynamic of what the listeners and the presenter do or don't *pretend*. So, when an actor goes onstage, he pretends the audience isn't there. And the audience, in turn, pretends that the actor can't really see them. But when a storyteller steps onstage, he addresses the audience directly—and the audience expects the storyteller to look at them rather than pretend he can't see them. Neither pretends.

It was an illuminating insight that has helped me better connect with listeners over the years.

Related to this is the topic of eye contact.

Many of us have heard the sage advice to use "good eye contact" with our listeners. But what does that mean, exactly? Does good eye contact mean looking at everyone in the audience? Or staring over their heads, as some people recommend?

Ed taught me that to understand good eye contact, you need to first understand a little bit about the way stories work. When we tell stories, we sometimes take on the role of the narrator and explain what's happening in the story. For example, if you were telling the story of the time when you had a crush on your high school teacher, you might begin by saying, "I was fourteen years old and I was in love with my English teacher. She was everything I could ever hope for—except for being twice my age."

That's *narration*.

At other times, however, you might step into the role of one of the characters and talk as if you actually were that character: "I'd like to see you after class today." "Who, me?" "Yes. Just for a few minutes. There's something I need to talk to you about." "Oh. Okay."

That's *dialogue*.

See the difference? When the storyteller is narrating, he's addressing the audience. When he's engaged in dialogue, he's actually talking to the other characters in the story.

Here's the secret to good eye contact: always look at whoever you're speaking to. When you're narrating, look at the audience. When you're engaged in dialogue, look at the other characters in the story.

"Wait a minute . . ." I can hear someone say. "The other characters aren't really there!"

That's right. They're imaginary, but they're still present in the story. So, you'd look, let's say, to your left to address the student, and then back in the other direction to talk to the teacher. You don't look at the audience—rather, both you and the audience direct your attention to the place onstage where the other character would be standing if he or she were there.

Practice having a conversation like this with yourself. Pretend you're arguing with your friend about who the best basketball player of all time was. Go ahead: find a place where no one will think you're crazy if they hear you, and give it a try.

To summarize, good eye contact is natural, genuine, and directed at whoever the storyteller is addressing—either the audience or the other characters in the story.

By the way, when you do look at the audience, avoid staring at any individual person for too long. If you stare too long, they'll begin to feel uncomfortable and the attention of the rest of the audience will shift from you to the person you're looking at. On the other hand, if you find someone who's really enjoying your story, glance at that person often for encouragement that you really are doing a good job.

Instrument #4—Posture

Believe it or not, you communicate an awful lot just by the way you stand and hold your body.

If your shoulders are slouched too far forward, people might think you're sad, depressed, or shy. If you hold your shoulders too far back, they might presume that you're overly confident, proud, or even stuck-up. If you stand straight and tall with your shoulders comfortable and natural, people will think you're confident and at ease with them.

To become more aware of how posture communicates, do some people-watching on a busy street, on the subway, or in the lobby of your place of business. Watch how different people carry themselves and then evaluate what impression it gives you. Be aware of how stiffly or loosely they stand, how straight or crookedly they walk, and if they lean forward or backward when they stop. Notice how they hold their weight and position their head, back, arms, and legs.

As you tell your stories, you may wish to let your posture naturally reveal personality traits of the characters you're portraying. How do you think an embarrassed character might stand? What about someone who is conniving? Menacing? Deceptive? Brash and impulsive? Confident and self-assured?

Finally, be aware of your own posture as you stand in front of your listeners. If you sit when you tell your stories, notice the difference between tilting backward, sitting upright, or leaning forward. Each posture communicates a different level of formality with your listeners.

Practice standing or sitting with your shoulders in a relaxed, neutral position. It'll help you stand comfortably and confidently as you deliver your stories.

Instrument #5—Movement

At the beginning of my storytelling career when I was studying mime and physical movement in storytelling, my instructor watched me walk across the stage. The first time as a monkey, then as a baby, then as a stork. He shook his head in frustration. "You don't have a very big vocabulary."

"What do you mean?"

"Do something different!" he demanded. "It's like you're a two-year-old and you keep repeating the same few phrases over and over!"

He meant that I had a very limited movement vocabulary. I had a few moves that I knew, but I'd never trained to understand my body as a means of communicating. I was still like a young child learning my words.

The more you explore the language of movement, the more comfortable you'll become in expressing new and interesting words with your body.

The way you move through space can be used to communicate many things. Some storytellers are comfortable jumping around onstage, skillfully changing their bodies into the shapes of all sorts of different characters and creatures. They practically dance their way through the story.

Other tellers are more comfortable sitting in a rocking chair or on a stool, elegantly weaving their tale simply by using well-chosen words—without any movement at all. Do what's most comfortable for you and appropriate for your story and your listeners.

The amount of body movement you include in your story will depend on:

- Audience—How many people are in attendance. (Typically, the more people, the more movement.)
- Proximity—How far you are from your audience. (Typically, the more distance, the more movement.)
- Story content—How much movement naturally occurs in the story.
- Your personality—How at ease you are in using movement to tell your stories.

Movement should grow from your own comfort level rather than what you think you're "supposed to look like." Experiment with different ways of moving during your story to find the balance that works best for you.

Instrument #6—Gestures

Closely related to the way you stand or move your body are gestures—the way you move your arms and hands. Most people gesture as they speak. It's natural. Some people are so used to "talking with their hands" that they even do it while they're speaking on the phone or driving the car!

Many people get onstage and suddenly don't know what to do with their hands. They often stand there with their hands clasped in front of their groin.

In public-speaking circles, we refer to this as "the fig leaf position." Clasping your hands behind your back is the reverse fig leaf position. Some people will just stand there going back and forth—fig leaf to reverse fig leaf to fig leaf again. It can be entertaining to watch as they subconsciously try to hide.

So, how should you stand?

Naturally, with your hands to the side, or, if the social context calls for it, you might put one hand in your pocket and gesture with the other.

Make your gestures consistent and committed. Don't hesitate. Don't do them half-heartedly. They should be done like the rest of the story—with confidence, sincerity, appropriateness, and authenticity. Gestures are most effective when they're done from the elbow or shoulder, rather than the wrist.

If you're speaking to a large group and there are no video screens that show your face, you'll typically want your gestures and expressions to be a bit more animated than usual so people in the back of the room can see them. (Tom covered video and visuals in depth in chapter 9.)

If you're going to use gestures when you tell your story, use them when you practice the story. That way, they grow organically out of the story and aren't awkwardly grafted in at the end. Don't try to "act out" every word. Rather, look for a way to naturally *embody* the story and the characters as you tell it. As authors Haddon W. Robinson and Torrey W. Robinson put it in their book, *It's All in How You Tell It*, "Eye contact, movement, and gestures will all be more natural if you *relive* the story rather than *retell* it."

Be careful not to contradict the world you create when using gestures or action. So, for instance, if you reach for an imaginary doorknob, make sure it's in the same place onstage each time you open and close the door. Some speakers interact with the imaginary objects around them in a different way each time they pick them up or set them down. This disrupts the imaginary world that's been created onstage and will distract and even frustrate your listeners.

When practicing your story, try telling it different ways—as if you're having a conversation, as if you're speaking to an auditorium full of people, while sitting, or using only gestures and no words. Then, after brainstorming (or would it be bodystorming?) your way through the story, keep the ideas that work best for you.

As you experiment with telling your story, explore how you could communicate the ideas within it simply by the way you stand, move, and gesture. If you're careful to observe and respond to the movements, you'll discover new and interesting ways to use your body while storytelling.

Sometimes, people practice a specific gesture so much that when they tell the story, the gesture looks "rehearsed" or "canned" rather than natural. Avoid that. Let your gestures flow naturally from the story rather than distract from it.

Instrument #7—Imagination

If voice is the way a storyteller relates to the audience, imagination is the way a storyteller relates to the story. As we emphasized earlier, effective storytellers remain observant while they tell their stories. They're using their imagination to see the story, and then responding to the images and their listeners' reaction as they tell the story.

When my daughters were young, I told them a continuing bedtime story that, to the astonishment of all of us, ended up lasting more than ten years. During that time, we tracked the adventures of a boy (Tirean) and a girl (Perea) in a magical land full of flying unicorns, dragons, wizards, and talking animals. There was the evil Witch of Pacoland, the Shadow People (who could turn you into a shadow if they touched you), and a giant polka-dotted rhinoceros who could break through anything (aptly named Rhino Polkalarge), and many more colorful characters.

Every night, I'd build the story up to an exciting moment and then say, "I'll tell you more tomorrow." Then, the following night, I'd pick up the story by recalling where we left off: "As you remember . . ." That gave me the chance to review the story and get some mental momentum for the next adventure.

Thinking back now on all of those thousands of stories, it seems like an overwhelming task that I can't believe I actually pulled off. If you would've asked me at the time if I thought I could tell three thousand episodes of a bedtime story, I would've said, "No way!"

But, in truth, the process that I followed each night wasn't really some arcane, dusty secret handed down from ancient storyteller to storyteller through the ages. It was just a process of tracking what would naturally happen within a story. I would simply review the context, introduce a character my daughters would care about, give him a desire, make something go wrong, and then allow him to use his special skills to try to solve it in an unexpected way.

(By the way, sometimes I did get tired of the story and I would simply say to my girls, "And they all lived happily ever after." And they would say, "No, they didn't!" "Oh, yes," I'd tell them. "Trust me. They did. They all lived happily ever after." And my daughters would shake their heads vehemently. "No, they didn't! *Something went wrong!*" Even as four- and five-year-olds, they understood that for a story to go on, something needs to go wrong—and they wanted their special story to go on . . . and on . . . and on.)

Many of us feel like story creation is beyond us, that other, more creative people are more qualified to do it than we are.

But tapping into imagination is not the exclusive domain of the creative elite.

Back in 1921, in *Back to Methuselah*, George Bernard Shaw wrote, "Imagination is the beginning of creation. You imagine what you desire; you will what you imagine; and at last you create what you will."

Applying imagination to a story—whether you're creating it on the spot from scratch, or picturing it as you retell it—will help your listeners imagine it as well. Enter it. Go ahead. Let the story enfold you and then unfold around you as you speak it into existence.

Instrument #8—Presence

The story is told in India that there was an old man outside of the village who sat beside a large pot filled with mud. There, he would mix the mud with a heavy stick all day—and every couple of days, he would reach into the pot and pull out a chunk of gold.

Well, everyone was amazed by this, and a young man said to himself, "I need to learn the secret to this so I can have gold myself!"

So he went up to the old man and asked him the secret.

"Well, it's quite simple, really," the old man replied. "Just take a pot and put some dirt in it. Add water, then mix it with a stick for three days and reach in and pull out the gold."

The young man immediately did as the old man had said. He mixed the mud for three days and reached in, but there was no gold.

He went through the process again. Then a third time, but each time there wasn't any gold. At last, he returned to the old man and said, "I've done exactly what you said, but there's never any gold."

"Tell me what you did."

"I took a pot, put some dirt in it, then added water and mixed it with a stick for three days. I reached in and there was no gold."

"Ah, yes!" said the old man. "There's one thing I forgot to tell you. While you're mixing the mud, you can't be thinking about the gold."

Be present in your story. Avoid dwelling on what people might or might not think of you later. Don't worry about accolades and applause. Instead, mix the mud, immerse yourself in the moment, and enjoy the process—producing the best work you can right now—without being distracted by thinking about the possible outcome, or you'll miss out on the treasures that this present moment is offering you.

SUMMARY

Remember, the key is orchestration. The more you develop expertise in each of these eight areas, the better your story will be as you add just the right amount of each "instrument" to serve the story as a whole.

Study any professional speaker, and you'll likely find something that he or she does "wrong." Maybe they pause too long, don't make good eye contact, or slouch too much—but often, despite not following the "rules," the story works. Why? Because those tellers know that the tools of the storyteller are there to serve the story, not the other way around.

With a story, the whole is greater than the sum of its parts.

Just as a moving melody is more than simply a mixture of cello and drums and violin and guitar, a good story is more than a well-trained voice, natural gestures, good timing, and appropriate eye contact. While all of these are important, how good the song sounds (that is, how well your story impacts your audience) is even more vital.

As you work on developing your story by mixing together the instruments mentioned in this chapter, keep your listeners in mind and look for ways to help them connect with this story you're telling them, here, now, today.

Key Points to Remember

- Use the instruments of your voice, your body, your gestures, and your movement to shape and tell your stories—naturally.

- Face whoever you're talking to—whether that's the audience or the various characters within the story.
- Use eye contact to develop and maintain your relationship with the audience.
- Lean into your imagination as you share your story, develop wonder, express passion, exhibit your own individuality, and continue to remain responsive to the audience's reaction.
- Enjoy the story's formation and don't let anticipation of what might come later steal away the golden moments the creative process is offering you right now.

CONCLUSION

Here's something you might find interesting: Tom and I wrote this book backward.

First, we tapped into our experience as public speakers, authors, and storytellers. Between the two of us, that amounted to tens of thousands of hours of writing, shaping, presenting, and teaching stories and storytelling.

I'd done plenty of research on the essence of story twenty-five years ago when I was pursuing a graduate degree in storytelling (and later while writing two books on the craft of fiction writing), but for the most part I've been so consumed with writing stories over the ensuing years that I haven't really taken the time to step away and re-research what makes them work. So, after Tom and I wrote this book, I said, "I ought to see if there's any research out there to support what we're saying."

Tom was more than happy that I was the one signing up for that job. "Remember, you're reading for two now," he said.

"Um. Thanks."

So I dove in, devouring dozens of books from different disciplines—storytelling, writing, education, leadership, preaching, public speaking—and I kept finding the same things over and over again: stories truly are one of the most powerful ways to connect with, captivate, inform, and persuade audiences. Stories engage both sides of the brain, build empathy, and foster greater understanding. A story that's told well can inspire entire generations in the way to live. Stories don't just reflect culture; they actually help to reshape it. As a proverb often attributed to the Hopi people puts it, "The one who tells the stories rules the world."

So, even though most writing projects might begin with research, ours ended with it. And maybe that's not such a bad approach after all.

We've seen these principles and techniques work throughout our lives with millions of listeners and readers. And now we know why stories work so well—it's how people are wired.

We hope you'll take these ideas and apply them in your own storytelling ventures. New stories are waiting to be told. New listeners are waiting to be impacted. New paths are waiting to be traveled, paved with the tales we tell and listen to together.

—Steven James

ACKNOWLEDGMENTS

We'd like to thank our literary agent, Steve Laube, for his honesty, commitment, and encouragement along the way—and for the occasional kick in the seat of the pants when we needed it. Also, we extend our deepest gratitude to Tim Burgard and all of the folks at HarperCollins Leadership for believing in this project and giving it the green light. Thanks, also, to Jeff Farr and his team, and to Sarah Haskins for their editorial insights and input.

Some unsung heroes of this work are Kevin Kern, Nicole Carroll, and the rest of the team at the Walt Disney Archives, who were kind enough to review our entire manuscript with an eye toward historical accuracy in our Disney references. Two others are Margaret Adamic and Max Raley of The Walt Disney Company Legal team, who pursued and helped us secure permission to use credited Disney content in this work. True to the Disney brand, Kevin, Nicole, Margaret, and Max were cheerful and encouraging every step of the way.

Once again, just as with all of our books, our wives deserve our thanks for giving us the space and time to work on this manuscript— and remaining married to us throughout the process.

Finally, we'd like to thank all of the listeners who've been in our audiences around the world over the last three decades. Sometimes we've said the right things, sometimes the wrong ones. Thanks for giving us a chance to share our stories with you, for your patience when we mess up, and for your laughter, graciousness, and appreciation through it all. We hope that this book will draw all of us closer together in this grand, wondrous, and mystifying circle of—and story of—life.

APPENDIX A

TEN SUREFIRE WAYS TO COME ACROSS AS AN AMATEUR

Here's a helpful list of ten ways to undermine your message, annoy your listeners, and make you appear unprepared. Enjoy!

1. **Check your mic while there are people in the room. Be sure to say, "Testing one, two, three."**

What to do instead: Arrive early, before your listeners do, and work with the sound technicians to test the mic yourself. When checking it, keep the mic at the same distance from your mouth that it'll be at when you present; the techs will be adjusting it to perform well in that position.

During the test, rather than counting aloud, tell part of your story. Speak naturally and clearly into the microphone. Trust it to carry your voice. Walk to the parts of the stage you'll be using during your presentation to make sure there isn't any feedback. Become familiar with the mic, identifying if it has an "on" button, a "mute" button, and so on. Finally, take this opportunity to verify that the battery level is adequate.

Be patient with and considerate to the sound techs, and thank them when the event is over; while the audience may never see them, these people are the "backup band" for your presentation.

2. When you get onstage, blow into your mic or tap it with your finger and say, "Is this on? Can you hear me?"

What to do instead: Begin your talk right away. Since you already did your sound check, you know the mic is working. The audience is waiting. Go ahead and start your story. By the way, the microphones used by some venues may have price tags reaching into the thousands of dollars (seriously), and the technicians will not appreciate it if you bang on, tap, or drop them for effect. They may even bill your host organization for damages, which strongly diminishes your chances of being invited back again.

3. Squint at the spotlights and complain about how you can't see the audience because the lights are in your eyes.

What to do instead: Avoid drawing attention to the fact that you're standing in the lights (your listeners already know that) or that it's hot up there onstage in the spotlights. Ideally, when you do the sound check you'll be able to check the stage lighting as well. Ask the person in charge of the lighting to set it to "show lighting"—i.e., what it'll be like *while you are speaking*. Then, use that to gauge where to stand to best be seen by your listeners.

4. Make sure that the stage is the least lit area in the room. It's especially helpful if there's more light in the back of the room.

What to do instead: Remember, light draws attention. If you're up front in the dark and the back half of the room is in bright light, it'll diffuse the audience's "energy" through the room. The people in attendance will tend not to laugh at your humor. They might very well disengage, start checking their phones, and even talk to each other. Of course, if you're doing a slide presentation at the front of the room, the front will need to be darkened. If that's your preferred approach, find a place onstage that has light directed at you.

Remember, stand where you can be seen. You don't want to be talking to your listeners from the shadows.

5. If something goes wrong, blame someone else.

What to do instead: Let's say that the microphone stops working. Handle it like a pro. Say something like, "It looks like we're going to need a different mic up here." Then, thank the sound techs when they bring you one or fix the problem. Don't complain about them, sigh heartily, shake your head, roll your eyes, or say, "This always happens to me every time I come to this conference center."

6. Leave the stage in your quest to get close to the audience. Wander throughout the crowd.

What to do instead: Stay on the stage. Presenting your talk while you're walking up and down the aisles is a great way to make your listeners feel uncomfortable. Once you leave the stage, they won't know if they're supposed to turn around and watch your back as you pace the aisles, or what they should do. Most of the time, they'll keep watching the empty stage. *Soooo* awkward. Stay in the place where everyone can see you. That's what the stage is there for. If you want to make it seem more intimate, just move to the house side (front edge) of the stage.

7. Let people see the home screen on your computer when you're doing your slide presentation.

What to do instead: Your audience doesn't want to see your home screen. It screams, "Unprepared!" Arrive early enough to set up the computer, plug in the correct adapters, and prepare to play your presentation before anyone else is present. I've lost count of how many times I've seen presenters fumble around with their computer, trying to find the right cords or connectors after the program was supposed to have started.

When it comes to props, slides, and visuals, anything that doesn't add to your talk will detract from it. Strive to use visuals as (1) reminders of your key point, (2) revelations of something unexpected, (3) bridges to the application you're teaching, or (4) sparks to ignite curiosity about what you're saying or where your talk is going.

Although slides can become a distraction, in some contexts they're required. If you do use them, make sure you rehearse with them, just as you would practice a story that you're telling without any visual aids. Also, include a duplicate of the last slide so if you mess up and click past your last slide, you won't land on that distracting and unprofessional home screen.

8. Have the person who's introducing you read the same introduction that appears in the conference folder that everyone already has a copy of.

What to do instead: Before the presentation—with enough time left so that the emcee can make changes if necessary—simply ask her what she will be saying. Have her read the introduction to you, aloud.

Not only will this help you understand how she'll be setting the listeners' expectations, but it'll also give you the chance to change or clarify anything if necessary. For instance, "Please don't say I'm going to get everyone up and moving around," or "You can just tell them I'm the president of Tech World Giants, Inc.—you don't need to list all the other places I've worked." (For more tips on emceeing, see Appendix B.)

9. Correct the emcee after she's done and you have the microphone. For instance: "Actually, I've written twenty-eight books, not twenty-five."

What to do instead: Accept what's said unless it's absolutely vital that you correct it: "Well, I haven't actually had a *New York Times* bestselling book yet, but that is certainly one of my goals!"

10. Read to the listeners from your handout or your slide presentation.

What to do instead: Use the slides to enhance what you're saying with their visuals and summary points, but don't read them to the people you're speaking to. A good rule of thumb is to think of the slides as playing "harmony" to the "melody" of your talk.

If you're not using your own laptop for the presentation, but are using the venue's computer, make sure it has all of the fonts that you're using in its font library, and that they'll appear the same way that they do on your personal computer.

Before you present, verify that the font size is large enough for the audience to read and that the words will be visible to everyone, even those in the back of the room.

If you decide to give printed notes to your listeners or send them PDFs of the material, do so at the end as summaries or for review. Don't distribute them at the beginning and then read them to everyone. Why should the attendees listen to you when they can just read everything you're going to say?

APPENDIX B

EMCEEING MADE SIMPLE

Emceeing can be tricky. You're not the warm-up act for the main speaker. You're not here to show off your stuff, do your schtick, or end up "stealing the show." Instead, you're here to serve the needs of the person you're introducing, prepare the listeners, remove distractions, and hand off the mic to the next person onstage.

Here are ten steps to becoming a proficient and professional emcee.

1. Do your homework beforehand. Go to the speaker's website and prepare what you're going to say. Don't simply read the person's bio from the program booklet that the attendees have in front of them. That speaks to a lack of preparation.

2. If the presenter has provided you with a written introduction, respect that and don't reword or improvise on the podium. If their intro is poorly written or too long, politely ask if you can condense or rephrase it—then do so before you get onstage. Also, make sure you know how to pronounce everything in the bio.

3. Greet the presenter a few minutes beforehand, and explain that you'll be introducing them. Run through the introduction with them and see if they have any corrections: "No, actually, I don't live in Denver anymore. We moved to San Diego."

4. Audiences like to know where someone is from and a snippet of inside info about him or her: "Coming to us all the way from Death Valley, where she teaches tai chi to dogs in her spare time, our speaker today . . ." Or, "Good morning and welcome, everyone. We're honored today to have one of the country's top experts on tax law with us today. He's also a hot air balloonist who was featured in the recent documentary *You're Full of Hot Air . . .*"

5. As soon as you say the presenter's name, attendees will think they're supposed to clap. Because of that, it's usually best to leave mentioning their name until last rather than starting with it. This also keeps audience members from whispering to one another, "Who is this again?" as you're delivering the crucial opening lines of your remarks. For example, "Our presenter today has sold ten million books and shared his unique approach to fostering a creative mindset for more than twenty years, all over the world . . . [*Insert a fascinating fact here*] . . . Please join me in welcoming Joe Famousguy!" Then applaud so the audience knows they are to do so as well.

INTRODUCTION CHECKLIST

- Welcome the audience.
- Note the speaker's qualifications.
- Add a fascinating fact.
- Mention where she's from.
- Close with her name and an invitation to applaud.

---

6. Your intro is about the person you're introducing, not about you, so avoid making it seem like the two of you have a special friendship or share an inside joke that the audience isn't a part of. You don't want the listeners to feel left out, but rather welcomed in. (By the way, also, avoid commenting on the quality of the talk: "He's hilarious and you're gonna keel over from laughing so hard . . ." "She's super-motivating and is gonna get you *so* excited about our sales event . . ." "This guy is the smartest person who's ever graduated from MIT—you'll be blown away . . .") Listeners know that this person is qualified to be there—obviously they are, since they're the featured speaker. So, you might say this: "Our guest speaker today has written fourteen books, hiked the Appalachian Trail barefoot, and comes to us all the way from Las Vegas, Nevada. Please join me in welcoming Joe Famousguy!" Instead of this: "Our guest speaker today is Joe Famousguy! He's the funniest person I've ever met. We go way back, Joe and I . . ."

7. Take into account what time of day it is. So, if this is the first seminar of the morning, welcome people. If it's the last one of the day, you might wish to say something like, "This has been a day packed full of great info. If you're like me, your brain is buzzing with new leadership strategies that you can't wait to implement. But don't tune out yet—we have one more stellar presenter for you today . . ."

8. Be brief. Just a few sentences is all you need. Speak clearly, set the audience at ease, and don't give the impression that things are hurried, rushed, behind schedule, or frantic.

9. Don't say, "This person needs no introduction." Of course they do—that's what you're onstage to provide. (By the way, also, don't end with, "Without further ado." There's no need to say that.) No matter how famous the person is, you'll want to find something unique or a hidden little gem about them: "Many of you are familiar with Joe Famousguy's acting career, but did you know that when he's

not starring as an A-list actor in Hollywood he also volunteers at a reptile recovery center for homeless lizards? Please give it up for Joe Famousguy!"

10. Put it all together. Walk onstage, greet the audience, and get right to it. Usually four to five sentences is plenty: "Today, we're honored to have as our guest speaker one of the world's foremost authorities on underwater basket weaving. He has taught his wet-weaving techniques to more than one hundred thousand people over the years, and his baskets appear in museums throughout Europe and North America. When he's not underwater, you'll find him high above it, climbing frozen waterfalls in his home state of Alaska. Let's all welcome Joe Famousguy!"

APPENDIX C

365 STORY STARTERS

1. You saw a bridge emerge between two things, ideas, or people.
2. You looked into someone's eyes and realized something.
3. You felt pain over the loss of a loved one.
4. You experienced joy over seeing a loved one.
5. You witnessed a teacher bring about peace.
6. You were afraid of dying.
7. You felt rejection.
8. You peeled off a mask you were wearing.
9. You tried to forgive, but couldn't.
10. You stood up for someone else.
11. You abandoned the rat race.
12. You redefined your view of success.
13. You were lost.
14. You were found.
15. You were almost killed.
16. You witnessed new life.
17. You flirted with death/disaster.
18. You were given a second chance.
19. You weren't caught doing something wrong.
20. You experienced discrimination.
21. You had butterflies in your stomach.
22. You knew you were going to panic.
23. You felt paralyzed.
24. You were uptight.
25. You were angry at injustice.
26. You witnessed hypocrisy.
27. You realized people don't spend time on important things.
28. You fit in when you should have stood out.

29. You stood out when you should have fit in.

30. You longed to make up for a wrong you'd done.

31. You wished there was somewhere to turn.

32. You found out it was too late to help someone.

33. You wished you were someone else.

34. You felt rejected by those you loved.

35. You felt loved by those you rejected.

36. You felt alone in the midst of many people.

37. You were proud of an accomplishment.

38. You saw inspiration flash into someone's eyes.

39. You felt helpless.

40. You were thankful to be alive.

41. You did something completely spontaneous.

42. You realized you are unique.

43. You were in the right place at the wrong time.

44. You were embarrassed for someone else.

45. You didn't care when you should have.

46. You were the recipient of a gift you didn't deserve.

47. You went on an incredible trip.

48. You were followed by a strange person.

49. You fell in love.

50. You wished for something magnificent.

51. You dreamed an impossible dream.

52. You sought adventure.

53. You were falsely accused of wrongdoing.

54. You met someone very famous and weren't impressed.

55. You met someone unknown and were astonished.

56. You saw compassion in action.

57. You stopped to smell the roses.

58. You heard a funny joke, but couldn't remember it.

59. You experienced a broken heart.

60. You were healed of your hatred or anger.

61. You let go of bitterness.

62. You resisted an urge.

63. You discovered the meaning of life.

64. You saw the most beautiful or sublime thing in the world.

65. You struggled with temptation.
66. You learned an important lesson.
67. You were wounded, but grew as a result.
68. You strove for something you couldn't attain.
69. You lost your innocence.
70. You were overcome with emotion.
71. You discovered a new way of looking at life.
72. You were afraid for someone you loved.
73. You struggled with yourself.
74. You wrestled with your conscience.
75. You gave in to pride.
76. You wanted to fight.
77. You saw someone give up on life.
78. You had the power to harm someone.
79. You were lured by power.
80. You had to humble yourself and admit your mistake.
81. You asked for mercy.
82. You sawed off the branch you were sitting on.
83. You changed your mind.
84. You began to respect someone you didn't like.
85. You wanted to hide but there was no place to go.
86. You were helpless and needed to be rescued.
87. You realized there was no excuse and no escape.
88. You were falsely accused.
89. You were deceived into believing a lie.
90. You approved of wrongdoing.
91. You had a brush with fame.
92. You struggled with rejection.
93. You let go of a loved one.
94. You were hurt and it was hard to trust again.
95. You grew roots and they were hard to pull up.
96. You walked to the edge of the cliff to see how close you could get.
97. You went along with the crowd.
98. You turned your back on someone in need.
99. You found out what it feels like to be genuine and sincere.
100. You didn't feel like being good any longer.
101. You desired something you shouldn't have.

102. You drifted away from your moral foundation.
103. You ached for someone you didn't know.
104. You discovered you couldn't make up for a wrong.
105. You were provoked.
106. You awakened to a new day.
107. You agonized over the problem of pain.
108. You couldn't help but be discouraged.
109. You realized the evil you are capable of.
110. You learned how vulnerable you are.
111. You learned how valuable you are.
112. You betrayed a trust.
113. You were overcome with frustration.
114. You were refreshed.
115. You met someone you'll never forget.
116. You found an unusual treasure.
117. You saved something no one else would have saved.
118. You changed your attitude.
119. You didn't care when you should have.
120. You didn't take time for yourself.
121. You gave thanks.
122. You were charmed into believing a lie.
123. You tried your hardest, and failed.
124. You redefined failure.
125. You passed a test you'd previously flunked.
126. You searched, but never found.
127. You went off to seek your fortune.
128. You were prepared for battle.
129. You became a captive to your desires.
130. You finally obtained what was rightfully yours.
131. You turned over a new leaf.
132. You recovered something (or someone) precious.
133. You kept a secret too long.
134. You were thankful that life isn't fair.
135. You were the bearer of bad news.
136. You faced the hardest decision of all.
137. You chose the path of healing.
138. You made a fatal mistake.

139. You believed the unbelievable.
140. You did things "their" way for once.
141. You let anger tell you what to do.
142. You got into trouble.
143. You needed to be punished.
144. You didn't care what happened.
145. You were glad you got caught.
146. You should have been bolder.
147. You admitted you were weak.
148. You loved and lost.
149. You were in the eye of someone else's storm.
150. You were no longer content.
151. You went from rags to riches.
152. You had faith in the wrong thing.
153. You didn't take responsibility for your actions.
154. You experienced inner peace.
155. You learned something about holiness.
156. You turned your back on your old life.
157. You experienced inner poverty.
158. You forgave but you didn't forget.
159. You hurt the one you loved. Again.
160. You took action before it was too late.
161. You became a victim of your own desire.
162. You tricked your way out of a blessing.
163. You opened your big mouth.
164. You prayed for your enemy.
165. You learned by example.
166. You felt abandoned.
167. You were ignored. And it was okay.
168. You gave advice instead of listening.
169. You faced the consequences of your actions.
170. You went on a quest to discover yourself.
171. You dared to go someplace new.
172. You knew you were boxed in.
173. Your job became a calling.
174. Your feelings were hurt.
175. Your dreams turned to dust.

176. Your loved ones turned their backs on you.
177. Your friends betrayed you.
178. Your curiosity had brutal consequences.
179. You were rescued at just the right moment in a way you could never have anticipated.
180. Someone helped you withstand the pressure.
181. Life overwhelmed you.
182. A burden was lifted.
183. Worry made you tremble.
184. The strong flower wilted.
185. Rumors destroyed a friendship.
186. One person became a majority.
187. Stormy seas were finally calmed.
188. The outcast was accepted.
189. Unexpected news stunned you.
190. You received an awkward blessing.
191. Restlessness stirred your soul.
192. Suffering and sadness gripped you.
193. Vengeance seemed more important than love.
194. Mourning turned to dancing.
195. Joy came in the morning.
196. Ambition blinded you.
197. Favoritism hurt you.
198. Seduction came knocking at your door.
199. Encouragement came from nowhere.
200. You were finally free.
201. Reinforcements arrived.
202. Life didn't make sense.
203. A "ghost" from the past pursued you.
204. Everyone laughed at you.
205. A promise was kept.
206. A promise was broken.
207. A prayer seemed to go unanswered.
208. A prayer was answered in an unexpected way.
209. Something you said was taken the wrong way.
210. The pain of regret was healed.
211. An old wound was reopened.
212. An injustice occurred in front of you and you were helpless to change it.
213. A child reminded you of something vital.
214. The good guy didn't win.
215. The underdog had a big finish.
216. The person you looked up to let you down.

217. Life became boring and routine.
218. Life became adventurous and wild.
219. Your house became a home.
220. The dark cloud lifted.
221. A simple thought changed your life.
222. Love replaced infatuation.
223. Zeal consumed you.
224. Joy bubbled out of your soul.
225. Relief finally came.
226. Everything you believed in crumbled.
227. Time seemed to stand still.
228. Courage seemed impossible.
229. Disaster seemed imminent.
230. Everyone accepted you.
231. No one seemed to care.
232. Someone overlooked the past.
233. Feelings dictated your actions.
234. The joke was on you.
235. Inspiration came at last.
236. Amusement made up for disappointment.
237. Quitting seemed like the only option, but you persisted.
238. No one seemed to notice your effort.
239. Opportunity knocked.
240. Wisdom outshone knowledge.
241. A small deed changed your life.
242. Both of the options were acceptable.
243. Everything fell into place.
244. A friend brightened your day.
245. A stranger appeared at just the right moment.
246. Good news finally arrived.
247. Things went better than expected.
248. Clouds parted enough to reveal a rainbow.
249. It felt good to go home.
250. The secret was finally revealed.
251. The confession was finally made.
252. Even your friends seemed far away.
253. Hope came knocking at your door.
254. A new pathway suddenly appeared.
255. Saying goodbye was the hardest thing to do.
256. Faith was a source of strength.

257. Laughter exploded out of you.
258. The letter you'd been waiting for arrived.
259. Something unpredictable happened.
260. Hope reappeared.
261. Tragedy struck.
262. The imitation seemed like the real thing.
263. The look in a child's eye made life seem "okay."
264. Bliss came from an unexpected place.
265. A prediction came true.
266. A person from you past reentered your life.
267. A family heirloom was passed down.
268. The brevity of life became apparent.
269. An accident happened and you were there to help.
270. Truth became crystal clear.
271. Neither option seemed acceptable.
272. A big move caused you to reevaluate your life.
273. The urgent overshadowed the important.
274. Only one thing mattered.
275. Embarrassment opened a door.
276. A friend from the past reappeared out of nowhere.
277. A regret that you've lived with resurfaced.
278. Shame clouded your reasoning.
279. Innocence was betrayed.
280. Guilt became overpowering.
281. Opportunity knocked, but you weren't home.
282. Peace surpassed understanding.
283. Because of foresight, a crisis was narrowly avoided.
284. Wisdom came from an unexpected source.
285. A new challenge arose.
286. Wounds were healed.
287. The future seemed bright.
288. The past became significant.
289. Seeing wasn't believing.
290. Peace flooded your life.
291. Wonder and awe filled your heart.
292. Desperate measures were called for.
293. Grief made joy impossible.
294. Love made grief bearable.
295. A heart was broken.
296. Shame caught up with you.

297. The world seemed cold and uncaring.
298. Darkness moved in.
299. A little white lie grew into a betrayal.
300. A misunderstanding led to hatred.
301. It was hard to break free of a habit.
302. Memories of good times caused you to cry.
303. Forgiveness was the only option.
304. Two roads diverged and you had to choose.
305. Jealousy became easier and easier.
306. Something insignificant became valuable.
307. A gift changed everything.
308. Someone touched you with a kind word.
309. A long struggle finally ended.
310. The mystery was suddenly solved.
311. You doubted and were reassured.
312. Greed blinded you.
313. Someone took your place.
314. The ladder you were climbing was leaned against the wrong building.
315. Selfishness became a way of life.
316. Evil seemed to have the upper hand.
317. Someone else's success made you envious.
318. Life didn't seem fair.
319. Strife in your family made life difficult.
320. A rival was successful at your expense.
321. An obstacle was overcome.
322. The guilty person walked away unpunished.
323. Peace surpassed understanding.
324. The world seemed like a cruel place to raise a child.
325. The story had a happy ending.
326. Pleasure was ruined by passion.
327. Purity was lost.
328. Purity was regained.
329. A warning came from an unusual place.
330. The champion gave up on his cause.
331. A disguise came off and you saw the real person.
332. Two enemies were reconciled.
333. The effects of past choices became evident.

334. A debt was paid.
335. Everything was turned upside down.
336. A hero emerged.
337. An honorable sacrifice was made.
338. A warning was not heeded.
339. A curse became a blessing.
340. A blessing became a curse.
341. You discovered something you wish you hadn't.
342. The forbidden seemed safe.
343. Obligation drained your enjoyment.
344. A quarrel broke out.
345. Controversy erupted.
346. A rivalry separated good friends.
347. The victim sought revenge.
348. You were powerless to prevent something awful.
349. A dark desire sprang up inside your soul.
350. Duty called.
351. Suspicion arose.
352. Insult was added to injury.
353. The punishment didn't fit the crime.
354. Life imitated art.
355. Danger complicated matters.
356. Respect deteriorated.
357. Hard work didn't pay off.
358. Perseverance did pay off.
359. Hope sustained you.
360. Love was more than a feeling.
361. Someone else's success brought you discontent.
362. Devotion prevented disaster.
363. Sorrow overwhelmed you.
364. Wisdom saved the day.
365. A wish came true.

NOTES

CHAPTER 1
The Unparalleled Power of Story

Page 10: Kendall Haven, *Story Proof: The Science Behind the Startling Power of Story* (Libraries Unlimited, 2007), 7.

Page 10: Antonio Damasio's research is summarized in *Everyday Business Storytelling: Create, Simplify, and Adapt a Visual Narrative for Any Audience* by Janine Kurnoff and Lee Lazarus (Wiley, 2021), 12.

Page 14: Peter Guber, *Tell to Win: Connect, Persuade, and Triumph with the Hidden Power of Story* (Crown Business, 2011), 22.

Page 23: Richard L. Thulin, *The "I" of the Sermon* (Augsburg Fortress, 1989), 52.

CHAPTER 3
The Three Questions That Will Change Everything

Page 50: Lisa Cron, *Story or Die: How to Use Brain Science to Engage, Persuade, and Change Minds in Business and in Life* (Ten Speed Press, 2021), 16.

Page 57: Carmine Gallo discusses Uri Hasson's findings in *Talk Like TED: The 9 Public-Speaking Secrets of the World's Top Minds* (St. Martin's Press, 2014), 49–51.

CHAPTER 5
Shrinking the Space Between Us

Page 81: Nancy Duarte, *DataStory: Explain Data and Inspire Action Through Story* (Ideapress Publishing, 2019), 33.

CHAPTER 6
The Chemistry of Storytelling:
Hugging the Audience with Story

Page 94: Stephen Denning, *The Leader's Guide to Storytelling: Mastering the Art and Discipline of Business Narrative* (Jossey-Bass, 2005).

CHAPTER 7
The Six Most Common Mistakes Speakers Make
(and How to Avoid Them)

Page 111: Dave Barry, *Babies and Other Hazards of Sex: How to Make a Tiny Person in Only 9 Months, with Tools You Probably Have Around the Home* (Rodale, 1984), 79.

Page 113: Mike Yaconelli, "Youthworker Roundtable: The Ethics of Public Speaking," *Youthworker: The Contemporary Journal for Youth Ministry* (Fall, 1990), 43.

Page 118: Michael Hauge, *Storytelling Made Easy: Persuade and Transform Your Audiences, Buyers, and Clients* (Indie Books International, 2017), 87.

CHAPTER 9
The Story That Changed an Industry

Pages 152–53: Bob Thomas, *Walt Disney: An American Original* (Disney Editions Deluxe, 2017), Kindle Edition.

CHAPTER 10
Humor: Adding a Light Touch
to the Stories You Tell

Page 168: Kim Johnson, *Truth in Comedy: The Manual for Improvisation* (Meriwether Publishing, 1994), 9.

Page 184: Margot Leitman, *Long Story Short: The Only Storytelling Book You'll Ever Need* (Sasquatch Books, 2015), 3.

CHAPTER 12

The Kung Fu Lesson, the Llama Sweater, and the Ice Cream Cookie Stack

Page 208: The story of the birds and the beasts is based on an excerpt from Steven's novel *Every Wicked Man* (Penguin Random House, 2018), 44–45, in which the villain uses the fable to encourage a young woman to choose which side she is going to fight on. And she does not choose wisely . . .

CHAPTER 14

Transformative Techniques to Improve Your Delivery

Page 237: Kendall Haven, *Story Proof: The Science Behind the Startling Power of Story* (Libraries Unlimited, 2007), 124.

Page 245: Tony Montanaro, *Mime Spoken Here: The Performer's Portable Workshop* (Tilbury House, 1995), 68–69.

Page 246: Flannery O'Connor, *Mystery and Manners* (Farrar, Straus and Giroux, 1970), 96.

CHAPTER 15

Dusting Off Your Memories: Crafting Personal Experience Stories

Page 259: Webb B. Garrison, *The Preacher and His Audience* (Fleming H. Revell Company, 1954), 127.

Page 259: Helmut Thielicke is quoted by Eugene L. Lowry in *The Homiletical Plot: The Sermon as Narrative Art Form* (John Knox Press, 1980), 45.

Page 260: Matthew Dicks, *Storyworthy: Engage, Teach, Persuade, and Change Your Life Through the Power of Storytelling* (New World Library 2018), 112.

CHAPTER 17

Steps to Growing Your Own Tale

Page 294: Jim May, *The Storyteller's Guide* (August House, 1996), 54.

CHAPTER 18
Orchestration: Bringing It All Together

Page 314: Haddon W. Robinson and Torrey W. Robinson, *It's All in How You Tell It: Preaching First-Person Expository Messages* (Baker Books, 2003), 64.

ABOUT THE AUTHORS

STEVEN JAMES is an award-winning author, keynote speaker, and professional storyteller with a master's degree in storytelling. Since 1996, he has appeared more than two thousand times, presenting his stories and teaching writing and storytelling at events spanning the globe.

With more than one million copies sold, his books have won or been shortlisted for dozens of national and international awards. Best known for his psychological thrillers, his novels have garnered wide critical acclaim from sources including *Booklist*, *Library Journal*, the Associated Press, the New York Journal of Books, and many others. *Publishers Weekly* has called him a "master storyteller at the peak of his game."

In addition to his writing and speaking, Steven hosts the weekly podcast *The Story Blender*, on which he has interviewed hundreds of the top storytellers and writers in the world (including Tom!).

■ ■ ■

TOM MORRISEY is deeply in demand as one of the world's top speechwriters and executive-engagement specialists. He has spent more than three decades as a Fortune 500 speechwriter and communications consultant, working with companies such as Chrysler, Ford Motor Company, General Motors, and The Walt Disney Company.

He is also a popular conference speaker who has taught storytelling techniques (and the science underlying them) on both sides of the Atlantic. Tom currently works in public affairs management for The Walt Disney Company, where he mentors speechwriters and storytellers on three continents. When not writing speeches, he pens thrillers and literary fiction.

▪ ▪ ▪

For the last twenty-five years, Steven and Tom have taught presentation skills and storytelling techniques to thousands of speechwriters, speakers, authors, executives, and educators around the world.

To invite us to speak to your group and for bonus material and more information about our presentations, please visit our website, www.storytellingkeys.com. We always enjoy hearing from readers. Drop us a note through the contact form on the website. We hope that one day our paths will cross in person and that we'll get to hear the stories you have to share.